JUSTICE IN JEOPARDY

REPORT OF THE
AMERICAN BAR ASSOCIATION
COMMISSION ON THE 21ST CENTURY
JUDICIARY

July 2003

Alfred P. Carlton, Jr.

American Bar Association President, 2002-2003

PRINTING OF THIS REPORT WAS MADE POSSIBLE WITH THE GENEROUS SUPPORT OF LEXISNEXIS™, A DIVISION OF REED ELSEVIER INC.

American Bar Association
Commission on the 21st Century Judiciary

CHAIR
Edward W. Madeira, Jr.
Pepper Hamilton LLP
Philadelphia, Pennsylvania

HONORARY CO-CHAIRS

Hon. Abner Mikva
University of Chicago Law School
Chicago, Illinois

Hon. William S. Sessions
Holland & Knight, LLP
Washington, District of Columbia

MEMBERS

Julius Chambers
Ferguson Stein Chambers
Charlotte, North Carolina

Henry C. Duques
First Data Corporation
Sarasota, Florida

George Frazza
Patterson Belknap et al.
New York, New York

Representative Peter Gallego
Texas House of Representatives
Austin, Texas

Patricia Hynes
Milberg Weiss et al.
New York, New York

Chief Justice Margaret Marshall
*Supreme Judicial Court of
Massachusetts*
Boston, Massachusetts

Chief Justice Thomas R. Phillips
Supreme Court of Texas
Austin, Texas

Barbara Roberts
Former Governor of Oregon
Portland, Oregon

Thomas W. Ross, Sr.
Z. Smith Reynolds Foundation
Winston-Salem, North Carolina

Stephen N. Zack
Boies, Schiller & Flexner, LLP
Miami, Florida

ABA BOARD OF GOVERNORS
LIAISON

Jose C. Feliciano
Baker & Hostetler, LLP
Cleveland, Ohio

REPORTER

Charles Gardner Geyh
Indiana University School of Law
Bloomington, Indiana

David Giampetroni
Assistant to the Reporter

REPORTER

Luke Bierman
Director, ABA Justice Center

Katy Englehart
Staff Operations/Special Projects,
ABA Office of the President

Eileen Gallagher
*Director, ABA Standing Committee
on Federal Judicial Improvements*

Seth Andersen
*Project Manager, ABA Standing
Committee on Judicial Independence*

Marcia Kladder
*Associate Director, ABA Justice
Center*

American Bar Association
Commission on the 21st Century Judiciary

Special Advisory Committee

ABA Section Officers Conference
Bernard F. Ashe
Delmar, New York

ABA Section of Litigation
Michael J. Henke
Vinson & Elkins
Washington, District of Columbia

ABA Judicial Division
Hon. David Horowitz
Studio City, California

ABA Section of Tort Trial and Insurance Practice
Michael E. Mone
Esdaile, Barrett & Esdaile
Boston, Massachusetts

ABA Section of Legal Education
Dean Gene R. Nichol, Jr.
University of North Carolina
School of Law
Chapel Hill, North Carolina

ABA Standing Committee on Strategic Communications
Allan J. Tanenbaum
AFC Enterprises, Inc.
Atlanta, Georgia

American College of Trial Lawyers
Benjamin H. Hill, III
Hill Ward & Henderson PA
Tampa, Florida

Association of Trial Lawyers of America
Robert S. Peck
Center for Constitutional
Litigation
Washington, District of Columbia

Corporate Counsel
Louis L. Hoynes, Jr.
Wyeth Law Department
Madison, New Jersey

Defense Research Institute
Richard T. Boyette
Cranfill, Sumner & Hartzog
Raleigh, North Carolina

Hispanic National Bar Association
Duard D. Bradshaw
Roderick Linton LLP
Akron, Ohio

League of Women Voters
Patricia Brady
Springfield, Virginia

United States Chamber of Commerce, Institute for Legal Reform
James Wootton
Washington, District of Columbia

American Bar Association
Commission on the 21st Century Judiciary

Acknowledgements

Many people provided their time, talent and energy to ensure the success of this project. The Commission would like to extend its heartfelt thanks and appreciation to all those who assisted with the organization of the hearings, colloquium and meetings. While it would be impossible to list everyone who assisted the Commission in its work, we would like to acknowledge the contributions of the following individuals and organizations.

Funding for the Commission on the 21st Century Judiciary was generously provided by the Joyce Foundation, LEXIS-NEXIS, the Open Society Institute and the Z. Smith Reynolds Foundation.

The Detroit, Michigan hearing was held at Wayne State University College of Law. The Commission wishes to express its gratitude to Dean Joan Mahoney and Eleanor "Coco" Siewert for their gracious and comprehensive assistance throughout our inaugural hearing. The Commission is grateful to ABA President-Elect Dennis Archer for his hospitality during our stay in Detroit.

The Commission held its second hearing in Philadelphia, Pennsylvania at the James A. Byrne U.S. Courthouse. Joe Hartnett and Michael Kunz, Clerk of the Court, were invaluable to ensuring a successful hearing. The Commission also extends its gratitude to Chief Judge Edward Becker and Judge Norma Shapiro.

The third hearing was held in Portland, Oregon at the College of Urban and Public Affairs of Portland State University. Rod Johnson, Director of Special Events, Office of the Dean, provided excellent assistance to the Commission. The thoughtful assistance of Judge Ellen Rosenblum, Barbara Roberts, Karen Garst, and Kay Pulju paved the way for a successful hearing and a number of outstanding outreach activities.

In Austin, Texas, the Commission held its final hearing in the Old Supreme Court Chambers in the Texas Capitol. The Commission wishes to express its gratitude to Chief Justice Phillips and his wife, Lyn, for their gracious hospitality and assistance, and to Catherine Bartoli, Representative Pete Gallego and his entire staff, and Steve Hall for their efforts on behalf of the Commission.

Many individuals and organizations contributed to the success of the National Colloquium on the 21st Century Judiciary, held on March 14, 2003. The Commission thanks the leadership and staff of the North Carolina Bar Association (NCBA) for hosting the colloquium at the magnificent North Carolina Bar Center in Cary, North Carolina. Special thanks go to J. Norfleet Pruden III, NCBA President, Allyson Duncan, NCBA President-Elect, Allan Head, NCBA Executive Director, and staff members Michelle Frazier, John Lambeth, Russell Rawlings, Kim Vaughan and Betty Wood. North Carolina Chief Justice I. Beverly Lake welcomed participants to the colloquium, and former United States Senator Robert Morgan set the tone for a day of productive discussions on the Commission's draft recommendations.

In addition, Matt Leighninger and Melissa Wade of Study Circles Resource Center organized and facilitated Study Circle presentations in a number of cities to coincide with the Commission hearings. Paula Nessel and the ABA Coalition for Justice organized National Issue Forum discussions based on their "And Justice for All" issue book, moderated by Patti Dineen, in all of the cities where the Commission held a hearing. We are grateful for their efforts.

The Herculean efforts of Hazel Walker and her staff in the ABA Meetings and Travel Department ensured that each meeting and hearing of the Commission was as unique and enjoyable as it was informative. Seth Andersen and Eileen Gallagher spent countless hours editing and proofreading the final Commission report in preparation for publication.

We are grateful to all for their time, assistance and dedication to the work of the Commission.

Table of Contents

APPENDICES

Executive Summary

Justice in Jeopardy

Report of the American Bar Association Commission on the 21st Century Judiciary

Executive Summary

The judicial systems of the United States at the beginning of the 21st Century remain unparalleled in their capacity to deliver fair and impartial justice, but these systems are in great jeopardy. Our state courts play a critical role in preserving American freedom and democracy. Almost 100 million cases are resolved peacefully and with relatively little fanfare by some 30,000 state judges each year. Increased political involvement in the judiciary, diminished public trust and confidence in the justice system, and uncertain resources supporting the courts place burdens on the judiciary's capacity to provide fair and impartial justice. Indeed, the escalating partisanship and corrosive effects of excessive money in judicial campaigns, coupled with changes in society at large and the courts themselves, have served to create an environment that places our system of justice, administered by independent and impartial judges, at risk.

ABA President Alfred P. Carlton, Jr., convened the Commission on the 21st Century Judiciary to study, report and make recommendations to ensure fairness, impartiality and accountability in state judiciaries. The Commission held four public hearings, generating over 1,000 pages of testimony, and a national colloquium, attended by over 150 judges, lawyers, law and social science scholars, and members of the public. The hearings and colloquium focused on recent developments in the states that have politicized the judiciary and on demographic trends affecting how courts conduct their business.

The Commission recognizes that effective, independent and impartial judicial systems require the trust and confidence of the public, which must understand and care about its courts. A set of enduring principles underscores the importance of an independent, impartial judiciary to uphold the rule of law in a constitutional, democratic republic. Challenges to these enduring principles are identified. Recommendations serve as a framework for the ABA and the states to address and counteract the developments that are adversely affecting the fair and impartial administration of justice.

Eight enduring principles should be central components to each state's understanding of the role of the judiciary as a co-equal branch of government. These principles recognize that judges should uphold the rule of law and be impartial and independent, while possessing the appropriate temperament and character, as well as appropriate capabilities and credentials. Moreover, judges should have the confidence of the public and the justice system should be diverse, reflecting the society it serves. Finally, judges should be constrained to perform their duties in a manner that promotes public trust and confidence in the courts.

A number of factors and trends have led to the excessive politicization of state courts. Among these are the proliferation of controversial cases generally; the rediscovery of state constitutions as a basis to litigate constitutional rights and responsibilities; the increases in caseload; the interposition of intermediate appellate courts between trial courts and courts of last resort; the spread of the two-party system; the emergence of single-issue groups; and the presence of a skeptical and conflicted public. Additional challenges for the judiciary include changes in classes of litigants, including a trend towards pro se litigation and its impact on the role of the trial judge; changes in the demographic composition of America, with concomitant impact on the public's confidence in the courts; and changes in the role of the courts, including the rise of problem-solving courts.

These factors and trends contribute to increased politicization of the courts, placing the fair and impartial administration of justice at risk. Increasingly expensive state judicial campaigns focus on narrow issues of intense political interest, contributing to the public's perception that judges are influenced by their contributors. Some of the most partisan and misleading campaign related speech comes in the form of "issue advertising." The viability of judicial ethical standards are at risk, especially in light of recent judicial decisions, including that by the U.S Supreme Court in Republican Party of Minnesota v. White, limiting some ethics rules. The pronounced lack of diversity in the judicial system inhibits public trust and confidence in the courts, as do apparent trends in the relationships between courts and legislatures that too often have been problematic, manifested by attempts to cut the judiciary's budget, curb court jurisdiction, remove judges from office, and constrain courts' constitutional interpretations.

Thirty-one recommendations address the challenges threatening state courts at the beginning of the 21st Century. The first set of recommendations is designed to preserve the judiciary's institutional legitimacy by enhancing judicial qualifications, training, evaluation, ethical standards and diversity. The second set of recommendations is designed to improve judicial selection by encouraging appointment of judges who serve for long terms with limited opportunity for reselection while offering a number of alternatives for jurisdictions that continue to elect and retain judges. The final set of recommendations is designed to promote an independent judicial branch that works effectively with its coordinate branches of government.

An independent judiciary guarantees every citizen access to a branch of government designed to protect the rights and liberties afforded by federal and state constitutions and to resolve disputes peacefully and impartially. Fundamental to this unique role of the courts is the necessity for the judiciary to be distinct from the other two branches of government, functioning independently to ensure an effective role in the American tradition of a republican form of government. The differences unique to the judiciary, manifested in ethical restrictions on judges, judicial selection methods, and the nature of the judicial process, are vital aspects of maintaining balance among the branches of government. With the promulgation of a comprehensive set of recommendations, the Commission on the 21st Century Judiciary provides a call to action that will maintain independent, impartial state judiciaries, functioning as effective, co-equal branches of government, for generations to come.

AMERICAN BAR ASSOCIATION COMMISSION ON THE 21ST CENTURY JUDICIARY

PRINCIPLES AND CONCLUSIONS
AUGUST 2003

I. **ENDURING PRINCIPLES**

A. Judges should uphold the law.
B. Judges should be independent.
C. Judges should be impartial.
D. Judges should possess the appropriate temperament and character.
E. Judges should possess the appropriate capabilities and credentials.
F. Judges and the Judiciary should have the confidence of the public.
G. The judicial system should be diverse and reflective of the society it serves.
H. Judges should be constrained to perform their duties in a manner that justifies public faith and confidence in the courts.

II. **PRESERVING THE JUDICIARY'S INSTITUTIONAL LEGITIMACY**

A. **Judicial Qualifications, Training and Evaluation**

-   States should establish credible, neutral, non-partisan and diverse deliberative bodies to assess the qualifications of all judicial aspirants so as to limit the candidate pool to those who are well qualified.
-   The judicial branch should take primary responsibility for providing continuing judicial education, that continuing judicial education should be required for all judges, and that state appropriations should be sufficient to provide adequate funding for continuing judicial education programs.
-   Congress should fully fund the State Justice Institute.
-   States should fully fund the National Center for State Courts.
-   States should develop judicial evaluation programs to assess the performance of all sitting judges.

B. **Judicial Ethics and Discipline**

- The American Bar Association should undertake a comprehensive review of the Model Code of Judicial Conduct.
- The codes of judicial conduct should be actively enforced.

C. Diversification of the Justice System

- Members of the legal profession should expand their use of training and recruitment programs to encourage lawyers who reflect diversity to join their firms, they should include them fully in firm life, and they should prepare them for pursuing careers on the bench following their years in practice.
- Courts should promote a representative work force and diverse court appointments.
- Courts should act aggressively to ensure that language barriers do not limit access to the justice system.
- Courts should have in place formal policies and processes for handling allegations of bias.
- Information regarding diversity should be shared among the courts in a state and among the states.
- Measures should be adopted to improve and expand jury pool representation.

D. Improving Court-Community Relationships

- Courts should take steps to promote public understanding of and confidence in the courts among jurors, witnesses and litigants.
- Courts should engage and collaborate with the communities of which they are a part, by hosting trips to courthouses and by judges and court administrators speaking in schools and other community settings.
- The continuation of problem-solving courts as a means to promote public confidence in the courts.

III. IMPROVING JUDICIAL SELECTION

A. The preferred system of state court judicial selection is a commission-based appointive system, with the following components:

- The governor should appoint judges from a pool of judicial aspirants whose qualifications have been reviewed and approved by a credible, neutral, non-partisan, diverse deliberative body or commission.
- Judicial appointees should serve until a specified age. Judges so appointed should not be subject to reselection processes, and should be entitled to retirement benefits upon completion of judicial service.

- Judges should not otherwise be subject to reselection, nonetheless remain subject to regular judicial performance evaluations and disciplinary processes that include removal for misconduct.

B. Alternative Recommendations on Systems of Judicial Selection

- For states that cannot abandon the judicial reselection process altogether, judges should be subject to reappointment by a credible, neutral, non-partisan, diverse deliberative body.
- For states that cannot abandon judicial elections altogether, elections should be employed only at the point of initial selection.
- For states that retain judicial elections as a means of reselection, judges should stand for retention election, rather than run in contested elections.
- For states that retain contested judicial elections as a means to select or reselect judges, all such elections should be non-partisan and conducted in a non-partisan manner.
- For states that continue to employ judicial elections as a means of judicial reselection, judicial terms should be as long as possible.
- For states that use elections to select or reselect judges, states should provide the electorate with voter guides on the candidate(s).
- For states that use elections to select or reselect judges, state bars or other appropriate entities should initiate a dialogue among affected interests, in an effort to deescalate the contributions arms race in judicial campaigns.
- For states that use elections to select or reselect judges, state bars or other appropriate entities should reach out to candidates and affected interests, in an effort to establish voluntary guidelines on judicial campaign conduct.
- For states that do not abandon contested elections at the point of initial selection or reselection, states should create systems of public financing for appellate court elections.
- For states that retain contested judicial elections and do not adopt systems of public financing, states should impose limits on contributions to judicial candidates.

IV. **PROMOTING AN INDEPENDENT JUDICIAL BRANCH THAT WORKS EFFECTIVELY WITH THE POLITICAL BRANCHES OF GOVERNMENT**

- Standards for minimum funding of judicial systems should be established.
- The judiciary's budget should be segregated from that of the political branches, and it should be presented to the legislature for approval with a minimum of non-transferable line itemization.
- States should create independent commissions to establish judicial salaries.
- States should create opportunities for regular meetings among representatives from all three branches of government to promote inter-branch communication as a means to avoid unnecessary confrontations on such issues as court funding, judicial salaries, and structural reform of courts.

Chair's Introduction

Chair's Introduction

"The common task in which we [the bench and the bar] are all engaged — the great and sacred task — the administration of justice"
Justice Benjamin Cardozo

The thirty thousand state court judges who constitute the judicial branches of our fifty states conduct 98% of the country's legal business. Each state's judiciary has the function of providing able and impartial administration of the state's justice system and ensuring justice for all who come before its courts. The trust and confidence of the public are essential to the success of the judiciary.

In recent years state judiciaries have been the subject of several professional surveys to determine how they are viewed by the public. As might be expected the results are in some respects positive, some negative and occasionally inconsistent.

Given the far flung, diverse nature of the fifty states, it is inappropriate to generalize; however, a closer look at these surveys as well as more recent developments suggest that trust and confidence in our judicial systems are on the wane and apathy and dissatisfaction are on the rise, more so in some states than others. Unless checked and addressed, the ability of the state judiciaries to fulfill their constitutional obligations in a democratic republic will be in jeopardy, with deleterious effects for the American system of justice and experiment in self government.

Our tasks are to identify the factors contributing to these trends, suggest ways to improve the current environment in which courts operate, and draw attention to the ramifications if we do nothing. We have taken our tasks seriously, devoting many hours and much attention, guided by and taken advice from many persons with broad expertise and experience.

Despite the fact that the American system of justice remains the model for emerging democracies around the world, our exercise over the past few months reveals that there are storm clouds gathering that jeopardize the American judiciary's role as the template for establishing judicial organizations.

Whatever its historic rationale there can no longer be justification for contested judicial elections accompanied by "attack" media advertising that require infusions of substantial sums of money. These contested elections threaten to poison public trust and confidence in the courts by fostering the perception that judges are less than independent and impartial, that justice is for sale, and that justice is available only to the wealthy, the powerful, or those with partisan influence.

Present and anticipated state and municipal budget deficits have and will continue to impact adversely allocations to the judiciary resulting in reduction or even elimination of core judicial services.

Within communities of color—that together will comprise a majority of the American people by the middle of this century—concern that they receive unequal, inferior treatment in the courts is compounded by a lack of confidence due to the lack of diversity throughout the judiciary. The perception of two forms of justice— one for the wealthy and one for the poor — is widespread. Unless promptly addressed, one witness colorfully suggested that t "Equal Justice Under Law" should be sand-blasted from the Supreme Court Building.

Other constituencies are distrustful of the judicial system especially in jurisdictions that have become magnets for tort litigation as they perceive the playing field as not level.

The politics of crime imposes intense pressure on judges to decide criminal matters in a manner that satisfies popular expectations.

Judicial branches are increasingly viewed by Legislative and Executive branches as impediments to policy implementation rather than as a partner, a coequal branch of government, in doing the people's business, with negative impacts for allocation of adequate resources.

There is a growing concern that the courts are not meeting the public's expectations in areas involving domestic relations, family violence, juvenile justice and substance abuse.

There is political opposition to support structural changes in the judiciary that would increase economical and efficient judicial administration.

These trends provide cautions and concerns to which we must devote attention and resources – intellectual and financial. The promise of America is broken if the public thinks that judges are captured by special interests, controlled by the wealthy and powerful, and unconcerned about the rights of racial, ethnic and political minorities.   Our system of justice must contribute to fulfilling that promise.

The required ingredients for "able and impartial" administration of justice are qualified judges knowledgeable as to their roles and responsibilities and adequate resources supported by the coordinate branches of government to allow the judiciaries to meet, if not exceed, public expectation. It may be that these questions attract the most attention when addressing the problems affecting the judiciary.

But they are not the only issues that must be addressed in this area. The ABA's commitment to supporting judicial independence over the past few years reflects just how broad attention to these issues must be. President N. Lee Cooper convened the ABA Special Commission on Separation of Powers and Judicial Independence, which issued its report on July 4, 1997. Although focusing on the federal judiciary, the Commission noted that the challenges faced by the state judiciaries far outstripped those affecting the federal courts. Based at least in part on this assessment, President Jerome J. Shestack appointed a special committee on judicial independence, which had an immediate impact by encouraging ABA policy to assist those judges who found themselves on the wrong end of personal vindictive that impugned the trust and confidence of the public in the judicial branch. The response to this initiative from the states reflected the depth of concern about challenges to judicial independence at the end of the 20th Century.

The Association's commitment to these issues was strengthened when this special committee was transformed into a standing committee and President Philip S. Anderson appointed Alfred P. Carlton, Jr., as chair. During the next three years, this Committee, undertook important work, including the development of Standards for State Judicial Selection and a seminal proposal for public financing of judicial campaigns. These projects contributed to legislative proposals around the country to improve judicial selection processes, including the 2002 enactment in North Carolina of the nation's first full public financing law for judicial campaigns.

During this time, other improvements were encouraged. The ABA Model Code of Judicial Conduct was amended to limit bad effects from judicial campaigns upon recommendations from the ABA Task Force on Lawyers' Political Contributions. President Anderson convened symposia that encouraged new thinking about judicial independence and public trust and confidence in the justice system. Indeed, in cooperation with the League of Women Voters, the Conference of Chief Justices and the Conference of State Court Administrators, the ABA under President Anderson participated in a national conference addressing weaknesses in the public support for the justice system.

Our work builds on these past experiences but is necessarily forward looking. President Carlton, in convening this Commission, advised us on more than one occasion to be bold, to think creatively, and not to be timid. The commission members, and their helpful advisory committee, represent a variety of viewpoints, including those of lawyers, judges, legal scholars, legislators, business executives, and citizens. Our experiences are diverse but our commitment is singular and focused: to identify the enduring principles of an independent judiciary and the circumstances that are diminishing these principles and to recommend strategies to preserve an environment that is true to the ideals of Adams, Hamilton and other Founders for an independent judiciary in a democratic republic.

Our able reporter, Professor Charlie Geyh, commissioned experts in several aspects of state judiciaries who provided us with excellent "white papers" that both gave us extensive background and prepared us for our first hearing, which was held in Detroit a week following the 2002 ABA Annual Meeting. The white papers are reprinted as appendices to this report. We have proceeded from there — meeting regularly, challenging each other and devising new ideas. We held three additional public hearings in three other disparate regions of the country — Philadelphia, Portland (Oregon), and Austin. We heard from more than 25 witnesses, ranging from state chief justices, law school deans, law and politics scholars, citizen advocates, corporate general counsel, plaintiff trial attorneys, judicial ethics administrators, bar association presidents and others. The transcripts of these hearings encompass more than 1,000 pages. We invited and received submissions from many others interested in our proceedings and ABA staff provided literally thousands of pages of studies, reports, and other resources. The Commission was most well informed, from its collective experiences and the perspectives shared with us by those who participated in its many activities. Our collective thinking has been refined by a colloquium focusing on draft findings and recommendations, where those interested enough to travel to Raleigh, N.C., probed and examined the intricacies of the commission's draft report. The final report is better for that experience in the marketplace of ideas.

Our approach has been shaped by obvious but perhaps often overlooked aspects of efforts to improve the administration of justice in the state courts. We know that no system of judicial selection has yet been devised that is either criticism-free or free from potential political manipulation. We know that no system of justice will be able to satisfy the aspirations of all those citizens who are touched by a goal of equal justice under law. Yet we strive to do the best we can with the resources that are available. Our examination of how this is occurring at the beginning of the 21st Century has been hopefully broad and thorough.

Perhaps we can summarize the objective of those interested in improving the environment for equal justice under law by noting that the goal is to attract able, qualified persons for judicial office and to provide a climate for their continuance in judicial office that shields them from improper, outside influences. It is noteworthy that the founding fathers, most notably Adams and Hamilton, found little bases for debate as to a selection and tenure mechanism that would attract able and qualified persons, choosing presidential nomination and Senate confirmation with "good behavior" - basically lifetime tenure. Elections came into play in states in the early 19th century and debate has ensued ever since over the relative merits of the "best" means to select judges, with the result that there are varied and hybrid systems in place in states throughout the country and today there is agitation, if not organized initiatives, for change in many states.

If we were writing on a clean slate, based on what we now see in how judicial campaigns have come to be conducted and in light of the Supreme Court's recent decision in Minnesota Republican Party v. White, and its impact on the future, judicial elections would gradually be abandoned. Rather, in the 21st Century a preferred system of state court judicial selection would be a "commission-based appointive" system with components that are set forth in the report that follows.

But we write not on the clean slate but in recognition of the varied approaches of the citizens of the 50 states through their Constitutions have dealt and continue to deal with the conundrum of judicial selection. We offer recommendations as to changes in various existing election methodologies and urge that efforts to improve how judicial elections are conducted must continue, such as the trend to nonpartisan campaigns and the use of public financing mechanisms, in the face of difficulties to eliminate the use of judicial elections. Any selection system should be accompanied by a sound code of judicial ethics accompanied by effective, enforced judicial disciplinary procedures.

What follows is an effort to sound a warning bell. Our collective experiences confirm that the American judiciary is special, a work in progress to accomplish what had not been done before by ensuring that independent and impartial judges are motivated by the law rather than by fear or favor. Our collective examination confirms that the American judiciary is at risk, its capacity to provide impartial decision making as an independent branch sanctioned by the federal and state constitutions threatened by partisan and financial exigencies that are infiltrating a system based on the rule of law. As these trends in American life and law can be identified at the beginning of the 21st Century, it is time now to expend leadership to maintain a feature that is as indispensable to American life as any other American institution — the uniquely independent American judiciary.

Edward W. Madeira, Jr.
Philadelphia, Pennsylvania
August 2003

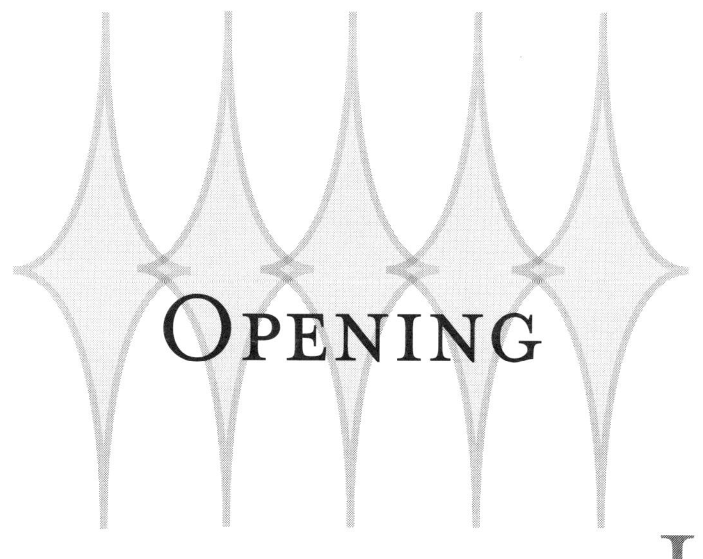

OPENING

SECTION I

Opening

The judicial systems of the United States remain unparalleled in their capacity to deliver fair and impartial justice. This report explores the serious challenges that confront our judicial systems in the twenty-first century and seeks ways to address them. The focus on problems that our judiciary faces should not obscure the Commission's enormous sense of pride in and commitment to our system of justice generally and our judicial systems in particular, which remain second to none in the world. It likewise should not be construed to impugn the dedication, integrity, or capabilities of the extraordinary women and men who are elected or appointed to serve our nation as judges. And in dwelling on the distance we have yet to travel, we must not forget the practicing lawyers who have brought us this far through their work in state and local bar associations. Their support, financial and otherwise, for qualified judges and judicial candidates, and their simple devotion to protecting and preserving an independent and impartial judiciary, must be acknowledged.

In short, ours is a great judiciary, and our goal is to make certain that it remains so. In that spirit, we must report that all is not well. Although our judicial systems have served us long and admirably, they are systems in serious jeopardy. They are being jeopardized by the corrosive effect of money on judicial election campaigns, in which some lawyers, businesses, and others interested in the outcomes of cases seek to gain advantage in the courtroom by influencing at the ballot box who will be judges. These infusions of campaign dollars have often been spent on attack advertising calculated to persuade a majority of the electorate that incumbent judges should be removed from office because they have made unpopular rulings in isolated cases or are beholden to their own campaign contributors. Not all states have experienced such problems, but the number that have is growing rapidly.

Such developments threaten to poison public trust and confidence in the courts by fostering a series of perceived improprieties: that judges are less than independent and impartial, that justice is for sale, and that justice is available only to the wealthy and powerful or to political and racial majorities. Within communities of color—that together will comprise a majority of the American people by the middle of this century—suspicion of the courts is compounded by a lack of diversity throughout the justice system. And these increasingly jaded views of the judiciary have begun to filter their way into the halls of state legislatures, where general assemblies often take a combative posture toward the judiciary when appropriating monies to fund court budgets and salaries.

The time has come to inoculate America's courts against the toxic effects of money, partisanship, and narrow interests.

An independent judiciary is essential in a democracy governed by the rule of law. In our system of government, the people create constitutions that identify their individual rights, empower legislatures to make laws consistent with the terms of those constitutions, and authorize governors to faithfully execute the laws that legislatures make. The laws that the people establish in their constitutions, that legislatures enact in statutes, and that governors execute are intended to protect everyone: the rich, the poor, the majority, the minority, the powerful, and the powerless. In order for that objective to be realized—that the law protect the one as well as the many—it is imperative that the administration of justice not become a popularity contest. We need judges who will tell us what the law is and how it applies in individual cases without regard to what the results of the latest opinion poll are, what the judge's campaign contributors think, or what the political agendas of influential public officials may be. In other words, we need judges who are independent enough to uphold the rule of law, even when the law is unpopular. If the constitution is flawed, the solution is for the people to amend it. If a statute is flawed, the solution is for the legislature to revise it. The solution is not to intimidate a judge into declaring that the law says something it does not because that will serve only to undermine the rule of law, upon which a constitutional democratic republic depends.

As important as an independent judiciary is to the rule of law in a representative democracy, public trust and confidence are equally so. The consent of the governed is a defining feature of democracy. Without it, democratic institutions must inevitably collapse. That is especially true of the judiciary, which controls neither the sword nor the purse and must depend on public acceptance for its continued existence as an independent branch of government. To the extent that significant segments of the public think that judges are captured by special interests, controlled by the wealthy and powerful, and unconcerned about the rights of racial, ethnic, and political minorities, our system of justice is in very serious trouble.

This is not the first time that our courts have been imperiled. The cyclical threats that our state and federal courts have weathered are familiar to many. Our nation was barely a decade old when the newly elected Jeffersonian Republicans sought to purge the federal courts of strident federal judges at the turn of the nineteenth century.[1] A generation later, Jacksonian Democrats attempted to control and, in some cases, defy state and federal courts. In the aftermath of the Civil War, Radical Republicans embarked on an aggressive program of court curbing. A generation later, populists and progressives pursued numerous strategies to subdue conservative, Lochner-era

---

[1] EMILY FIELD VAN TASSEL AND PAUL FINKELMAN, IMPEACHABLE OFFENSES: A DOCUMENTARY HISTORY FROM 1787 TO THE PRESENT 91-107 (1999).

courts on the state and federal levels, culminating in President Franklin Delano Roosevelt's court-packing plan. And two decades thereafter, hostility toward the Warren Court led to threats to defy its rulings and remove its justices.[2]

To say that our courts have been at risk before, however, is not to counsel complacency. To the contrary, it is only because those committed to the well being of the judiciary responded to crises by stepping into the breach and defending or reforming the courts that the judiciary's health has been assured. Nor does the recurrent nature of the challenges the courts have overcome imply that the problems the courts currently confront are no different from those of the past.

Ours is an ambitious project: to review the state of America's courts and to address their most pressing needs for the coming century. To accomplish such an objective, it may help to place our efforts in historical context. Nearly a century ago, the last great court reform movement began when Roscoe Pound gave an address titled "The Causes of Popular Dissatisfaction with the Administration of Justice" to the American Bar Association. In that address, Pound isolated four primary sources of dissatisfaction.

The first was "causes for dissatisfaction with any legal system." The second was "causes lying in our Anglo-American legal system." Unlike the first two sources of dissatisfaction, which Pound regarded as inherent in legal systems generally or our American system in particular, the third—"causes lying in American judicial organization and procedure"—he viewed as remediable. It is here that Pound focused his reform agenda.

The fourth and final source of dissatisfaction that Pound discussed was related to "causes lying in the environment of our judicial administration." Here, Pound called specific attention to "public ignorance of" and lack of interest in judicial systems; to the "strain" borne by law to replace "absolute theories of morals" that had "lost their hold" upon society; to the "putting of our courts into politics" and "compelling judges to become politicians," which had "almost destroyed the traditional respect for the Bench," and to the press for creating the "impression that administration of justice is but a game."

Pound regarded this final source of dissatisfaction as one that reformers could not remedy because it "inhere[d] in the circumstances of an age of transition." In some sense, it is a little odd that he should dedicate the entirety of his reform agenda to addressing the penultimate cause of dissatisfaction he identifies and closes not with a bang but a whimper by detailing a final cause of dissatisfaction that he viewed as unavoidable. It is prescient, however, in that this last cause of dissatisfaction with the courts that Pound left dangling is

---

[2]*Id.* at 54-59.

the one that confounds us most a century later and is the one to which we devote the bulk of our attention in this report.

It is perhaps understandable that Pound gave short shrift to problems within the "environment of our judicial administration" that he attributed to an "age of transition." He may have assumed that these problems would disappear once the transition was complete. But over the course of the past century, the pace of cultural, social, political, and technological change has accelerated to the point of placing us in a state of perpetual transition. The problems to which Pound referred—the politicizing of our courts; public apathy toward, distrust of, and lack of familiarity with our judicial systems; and friction over the roles played by courts and legislatures in what would become an age of legal realism—have not been transitory but have become entrenched. As a consequence, his assessment that these problems "will take care of themselves" has proved overly optimistic.

As the U.S. Supreme Court has observed, courts serve as "havens of refuge for those who might otherwise suffer because they are helpless, weak, outnumbered or because they are nonconforming victims of prejudice and public excitement."[3] Our judicial system is second to none in the world in upholding the rule of law for the benefit of majority and minority alike. But problems nearly a century in the making have recently worsened dramatically, driving that system to the brink of crisis. Now is the time to do something about it.

Commission Mandate

American Bar Association President Alfred P. Carlton Jr. has directed our Commission:

> To provide a framework and ABA policy that enable the Association to defuse the escalating partisan battle over American courts; to accommodate the principles of merit selection in a new model of judicial selection that minimizes the escalating politicization; to develop a set of guiding principles for an independent, accountable, and impartial judiciary in the twenty-first century; to involve broad-based constituencies of the legal and nonlegal communities in devising the necessary framework.

The first clause of our charge articulates the Commission's goal: to create a framework for addressing and alleviating the extent to which our courts have been excessively politicized. The remainder directs us to pursue this goal in three ways: by exploring how to improve judicial selection; by articulating principles to promote an independent and accountable judiciary; and by reaching out to the widest possible audience in developing recommendations for defus-

---

[3]Chambers v. Florida, 309 U.S. 227, 241 (1940).

ing the partisan battle over the courts and thereby preserving the principles that ensure judicial independence and accountability.

The logical starting point in the Commission's analysis is with the principles that ought to guide the twenty-first century judiciary—enduring principles underscoring the importance of an independent, impartial judiciary in a constitutional democratic republic that upholds the rule of law and maintains the trust and confidence of the people whom the judiciary serves. Once these principles have been enumerated in Part I of this report, we will describe in Part II recent developments among the states, including but not limited to events occurring in the context of judicial selection that have politicized the judiciary in ways that challenge some of those enduring principles. Finally, we offer in Part III a series of recommendations to serve as a framework for the ABA and the states to begin to address and counteract developments that have politicized the courts unnecessarily.

Enduring Principles

In 1780, nearly a decade before the United States Constitution was ratified, the Commonwealth of Massachusetts adopted a constitution of its own, drafted in large part by John Adams. The document begins with a declaration of rights, Article XXIX of which provides:

> It is essential to the preservation of the rights of every individual, his life, liberty, property, and character, that there be an impartial interpretation of the laws, and administration of justice. It is the right of every citizen to be tried by judges as free, impartial and independent as the lot of humanity will admit.

The aspirations Adams articulated for the fledgling judiciary of the late eighteenth century apply with equal force to the judiciary of the twenty-first century. Embedded in his simple declaration are several principles that should be isolated and emphasized.

Before launching into that discussion, however, it bears emphasis that while all states should strive to promote the following principles for all their judiciaries and judges, this is not to say that all states must employ the same means to promote those ends for all judges. Within any given state, the problems confronting the high court of a state may be significantly different in nature or severity from those confronting the trial courts, which may call for very different solutions. Among states, fundamental differences in constitutional structure, history, and culture may make certain reforms desirable and viable in some jurisdictions but not others.

For example, the Massachusetts constitution that John Adams devised sought to promote an independent and impartial judiciary by providing that its judges would be appointed to serve during good behavior. Beginning roughly fifty years later, a number of states concluded that they could better serve the ends of judicial independence (in addition to other objectives) by selecting their judges in partisan elections on the theory that judges who derived their authority directly from the people would be stronger and more independent than those who had been appointed by the governor. Another fifty years thereafter, around the turn of the twentieth century, several states determined that partisan elections made judicial candidates too dependent on the political parties for their nomination and sought to make judges more independent by opting for nonpartisan judicial races. And beginning in the early part of the twentieth century, yet another group of states began to decide that contested elections did not adequately promote a capable, qualified, and independent judiciary and devised a system of appointment based on "merit," in which voters would later have an opportunity to retain or oust the judge in retention elections.

We thus confront a patchwork of judicial selection systems across the states, each of which is designed to achieve the same goal of promoting an independent, impartial judiciary. While generalizations concerning the desirability of particular reforms are sometimes possible, respect for state autonomy and an appreciation for interstate differences counsel caution in that regard.

That much said, it bears emphasis that each of the approaches to judicial selection described above was the product of a different movement emerging over the course of our history. It has been close to a century since the last of those movements began its course. The time is ripe for a fresh look at an old problem.

Principle 1: Judges should uphold the rule of law.

In our system of government, "we the people" ordain, establish, and, in so doing, consent to be governed by organic laws known as constitutions. The U.S. and state constitutions structure the federal and state governments and enumerate the rights of the people that the government must respect. Those constitutions have structured our governments as representative democratic republics, in which the people elect representatives to make and execute statutory laws that govern them.

Representative democratic republics depend for their success upon the rule of law in two critical respects. First, the rules of law that the people's representatives have embodied in statutes will serve their purpose only if they are honored through observance and enforced when they are broken. Second, those who make and implement the statutory law must respect both the limits on their own power and the rights of the people as required by the higher law of the constitution.

The all-important task of upholding the rule of law by determining what the constitutional and statutory law requires and bringing it to bear in individual cases is one that our constitutions have delegated to judges. When constitutional or statutory law supports the position of an unpopular litigant or group, judges are required to uphold the law in favor of the minority, despite majority opposition. Thus, Adams was not overstating his point by declaring that if the "rights of every individual" are to be protected, it is "essential" that judges be willing and able to interpret and uphold the laws preserving those rights.

To say that judges should uphold the rules of law that the people and the political branches make warrants qualification. Under the common law, for instance, judges remain responsible for lawmaking. More importantly, the notion that constitutional or statutory law is sufficiently fixed and clear that judges can invariably divine its meaning uninfluenced by their personal or political experience is increasingly unrealistic. However, one can concede that constitutional and statutory law is sometimes subject to differing interpretations and still recognize that ambiguous law is nonetheless law, which judges have a duty to interpret and uphold. Indeed, it is ambiguity in the law and its application to specific cases that makes judges indispensable to the operation of government and the ultimate triumph of the rule of law.

Principle 2: Judges should be independent.

Governors and legislators are not expected to be independent of the people; to the contrary, these officials are expected to represent their respective constituencies by acting on the policy preferences of those who elected them. Judges, however, are different. Once voters' policy preferences are enacted into rules of law, it is up to judges to ensure that those rules of law are faithfully interpreted and upheld—an all but impossible task if judges are subject to the influence of threats, favors or constituencies that could endanger their unbiased judgment. Put another way, the rule of law would be corrupted if interest groups, public officials, powerful private citizens, or fleeting majorities of the public could intimidate a judge into interpreting a law to their liking or reading a law out of existence altogether. Unlike governors and legislators, judges must be, as John Adams urged us, as "independent as the lot of humanity will admit."

Although Adams extolled the virtues of judicial independence generally, it is possible to subdivide judicial independence into two distinct forms, both of which are instrumental to upholding the rule of law. First, judges must be independent enough individually to resist external efforts to influence inappropriately their decision making. In this regard, it is essential that a judge's interpretations and applications of law be controlled by what she construes the law to mean, and not by what others would coerce or cajole her into saying it means.

Second, judges must be independent enough collectively as a branch to resist institutional encroachments from the other branches of government that could place the judiciary—and the decisions its judges make—under the control of a political branch. On this point, the adequacy of judicial salaries, budgets, and working relationships with the other branches of government, among other concerns, may be critical to the judiciary's capacity to preserve its strength and institutional integrity. In sum, it is important that judges and the judiciary possess decision-making and institutional independence.

Principle 3: Judges should be impartial.

A primary goal of judicial independence, as Adams recognized, is "impartial interpretation of the laws." Judges occupy the role of umpires in an adversarial system of justice; their credibility turns on their neutrality. To preserve their neutrality, they must neither pre-judge matters that come before them, nor harbor bias for or against parties in those matters. They must, in short, be impartial if we are to be governed by the rule of law rather than judicial whim.

Judicial independence is necessary but alone may be insufficient to ensure impartiality. It is necessary because a judge who is not independent may be unable to remain impartial. If he is subject to external manipulation or control of his decision making, he may lack the capacity to be or remain open-minded and unbiased. Independence alone, however, is insufficient, because independence provides no guarantee of impartiality; a judge can be entirely independent but nonetheless biased and closed-minded. If independence alone is not enough to assure impartiality, the question becomes, What more is necessary?

Principle 4: Judges should possess the appropriate temperament and character.

If judges are to be impartial, they must not only be independent but also possess the appropriate judicial temperament. They must be committed to the rule of law. They must be women and men of integrity, who are evenhanded, open-minded, and unyielding to the influence of personal bias. They must be strong-minded and tolerant of criticism, yet resistant to intimidation. Then, and only then, can we be certain that an independent judge will be a truly impartial judge.

Principle 5: Judges should possess the appropriate capabilities and credentials.

Up to this point in the discussion, the focus has been on those principles that will assist in discouraging judges from consciously ignoring the rule of law because they are less than independent, are less than impartial, or lack the necessary judicial character or temperament. All of this assumes, however, that the judge is capable of ascertaining what the law is and how it should be enforced on a case-by-case basis. For this to be a safe assumption, however, the judge must possess the requisite intelligence, legal training, and experience.

The relevance of judicial temperament, character, capabilities, and credentials underscores the importance of the relationship between judicial selection and the rule of law. Judicial systems can and should be structured to provide judges and the judiciary with institutional and decision-making independence. But independent judges may not be impartial judges who will uphold the rule of law unless the pool from which their selection is made is carefully limited to those who possess the necessary temperament, character, capabilities, and credentials. That, in turn, may underscore the role that independent, deliberative bodies can and should play in defining the pool from which judicial candidates are elected or appointed.

Principle 6: Judges and the judiciary should have the confidence of the public.

The first five principles focus on those attributes needed to enable judges to uphold the rule of law. Even if judges follow the rule of law admirably and to the letter, however, it is also important that the public perceives them as doing so. When it comes to judges and the judiciary, appearances matter. That is why Canon 2 of the *Model Code of Judicial Conduct* declares that "a judge shall avoid . . . the appearance of impropriety in all of the judge's activities," and specifies in Canon 2(A), that a judge "shall act at all times in a manner that promotes public confidence in the integrity and impartiality of the judiciary." And that is why, in the federal system, judges must recuse themselves not only when the judge "has a personal bias or prejudice concerning a party," but also when a judge's "impartiality might reasonably be questioned."

Appearances matter because the public's perception of how the courts are performing affects the extent of its confidence in its judicial system. And public confidence in the judicial system matters a great deal for at least two reasons. First, and perhaps foremost, public confidence in our judicial system is an end in itself. A government of the people, by the people, and for the people rises or falls with the will and consent of the governed. The public will not support institutions in which they have no confidence. The need for public support and confidence is all the more critical for the judicial branch, which by virtue of its independence is less directly accountable to the electorate and, thus, perhaps more vulnerable to public suspicion.

Second, public confidence in the courts is a means to the end of preserving an independent judiciary. If the public loses its faith in a judiciary it perceives to have run amok, the obvious solution will be to bring the judiciary under greater popular control to the ultimate detriment of judicial independence and the rule of law that judicial independence makes possible.

The importance of public confidence in the courts is difficult to overstate. The ability of the courts to serve their purpose in a constitutional democratic republic turns on the public's acceptance and support. Without it, an otherwise sound judiciary cannot long endure.

Principle 7: The judicial system should be racially diverse and reflective of the society it serves.

Principle 7 follows naturally from Principle 6. The courts are required to protect all the people, and not just popular majorities, and, for that reason, an assessment of the extent of public confidence in the courts must go beyond cursory reviews of general public opinion surveys. If certain segments of the public—defined along racial, ethnic, economic, or other lines—do not share the majorityty's faith in the judiciary, it is a problem that must be addressed. Principle 5 underscored the importance of a judge's qualifications and credentials, while Principle 6 emphasized the need for public trust and confidence in the judicial system. Given the need for promoting public confidence in the judiciary within segments of the community that have become increasingly suspicious of the courts, efforts to diversify the bench may fairly be regarded as a qualifications issue, as well as one germane to promoting public confidence.

A multitude of witnesses testified before the Commission as to the relationship between the need for greater racial and ethnic diversity in the justice system and the institutional legitimacy of that system. For instance, polling data that reflect dramatically lower levels of public confidence in the courts among African American citizens signal a very serious problem that will only get more acute as our population becomes increasingly diverse, unless something is done about it now.[4] For these reasons, the Commission has devoted considerable attention to this issue.

Much of what the Commission has said with respect to diversification of the judiciary along racial and ethnic lines applies to gender and other aspects of diversity as well. The battle to diversify the judiciary along gender and other lines is likewise tied to the institutional legitimacy of our courts, and we would be remiss not to call attention to it. For example, state and federal courts have commissioned gender bias studies that reveal serious issues with respect to the manner in which female lawyers, witnesses, jurors and court personnel have been treated by judges, lawyers and court staffs.[5] While women are achieving greater entry into the ranks of the bench and bar, much improvement is still needed to ensure that women are appropriately represented at all levels of the justice system. As women continue to gain ground within the justice system generally and the judicial sys-

---

[4] National Center for State Courts, HOW THE PUBLIC VIEWS THE STATE COURTS: A 1999 NATIONAL SURVEY, at 7.

[5] The Unfinished Agenda: Women and the Legal Profession, American Bar Association Commission on Women in the Profession, 7 (2001).

tem in particular, the watchword must be vigilance, not complacency, to ensure that progress toward greater diversity continues.

We are becoming a more and more diverse people. Our judiciary and the judicial system (including judges, clerks, staff, lawyers, and juries) should reflect the diversity of the society in which we live. If they do not, the legitimacy of the courts and the judicial system will be called into question with increasing frequency.[6]

Principle 8: Judges should be constrained to perform their duties in a manner that justifies public faith and confidence in the courts.

Judicial independence has its limits. While we do not want judges to be dependent on any individual or group that might impair their capacity to apply the law fairly and without favoritism, neither do we want judges to exercise power arbitrarily. The judge who acts arbitrarily undermines both the rule of law and the public's confidence in the judicial system.

Judicial independence, then, must be tempered by judicial accountability. We are mindful that the phrase "judicial accountability" is subject to misuse. It can be employed in the service of those who would, in the name of "judicial accountability," obliterate judicial independence and the rule of law altogether by intimidating judges into contorting the law to reach results that are popular with temporary majorities of the public. In our view, however, accountability should be defined more narrowly, to serve the principles of a good judicial system that we enumerate here.

Principle 1, for example, declares that judges should uphold the rule of law; those who do not should be accountable to an appellate process that corrects judicial error. Principle 2 declares that judges should be independent; those who compromise their independence by taking bribes should be held accountable to criminal and impeachment processes. Principle 3 declares that judges should be impartial; judges who exhibit bias in individual cases should be held accountable to a recusal process. Principles 4 and 5 declare that judges should maintain the appropriate temperament and competence; if they do not, they should be accountable to a disciplinary process.

Taken together, then, these processes for promoting this eighth principle of accountability advance the goals of principles 1 through 5. At least as important, if not more, these processes will further the cause of Principles 6: enhancing public confidence in the courts.

---

[6]The American Bar Association House of Delegates adopted a principle addressing diversity in broader terms. (See Appendix A for policy adopted by the ABA.)

Recent Developments

SECTION 2

Recent Developments

Having spelled out some of the principles that have guided our state and federal judiciaries in the past and, in the Commission's view, should continue to guide them in the future, we turn now to the task of describing recent developments that have politicized the American judiciary. "Politicize" is an amorphous term. The self-evident definition of "politicize" is "to make political," and if "political," is defined innocuously to mean pertaining to the "structure or affairs of government,"[7] then a "politicized judiciary" is an untroubling truism. When we speak in terms of making the judiciary more "political," however, we typically mean to say making judges more like politicians, and the judiciary more like the political branches. Even then, a "politicized" judiciary is not invariably problematic. The judiciary, like the political branches, should be answerable for its budget, subject to improvements in the efficiency of its operations, and open to criticism. Moreover, to the extent that judges are asked to uphold the rights of the politically unpopular and are subject to intense criticism when they do, this additional pressure that judges bear may be part of the price we pay for the rule of law. It is only when the courts are politicized in ways that undermine the defining principles of a good judiciary enumerated in the preceding part of this report that problems arise.

A. The Politicizing of State High Courts

Although the recent developments this report discusses are categorized in terms of their application to lower courts and high courts, this is at best a rough means of classification. As we emphasize again later, many of the problems we describe here in our discussion of appellate courts also apply to lower courts. By the same token, some of the problems we elaborate upon later in our discussion of lower courts—such as the lack of diversity within the judiciary—apply equally to the appellate courts.

1. Trends Contributing to the Politicizing of State High Courts

A confluence of trends has contributed to making state high courts more politicized. Some of these trends are generations in the making and reflect fundamental changes in the role of American courts over time. These trends, described in this subsection, have created an environment conducive to the emergence of problems to which we turn in the subsection that follows.

a. *The proliferation of controversial cases generally*

Commission consultant G. Alan Tarr reports on "the increasing involvement of courts, particularly in recent decades, in addressing

---

[7] The American Heritage Dictionary 960 (2d Coll. Ed. 1982).

issues with far-reaching policy consequences," which he characterizes as a "major development with implications for judicial independence."[8] Professor Robert Kagan noted the beginnings of this trend a generation ago, when he observed that courts had recently become "less concerned with the stabilization and protection of property rights, more concerned with the individual and the downtrodden, and more willing to consider rulings that promote social change."[9] Consistent with Professor Kagan's observations on state courts, in the federal system only 296 civil rights suits were commenced in 1961, as compared to 34,027 cases thirty years later.[10] The expanding civil rights docket is one manifestation of a trend toward increased judicial involvement with policy-laden social and political issues that has embraced a wide range of subjects—from environmental protection to the rights of criminal defendants, abortion, political apportionment, education funding, and the liability of entire industries for toxic torts..[11] It bears emphasis that our intent is not to criticize these developments as deleterious but to describe the confluence of events that have contributed to the political pressure under which our courts operate.

Explanations for this trend are many, varied, and sometimes contradictory. Some attribute it to lawyers who have encouraged litigation into controversial arenas.[12] Others point to judges and their alleged propensity toward greater judicial activism.[13] Still others, such as former Chief Justice Warren Burger, have argued that the people themselves labor under a "mass neurosis," which leads them to "think that courts were created to solve all the problems" of society.[14] And still others explain the development in terms of a "law explosion" in which legislatures have expanded the range of statutory remedies available to litigants.[15]

It is beyond the scope of our project to divine the root cause for this trend toward increased judicial decision making on politically sensitive subjects or to applaud or condemn it. Suffice it to say that while the courts have always heard cases on highly controversial

---

[8] G. Alan Tarr, *State Judicial Selection and Judicial Independence, in* JUSTICE IN JEOPARDY: REPORT OF THE ABA COMMISSION ON THE 21ST CENTURY JUDICIARY, Appendix D, at 6 (2003).

[9] Robert Kagan et al., *The Business of State High Courts, 1870-1970,* 30 STAN. L. REV. 121, 155 (1977).

[10] Elizabeth Norman & Jacob Daly, *Statutory Civil Rights,* 63 MERCER L. REV. 1499, 1499-1500 (2002).

[11] Richard Birke & Louise Teitz, *U.S. Mediation in 2001: The Path that Brought America to Uniform Laws and Mediation in Cyberspace,* 50 AM. J. COMP. L. 181, 183-85 (2002) (discussing categories of cases contributing to the "litigation explosion").

[12] *See generally,* WALTER OLSON, THE LITIGATION EXPLOSION: WHAT HAPPENED WHEN AMERICA UNLEASHED THE LAWSUIT (1991).

[13] *See generally,* MAX BOOT, OUT OF ORDER (1998); THE GLOBAL EXPANSION OF JUDICIAL POWER (C. Neal Tate & Torbjorn Vallinder, eds.) (1995).

[14] Warren Burger, *Using Arbitration to Achieve Justice,* 40 ARB. J. 3, 5 (1985).

[15] Albert Alschuler, *Mediation with a Mugger: The Shortage of Adjudicative Services and the Need for a Two-Tier System in Civil Cases,* 99 HARV. L. REV. 1808, 1817-18 (1986).

issues, they may be doing so now more than ever, which places the courts in the middle of politically charged situations with unprecedented frequency.

b. The rediscovery of state constitutions

While federal and state courts both witnessed an upsurge in the controversial, policy-laden cases they were called upon to decide in the latter half of the twentieth century, this trend has become especially noticeable in state court systems. In her report to the Commission, consultant Emily Field Van Tassel observes "the politicization of state constitutional decision making coincides with the 'new federalism' of the Reagan era and the willingness of many state appellate courts to look to their own constitutions for guidance in many areas of law previously left to the federal constitution."[16] Professor Tarr concurs that this "rediscovery of state constitutions" called upon state judges to "shape the law of their states" and reports that this development was encouraged by social reform groups that "began to look to state courts as a new arena in which to pursue their goals" as the U.S. Supreme Court became increasingly unsympathetic to their agenda.[17]

As Tarr implies, state courts do not explore novel questions of state constitutional law on their own initiative but rule on such questions because litigants ask them to do so. As social reform groups began to shift the focus of their efforts toward the less familiar terrain of state constitutional law, state courts were called upon to explore this new frontier. Often times, state constitutions have been read no differently than their federal counterpart. In some instances, however, state courts have read the text of their constitutions differently than comparable text from the U.S. Constitution as construed by the Supreme Court. In other instances, state constitutions explicitly provide for the protection of rights that the federal constitution does not.

Our essential point here is not normative but descriptive. Whether these recent developments reflect a salutary change in which state courts are protecting rights too long neglected or a troubling one in which those courts are overstepping traditional bounds is well beyond the scope of our report. Our point is simply that state courts have become a new forum of choice for litigation of constitutional rights and responsibilities, which has placed them in the political spotlight with increasing frequency.

---

[16] Emily Field Van Tassel, *Challenges to Constitutional Decisions of State Courts and Institutional Pressures on State Judiciaries, in* JUSTICE IN JEOPARDY: REPORT OF THE ABA COMMISSION ON THE 21ST CENTURY JUDICIARY, Appendix E, at 3 (2003).

[17] *See also* William Brennan, *State Constitutions and the Protection of Individual Rights*, 90 HARV. L. REV. 489 (1977).

c. Increases in appellate caseload and the interposition of intermediate appellate courts between trial courts and courts of last resort

The National Center for State Courts (NCSC) reports that "starting in the 1950s and continuing through the 1980s, the number of cases filed in state appellate court systems grew to the point that caseloads were doubling nearly every ten years."[18] The center adds, that "[i]n response, states established two-tiered appellate court systems."[19] As of 1958, only thirteen states had established intermediate appellate courts.[20] Today they are in place in forty-one states.[21]

The success of intermediate appellate courts at reducing state high court workload has been mixed. Often, high courts have experienced temporary relief in the years after intermediate appellate courts were created but gradually returned to their earlier state of congestion.[22] To provide the state high courts with an additional means of docket control, many states have coupled the creation of courts of appeals with adjustments to the supreme court's appellate jurisdiction, which has given the highest court greater discretion to decline appeals from decisions of the intermediate courts.[23] This has put the high courts in a position to limit their caseload by allowing the courts of appeals to serve as courts of last resort in routine or "easy" cases and confine the cases they hear to important, difficult, and often controversial matters.[24] As a consequence, the percentage of the high courts' docket dedicated to politically sensitive cases is greater, and the likelihood that its decisions will more routinely generate political controversy is correspondingly higher.

d. The spread of the two-party system

Tarr identifies the spread of two-party competition throughout the United States as "one of the most dramatic changes during the latter half of the twentieth century." The relationship between this development and the politicizing of the judiciary is readily apparent. States without meaningful two-party competition typically foster less rancorous judicial races than states where competition between the parties is intense. The decline of single-party dominance in many states over the course of the past generation—particularly in the

---

[18] B. Ostrum and N. Kauder, Examining the Work of the State Courts, 1999-2000: A National Perspective from the Court Statistics Project 76 (2000).

[19] Id.; see also Robert Kagan et al., The Evolution of State Supreme Courts, 76 Mich. L. Rev. 961, 972-81 (1978).

[20] Victor Eugene Flango and Nora Blair, Creating an Intermediate Appellate Court: Does it Reduce the Caseload of a State's Highest Court?, 64 Judicature 75, 77 (1980).

[21] Peter Murray, Maine's Overburdened Law Court: Has the Time Come for a Maine Appeals Court?, 52 Me. L. Rev. 43 (2000).

[22] Flango and Blair, supra note 20, at 84.

[23] G. Alan Tarr et al., State High Courts in State and Nation 49 (1988); Ostrum and Kauder, supra note 18, at 76.

[24] Tarr et al., supra note 23, at 49.

south—has corresponded with increasingly fractious judicial campaigns in those jurisdictions. Heated campaigns of the past decade in Alabama, Florida, Georgia, Louisiana, Mississippi, North Carolina, and Texas are illustrative. Even states with ostensibly nonpartisan general elections for judges, such as Michigan and Ohio, have experienced highly politicized races when two-party competition is fierce and the party affiliations of the candidates are widely known.

e. The emergence of a skeptical and conflicted public

The preceding developments have not been lost on the general public, which shows signs of becoming increasingly skeptical of the view that judges are apolitical decision makers who simply interpret and apply the law. Tarr attributes this growing skepticism to two trends: a "general decline of confidence in the major institutions of American society" and the "lessons of legal realism," which have filtered down from the legal community to the general public and left it with a deeper appreciation for the law's indeterminacy and susceptibility to political influence. Attorney James Bopp Jr. made the point more bluntly in his testimony before the Commission: "[T]he secret is out . . . . Judges in the United States make law and the people in the United States know that."[25]

Survey data lend support to this observation. A New Mexico survey conducted in the mid-1990s revealed that 61 percent of respondents disagreed with the proposition that "[p]olitics do not influence court decisions in New Mexico."[26] More recently, a national survey commissioned in 2001 by the Justice at Stake Campaign asked whether the term "political" accurately described judges, and 76 percent responded that it described them "well" or "very well."[27]

It would be premature, however, to deduce from this survey data that the public simply rejects the notion that judges follow the rule of law and embraces the view that political considerations do or should be permitted to dominate judicial decision making. Although 76 percent of respondents in the Justice at Stake Campaign survey thought that judges were "political," 79 percent of that same group believed that judges were "dedicated to facts and law." When asked whether judges "make decisions based more on facts and law," or "more on politics and pressure from special interests," 58 percent answered the former. In short, the public is alert to the interplay between politics and law, believes that both are involved in judicial decision making,

---

[25]*ABA Commission on the 21st Century Judiciary*, Detroit, Mich. 234, (Aug. 21, 2002) (testimony of James Bopp Jr., Attorney). In light of the enduring principles that we have developed to guide the 21st Century judiciary, it all but goes without saying that we do *not* believe that judges do or should "make law" as legislators do. Our point is limited to one of public perception.

[26]State Bar of New Mexico & Admin. Office of the Courts, Community Survey of Lawyers and the Legal System, §16 at xi (1997).

[27]Justice at Stake Campaign, *National Survey of American Voters* (2002) *available at* http://faircourts.org/files/JASNationalSurveyResults.pdf.

and is divided as to which is more influential—with a relatively slender majority believing that law trumps politics.

f. The emergence of single-issue groups

Tarr discusses the emergence of single-issue groups and their relevance to politicizing the judiciary in his consultant's report. In the latter half of the twentieth century, interest groups formed to promote a specific political issue have become increasingly prominent in American politics generally and more recently have begun to involve themselves in judicial politics. Several consultants have reported to the Commission on roles played by such groups as the Florida Right to Life Committee, the Chamber of Commerce, Oklahomans for Judicial Excellence, Citizens for a Strong Ohio, and the National Rifle Association in seeking to influence the outcomes of judicial elections. The potential for single-issue groups to influence judicial races may be heightened by the general absence of voter interest and participation, insofar as it may then be easier for a comparatively small, highly motivated block of voters to affect the results.

By their very nature, these groups politicize judicial elections because they seek to link an incumbent's tenure in office to her position on a single, politically incendiary issue. It is unsurprising, therefore, that these groups have been at the center of several of the most troubling developments described below.

2. Specific Problems Arising out of Heightened Politicization of State High Courts

The trends described in the preceding subsection have created a politicized climate among state high courts in which a series of troubling developments have recently occurred.

a. State high court election campaigns are increasingly focused on isolated issues of intense political interest.

As state high courts began to decide more politically sensitive cases in a climate of increased two-party competition, with voters believing that politics influences judicial decision making, and with single-issue voter groups seeking to gain ground in judicial races, it was inevitable that high court campaigns would become more contested and that those contests would center on one or two "hot button" cases decided by those courts. In some instances, attempts to punish judges with loss of tenure for making unpopular decisions in these cases have been explicit. One notable example occurred in the aftermath of a retention election in Tennessee, in which the governor remarked: "Should a judge look over his shoulder [when making decisions] about whether they're going to be thrown out of office? I hope so."[28]

---

[28]Stephen Bright, *Political Attacks on the Judiciary*, 80 JUDICATURE 165, 166 (1997).

Without disputing the right of voters to elect whom they choose for whatever reason they deem persuasive, there is an obvious tension between this right and the preference of 78 percent of those polled in a recent survey, who believed that courts "should be free of political and public pressure."[29] As Florida Justice Ben Overton observed, "It was never contemplated that the individual who has to protect our rights would have to consider what decision would produce the most votes."[30] Putting judges in such a position complicates considerably the principles that a judge should be independent, impartial, and uphold the rule of law.[31]

It is worth noting that the problems posed by hinging the outcome of judicial races on one or two politically sensitive issues are most acute in the context of campaigns in which an incumbent is up for reelection or retention. To be sure, there may be problems associated with placing pressure on would-be judges to compromise their future impartiality by revealing how they would decide an especially incendiary issue. But it is incumbents who are put at future risk of losing their tenure when they uphold unpopular laws, invalidate popular laws, or protect the rights of unpopular litigants. In such cases, it is incumbents who are thus presented with the impossible choice of sacrificing either their careers or their independence and the rule of law.[32] In thinking about the relationship between politicized judicial elections and the threats they can pose to judicial independence, therefore, it is important to differentiate between the issues that arise in the context of initial selection and those that arise later in the context of retention or reelection.

The issue at stake in these hot-button cases has varied from jurisdiction to jurisdiction:

Criminal cases: Commission consultant Jeannine Bell[33] indicates that "state court judges around the country" have been challenged

---

[29]Justice at Stake Campaign, *supra* note 27.

[30]Bright, *supra* note 28, at 166.

[31]Note that such dilemmas potentially faced by judges are not limited to the election context. In Virginia, "an otherwise routine public hearing on judicial nominations" in the House of Delegates erupted into a heated interrogation when House Speaker S. Vance Wilkins, a staunch gun-control opponent, noticed that the judge before him had issued a controversial pro-gun-control ruling. While Wilkins foreswore any attempts to keep the judge off the bench, "the speaker's unusual personal interest" caused some to speculate whether "past rulings in gun-related cases could become litmus tests for reappointment to judicial posts." R.H. Melton, *House Speaker Presses Judge on Case*, WASHINGTON POST, January 25, 2002, at B08.

[32]By example, a West Virginia editorial, pointing to state judges' lack of life tenure as the reason the state's powerful coal and labor interests prefer state over federal venues, asks: "What [state] judge is going to take on the coal industry? . . . What are the chances that any three of any five Supreme Court justices ever in office would want to simultaneously take on both the coal industry and the labor movement?" Dan Radmacher, *State Courts Best for the Status Quo*, CHARLESTON, W.V. GAZETTE, May 4, 2001.

[33]Jeannine Bell, *The Politics of Crime and the Threat to Judicial Independence, in* JUSTICE IN JEOPARDY: REPORT OF THE ABA COMMISSION ON THE 21ˢᵗ CENTURY JUDICIARY, Appendix F, at 5 (2003).

because of their rulings in capital and other criminal cases. Among the examples Bell includes:

> • In 1992, Florida Justice Rosemary Barkett's retention was opposed by the National Rifle Association and a group of prosecutors and police officers on the grounds that she was "soft on crime."

> • In 1992, Mississippi Justice James Robertson lost his re-election bid on the basis of a death penalty decision the justice wrote.

> • In 1995, a sitting South Carolina justice was challenged for the first time in over a century, on the grounds that she was "soft on crime."

> • In 1996, The Tennessee Conservative Union and other groups successfully campaigned for the defeat of Tennessee Justice Penny White on account of a decision she joined overturning a death sentence. In the next election cycle, Justice Adolpho Birch Jr. resisted a challenge to his retention based upon his decision in the same case.

> • In 1999, a candidate challenged the Wisconsin chief justice's dissent from a decision upholding the constitutionality of the state's child predator law, suggesting that predators would be free to prey on children if the incumbent had her way.

> • In some cases, judges have been supported or attacked for their positions on criminal justice issues by groups concerned about other issues less likely to play well with voters. For example, one group whose Web page explained that it was launching a multistate advertising campaign in judicial races to "stop the tidal wave of new lawsuits," ran ads in Mississippi focused entirely on the victims' rights records of the candidates.[34]

> • It is also apparent that pressure on judges to decide criminal cases in certain ways is being brought to bear indirectly in the context of political, rather than judicial campaigns. In 2002, U.S. Senator Frank Murkowski, a candidate for governor of Alaska, delivered a campaign speech in which he criticized Alaska judges for "cuddling criminals," and he vowed to "alter" the judicial selection system to favor tough-on-crime judges."[35]

Civil cases: Commission consultants Carl Tobias and Andrew Spalding report to the Commission that in several jurisdictions, corporate defendants and their lawyers have been alarmed by a concentration of recent tort cases filed in a small group of counties in a handful of states that have yielded "spectacular" punitive damages

---

[34]Emily Heller & Mark Ballard, *Hard-Fought, Big-Money Judicial Races: U.S. Chamber of Commerce Enters Fray With Ad Money,* The National Law J., Nov. 6, 2000, at A1.
[35]*Tough on . . . Judges?,* Anchorage Daily News, August 16, 2002.

awards.[36] More generally, court decisions on issues of tort reform and defendants' liability in products and medical malpractice cases have occupied center stage in a number of judicial races. These decisions have prompted segments of the business community to lobby more aggressively for tort reform legislation. A number of states have responded by passing tort reform legislation, the constitutionality of which has then been challenged, often successfully. In turn, that has prompted the plaintiffs' trial bar and the business community to redirect their attention toward judicial campaigns. The net effect has been an escalating cycle of contributions and single-issue advertising campaigns in a number of jurisdictions around the country.

- In Alabama, a 1987 supreme court decision invalidating tort reform legislation has triggered an increasingly expensive battle for control of the court, in which some commentators have characterized judicial elections as "referenda on the trend of the court."

- In Illinois, business groups vowed to focus on the 2002 state supreme court race, amid predictions that the cost of the race could exceed $2.5 million. The catalyst for the business groups' interest was an earlier decision striking down tort reform legislation.

- The Commission heard testimony from several witnesses, including ABA President-Elect Dennis Archer and Michigan Bar Association President Reginald Turner, on the 2000 Michigan Supreme Court races, which featured multimillion dollar campaigns with ads attacking and defending justices regarded as business friendly.

- In the Commission's hearing in Detroit, Michigan, several witnesses, including Ohio Chief Justice Thomas Moyer, Dean Joseph Tomain of the University of Cincinnati College of Law, and political consultant Bill Burges alluded to the 2000 election campaign of Ohio Justice Alice Resnick, who was criticized in ads run by the Chamber of Commerce after writing the majority opinion in a case striking down tort reform legislation.

- A recent study reports that in Idaho, Louisiana, Ohio, and Michigan, "business groups . . . are preparing 'simplistic and misleading' evaluations of how judges vote in environmental and other cases and using the results as the basis for supporting the judges for re-election or targeting them for defeat."[37]

---

[36] Carl Tobias & Andrew Spaulding, *Civil Justice and Judicial Selection, in* Justice in Jeopardy: Report of the ABA Commission on the 21st Century Judiciary, Appendix G, at 3 (2003).

[37] Susan Finch, *Court Races Linked to Ecological Battles*, New Orleans Times-Picayune, October 31, 2000.

Additional constitutional and statutory issues: Van Tassel[38] reports on a number of additional races in which other discrete constitutional cases have served as a focal point in judicial races.

> • In the 1998 California Supreme Court elections, Chief Justice Ronald George and Justice Ming Chin withstood challenges to their retention based on their rulings in abortion cases.

> • In Florida, Justice Leander Shaw's retention was opposed on the basis of his ruling in an abortion case.

> • In Idaho, Justice Cathy Silak lost her re-election bid, in large part because of her decision in a federal water rights case.

> • In 1998, opposition to Ohio Justice Paul Pfeifer focused on his decision in a school-funding case decided under the Ohio Constitution (which was also an ancillary issue in the reelection battle of Resnick in 2000).[39]

b. Judicial races are becoming more expensive.

One natural consequence of judicial elections becoming more competitive and heated is that more money is spent on judicial campaigns. In 2001, the ABA Commission on Public Financing of Judicial Campaigns found that "[t]he cost of running judicial election campaigns is increasing dramatically across the country," and offered illustrations from eleven different states in support of that proposition. Since 1994, campaign expenditures by supreme court candidates have increased by over 100 percent, and by 61 percent between 1998 and 2000 alone.[40] In 1995-96, average spending for 116 judicial candidates was around $260,000. In 1997-98, it had risen to an average of over $340,000 for 95 candidates; and in 1999-2000, 116 candidates spent an average of $431,000.[41]

During the 2000 election cycle, more than a million dollars was spent on supreme court races in each of nine states, including Alabama, Illinois, Michigan, Mississippi, Nevada, North Carolina, Ohio, Texas, and West Virginia.[42] It bears emphasis, however, that there is tremendous variation among the states in campaign spending, with candidates in some states spending little or nothing.[43] One possible explanation for the variation may lie in the nature of the

---

[38]Van Tassel, *supra* note 16, at 5-7.

[39]Thomas Suddes, *Editorials and Forum*, CLEVELAND PLAIN DEALER, May 6, 1998, at 11B.

[40]Deborah Goldberg et al., *The New Politics of Judicial Elections* 4 (2002) *available at* http://brennancenter.org/resources/resources_books.html#ji.

[41]*Id.* In Montana, the 2000 race for Chief Justice of the state Supreme Court was "one of the state's costliest" election campaigns of any branch, with each candidate raising more than one-third of a million dollars. Erin P. Billings, *High Court Race Getting Expensive*, BILLINGS GAZETTE, May 23, 2000.

[42]Goldberg et al., *supra* note 40, at 4.

[43]*Id.*, at 5

issues at stake in the different campaigns. Lawyers and business interests constitute the two most significant sources of contributions to judicial races nationally, and it is therefore reasonable to assume that spending will be greatest in those states where the issues at stake are those of greatest importance to lawyers and business. Consistent with that assumption, the four states with the highest spending levels—Alabama, Illinois, Michigan, and Ohio—were states where the hot-button issue was tort-related liability, a matter of acute interest to plaintiff's trial lawyers, on the one hand, and the business community on the other.[44] In Illinois, for example, lawyers contributed more than $60,000 to Appellate Court Justice Melissa Chapman's campaign. Her opponent was able to raise only one-tenth as much money, with little of it coming from lawyers.[45]

It would be an overgeneralization to suggest, as some have, that these competing interests are driven simply by a crass desire of plaintiffs or defendants to "buy" judges in jurisdictions where they happen to sue or be sued. As Thomas Gottschalk explained from the perspective of General Motors, his company does business, hires employees, and litigates frequently in every state of the nation. As a "virtual… resident in the courts of most states," his company became concerned by the size of punitive damages awards in cases decided by courts in a limited number of jurisdictions and lobbied legislatures to reform their tort laws.[46] For its part, the plaintiff's trial bar challenged the constitutionality of tort reform legislation in states across the country and increased its contributions to judicial races, which in turn prompted increased contributions by business interests. The net effect was to create a cycle of escalating contributions from all concerned, driven less by a scheme to manipulate case outcomes than a mutual desire to level the playing field.

The spiraling cost of judicial campaigns may not in and of itself threaten the core principles identified in Part I of this report. It does, however, contribute to a series of related problems described below. As Tomain testified before the Commission:

> Money is the elephant in the room on judicial selection. It raises serious questions, such as how much money is required for judicial election, from whom does it come, what is the public perception, and so on.[47]

---

[44] *Id.*

[45] Kevin McDermott, *Lawyers Give Big to Judges' Campaigns*, ST. LOUIS DISPATCH, September 9, 2002.

[46] *ABA Commission on the 21st Century Judiciary*, Austin, Tex. 184-96 (Nov. 22, 2002) (testimony of Thomas Gottschalk, General Counsel, General Motors).

[47] *ABA Commission on the 21st Century Judiciary*, Detroit, Mich. 163 (Aug. 21, 2002) (testimony of Joseph Tomain, Dean, University of Cincinnati College of Law).

c. The public believes that judges may be influenced by their contributors.

As judicial races have become more expensive and hotly contested, the need to generate campaign contributions sufficient to cover escalating costs has become increasingly important. The sources of campaign contributions can be difficult to determine, although a 2002 study by the Brennan Center for Justice and the National Institute on Money in State Politics, The New Politics of Judicial Elections, has been able to ascertain the contributor interests associated with 76 percent of the contributions to high court races between 1989 and 2000. It found that 29 percent of total contributions came from lawyers; 19.8 percent from general business; 11.8 percent from political parties; 7.8 percent from the candidates themselves; and the remaining 7.6 percent of identifiable contributions from labor interests, small contributions, other ideological groups, public subsidies, and other contributors.

We should caution against making too much of these statistics. For example, one might assume that the lawyers who make contributions to the campaigns of supreme court justices would typically be state supreme court litigators, but that does not appear to be the case. In Michigan, for example, lawyers constituted 23 percent of all contributors, but 80 percent of those lawyer-contributors never appeared before the court during the eight years under study. Studies in Illinois and Wisconsin have yielded comparable results. And while 89 percent of the cases coming before the Michigan Supreme Court featured at least one participating contributor, the contributors participating in litigation before the court together comprised only 4.5 percent of all contributors to the campaigns of court members (and contributed only 6.2 percent of all funds).[48] Finally, there is no evidence to demonstrate that contributing to a judicial campaign increases the contributor's likelihood of success in cases before the court.[49]

A perception problem nonetheless remains. Lawyers and businesses—the two most significant sources of campaign contributions—have an obvious interest in the outcomes of cases decided by the judges whose campaigns they help finance. As judicial candidates become ever more dependent on campaign contributions from lawyers and business for their continuation in office, it is unsurprising that the public has come to suspect campaign contributions of influencing judicial decision making. One survey commissioned by the American Bar Association in 2002 found that 72 percent of

---

[48] *See* Samantha Sanchez, *Campaign Contributions and the Michigan Supreme Court: Report of the National Institute on Money in State Politics* (Jan. 2003) *available at* http://www.followthemoney.org/reports/mi/20020129/MI.phtml.

[49] Dawson Bell, *Good News About Judicial Fairness Gets Overlooked*, DETROIT FREE PRESS, May 25, 2002.

respondents were extremely, very, or somewhat concerned that "the impartiality of judges is compromised by the need to raise campaign money to successfully run for office."[50] Seventy-six percent of respondents in the Justice at Stake Campaign survey believed that campaign contributions exert some or a great deal of influence on judicial decisions.[51] Fifty-five percent went so far as to agree with the statement that judges were "beholden to campaign donors," and 52 percent agreed that judges were "controlled by special interests."[52]

These results are consistent with earlier surveys conducted in several states. In Ohio, a 1995 survey reported that nine out of ten residents believed that campaign contributions influenced judicial decisions.[53] In Pennsylvania, a 1998 poll sponsored by a special commission appointed by the Pennsylvania Supreme Court also found that nine out of ten voters believed that judicial decisions were influenced by large campaign contributions.[54] In Illinois, a 2002 survey sponsored by the nonpartisan Illinois Campaign for Political Reform showed that 85 percent of respondents agreed that campaign contributions influenced the decisions of judges.[55] In New Mexico, a poll conducted by the state's Administrative Office of the Courts revealed a strong perception that judges' decisions are influenced by "political considerations" and by "having to raise campaign funds."[56] And in Texas, a 1998 survey sponsored by the state supreme court found that 83 percent of Texas adults, 69 percent of court personnel, and 79 percent of Texas attorneys believed that campaign contributions influenced judicial decisions "very significantly" or "fairly significantly."[57]

According to a Kansas editorialist, "[t]he money that is being contributed to the election campaigns of judges in parts of Kansas is compromising the integrity of the courts. Inevitably, people expect something in return for their contributions."[58] This notion was echoed by a Maryland judicial candidate, attorney Stuart Robinson, who in his 2002 race refused to accept campaign contributions. Calling his stance "a battle for the conscience and soul of our system," Robinson stated, "[T]here's a perception that if you contribute

---

[50]Harris Interactive, *A Study About Judicial Impartiality,* Prepared for the American Bar Association (August 2002) *available at* http://www.abanet.org/media/aug02/shell/ppt.

[51]Justice at Stake Campaign, *supra* note 27.

[52]*Id.*

[53]T.C. Brown, *Majority of Court Rulings Favor Campaign Donors,* The Cleveland Plain Dealer, February 15, 2000, at 1A.

[54]*See* A.B.A., *Report and Recommendations of the Task Force on Lawyers' Political Contributions, Part Two,* at Appendix Seven, 124-126 (1998).

[55]Steve Neal, *State Needs Fairer Way to Pick Judges,* Chicago Sun-Times, September 4, 2002.

[56]*Take Partisan Politics Out of Justice System,* The Santa Fe New Mexican, June 20, 2000.

[57]Supreme Court of Texas et al., The Courts and the Legal Profession in Texas - The Insider's Perspective: A Survey of Judges, Court Personnel and Attorneys, Executive Summary (May 1999) *available at* http://www.courts.state.tx.us/publicinfo/publictrust/execsum.htm.

[58]*Keep Judges Out of Politics,* Kansas City Star, November 18, 2002.

money, there's a payback down the road."[59] Such perceptions are perhaps inevitable where, as in Nevada, "[a]ttorneys who appear before judges, and casino officials whose companies sometimes have millions riding on rulings, are the ones who write the checks."[60] In Washington, an executive from an industry that had contributed the bulk of one supreme court candidate's sizable campaign war chest, said candidly: "[B]usinesses have a lot to lose in this election if the right person . . . isn't elected."[61]

Moyer summarized the concern well in his testimony before the Commission. There is "a perception from the people," he explained, "that money contributions to judicial candidates do[] affect their decision[s]." He noted that public suspicion of the extent of influence will vary, depending on "how much money" is at issue, "how educated the people are," and "whether they've served on juries." Regardless of "whether it's true or not," however, "with the judiciary, the perception is almost as important as the fact."[62]

d. Some of the most politicized and misleading campaign related speech comes in the form of "issue advertising" developed by outside groups.

In addition to the support that judicial candidates receive from direct contributions, candidates are often supported indirectly by independent campaigns that run their own advertising. A study of the 2000 supreme court election cycle reveals that of the $10.7 million spent on television advertising, outside groups accounted for $2.8 million, as compared to $6.4 million by the candidates' themselves and $1.5 million by the political parties. Although most of the dollars spent on television advertising came from the candidates, Craig Holman reported to the ABA Commission on Public Financing of Judicial Campaigns that 76 percent of all "attack ads"—ads attacking opponents, as opposed to promoting or comparing the candidates— were produced by independent groups.[63]

It has been this downward spiral of attack politics often run by independent groups—most notably in Ohio and Michigan—that Commission witnesses have found most problematic. Burges described the negative advertising campaign against Resnick, who was his client, by the group called Citizens for a Strong Ohio. Burges noted the challenge posed by independent campaigns is that contri-

---

[59]Michael Olesker, *To Candidate, Contributions May Seem to Tip Justice's Scales*, BALTIMORE SUN, August 29, 2002.

[60]Steve Sebelius, *Tipping the Scales of Justice*, THE LAS VEGAS REVIEW-JOURNAL, May 30, 2002.

[61]Angela Galloway, *Builders Backing Top-Court Candidate*, SEATTLE POST-INTELLIGENCER, October 25, 2002.

[62]*ABA Commission on the 21st Century Judiciary*, Detroit, Mich. 107 (Aug. 21, 2002) (testimony of Thomas Moyer, Chief Justice, Ohio Supreme Court).

[63]AMERICAN BAR ASSOCIATION, REPORT OF THE COMMISSION ON PUBLIC FINANCING OF JUDICIAL CAMPAIGNS, 15 (2001).

bution and disclosure limits applicable to the candidates do not apply to such groups, making it "hard for a state legal system to get their hands around it."[64] Although the campaign backfired and Resnick won re-election easily, Tomain told the Commission that he found the experience quite troubling. The negative advertising, which "more than impl[ied] that Justice Resnick was receiving bags of money from special interests," made him rethink his earlier view that "matters of quality and independence are not dependent upon a particular judicial selection process" and led him to become increasingly skeptical of "the continued use of elections for judicial processes."[65]

Archer testified that in Michigan the supreme court candidates themselves did not "engage in any negative campaigning," but that outside supporters did, the net effect of which undermined respect for Michigan's system of justice.[66] Turner went further, describing the episode as a "debacle," that dealt "a serious blow to public confidence in Michigan's judicial system."[67]

It is important to note that such developments are by no means confined to states such as Michigan and Ohio, where media exposure of the problem has been greatest. In a 2002 primary election for the Idaho Supreme Court, for example, a group calling itself Idahoans for Tax Reform "dumped an estimated $75,000 into ads against Supreme Court Chief Justice Linda Copple Trout and for challenger Starr Kelso."[68]

e. The public is insufficiently familiar with judicial candidates, judicial qualifications, and the justice system.

The developments described above place the electorate in a very difficult situation. High courts are deciding more and more controversial questions. Those questions are of central importance in judicial campaigns. The information voters receive concerning those questions is communicated largely via advertising run either by the candidates themselves with money from contributors whom the public suspects of buying influence or by outside groups whose largely unregulated and often misleading negative campaigns have helped to undermine public confidence in the courts. Uninformed about the candidates' positions on relevant issues, uncertain about the candidates' qualifications or training, and unfamiliar with the candidates' job performance, voters are often unable to cast an informed ballot

---

[64] *ABA Commission on the 21st Century Judiciary*, Detroit, Mich. 194 (Aug. 21, 2002) (testimony of Bill Burges, political consultant).

[65] *ABA Commission on the 21st Century Judiciary, supra* note 47, at 163.

[66] *ABA Commission on the 21st Century Judiciary*, Detroit, Mich. 18 (Aug. 21, 2002) (testimony of Dennis Archer, President-Elect, American Bar Association).

[67] *ABA Commission on the 21st Century Judiciary*, Detroit, Mich. 83 (Aug. 21, 2002) (testimony of Reginald Turner, President, State Bar of Michigan).

[68] Wayne Hoffman, *Task Force to Look at Role of Money in Judicial Campaigns*, Idaho Statesman, June 8, 2002.

and so decline to vote in judicial races. It is, therefore, not uncommon to see less than 20 percent of the electorate voting in judicial races[69] and as much as 80 percent of the electorate unable to identify the candidates for judicial office.[70]

One manifestation of this phenomenon is voter "roll-off," in which voters go to the polls and cast ballots for political branch candidates at the top of the ballot but decline to vote in judicial races at the bottom of the ballot. For example, Turner told the Commission that in 2000 there were 900,000 voters who voted for governor, attorney general, or secretary of state but did not vote in the supreme court races on the same ballot.[71] Thus, there is an obvious relationship between voter knowledge, voter apathy, and the extent to which judicial elections can promote meaningful judicial accountability.

On a more general note, there may also be an extent to which lack of familiarity with the justice system and its operations corresponds with a lack of public confidence in the courts. A survey conducted by the American Bar Association in 1999 found that only 17 percent of respondents could name the chief justice of the United States; only 39 percent could identify all three branches of the national government; and when the questionnaire identified the three branches, many respondents exhibited considerable confusion as to their respective functions.[72] The survey then asked respondents about their confidence in the justice system and found that "people who are most knowledgeable are those who have the most confidence in the justice system." [73] Although this conclusion is not free from doubt,[74] it is corroborated by other studies.[75]

---

[69]Stephanie Gauthreaux, *Judicial Race Vote Turnout Running Low*, The Baton Rouge State Times, December 8, 1990 (reporting 13-15 percent turnout in Louisiana judicial race); Erich Smith, *Election Watchdogs Expect Low Turnout in Philadelphia*, Associated Press, May 17, 1997 (reporting an anticipated 12 percent turnout as a sign of "traditional voter apathy toward judicial races"); Sharon Theimer, *Lavish Campaign Spending Doesn't Lift Voter Turnout*, The Wisconsin State Journal, April 3, 1997 (reporting 21 percent turnout in state supreme court race); William Yelverton, *Low Turnout, But Voters Had Some Surprises*, Tampa Tribune, September 5, 1996 (reporting 17.5 percent turnout in local Florida judicial races).

[70]Gene Nichol, *Better Justice, By Appointment*, The Raleigh News & Observer, May 10, 2001 (citing exit polls in a neighboring state revealing that "over 80 percent of voters said they had no idea who the judges they had just selected were"); *People Want to Elect Judges But Don't Know Them*, The Birmingham News, March 26, 2000 (reporting that between 80-85 percent of Alabamians could not identify 11 of 12 Supreme Court candidates).

[71]*ABA Commission on the 21st Century Judiciary*, supra note 67, at 83.

[72]American Bar Association, Perceptions of the U.S. Justice System, 19-21 (1999).

[73]*Id.* at 10.

[74]For example, a 1999 survey conducted by the NCSC found that "respondents who reported a higher knowledge about the courts expressed lower confidence in courts in their community." National Center for the State Courts, How the Public Views the State Courts: a 1999 National Survey, at 7 (1999). There is, however, a difference between respondents who *reported* a higher degree of knowledge in the NCSC survey and those who *exhibited* a higher degree of knowledge in the ABA survey; moreover, the "knowledge" at issue in the ABA survey concerns factual knowledge about the justice system, as opposed to more general knowledge that may be derived from personal experience with the justice system.

[75]American Bar Association, supra note 72, at 7-8.

f. The recent decision of the United States Supreme Court in Republican Party of Minnesota v. White, 536 U.S. 765 (2002), creates considerable uncertainty surrounding the constitutionality of ethical limits on judicial campaign speech.

Historically, state codes of judicial conduct have imposed significant limits on what judicial candidates may say in judicial races. They may not comment on pending cases,[76] take positions that appeared to commit them on issues that may come before the court,[77] appear at political functions,[78] or make promises of conduct in office.[79] This may help to explain why so much of the negative, case-specific advertising in judicial races has come not from the candidates themselves but from independent groups. In Republican Party of Minnesota v. White, however, the U.S. Supreme Court left the continuing validity of some—if not all—of these restrictions in doubt, when it invalidated on First Amendment grounds Minnesota's so-called "announce clause," which forbade candidates from announcing their views on disputed legal issues. Numerous witnesses before the Commission emphasized the significance of the White decision and the extent to which it will change the rules of judicial ethics and judicial elections across the country.

Some argue that the decision liberates candidates to communicate more information directly to voters and thereby offset the impact of misleading attacks by outside groups and address the information shortfall that discourages voters from participating more actively in judicial races. Bopp, who represented the Republican Party in the White case, testified before the Commission that in his view "preventing judicial candidates from expressing their general views is . . . decided" and that the "judicial canons frankly require a major revision" to be compliant with White. He regarded this as a positive step that the ABA should encourage rather than resist:

> Incumbent judges are most likely to be vulnerable to attacks
> . . .and the question is, are they going to be hamstrung? . . .
> There are just massive restrictions on judicial candidates that
> make judicial incumbents particularly victims of the process.
> They need to be allowed to participate . . . fully.[80]

Burges concurred. "If we're going to elect judges, then these races need to be political," he argued, and the candidates "need to be able to talk" because "if they can't, too much is taken out of their hands and the interest groups . . . will take over the entire debate."[81]

[76] AMERICAN BAR ASSOCIATION, MODEL CODE OF JUDICIAL CONDUCT CANON 3(B)(9) (1990).
[77] AMERICAN BAR ASSOCIATION, MODEL CODE OF JUDICIAL CONDUCT CANON 5(A)(3)(d)(ii) (1990).
[78] AMERICAN BAR ASSOCIATION, MODEL CODE OF JUDICIAL CONDUCT CANON 5(A)(1)(d) (1990).
[79] AMERICAN BAR ASSOCIATION, MODEL CODE OF JUDICIAL CONDUCT CANON 5(A)(3)(d)(i) (1990).
[80] *ABA Commission on the 21st Century Judiciary, supra* note 25, at 243–44.
[81] *ABA Commission on the 21st Century Judiciary, supra* note 64, at 207.

Others, however, worry that the decision in White threatens to compromise judicial independence and impartiality. Moyer testified that White had created a "treacherous" situation for candidates. As the chief justice noted, the decision invalidated a rule that prohibited judicial candidates from taking positions on issues likely to come before them but did not address the validity of a related rule that prohibits candidates from promising to decide those issues in particular ways. That enables candidates to "pound the podium and say, I believe, I believe, I believe, and never . . . commit, never pledge, but . . . it's disingenuous to think people don't walk away thinking, if that issue ever comes by that candidate, he or she will probably vote that way."[82]

Illustrative of Moyer's point is a questionnaire that Bopp circulated to Indiana judicial candidates on behalf of Indiana Right to Life, shortly after he testified before the Commission. In the cover memo accompanying the questionnaire, Bopp carefully distinguished between candidates "speaking their minds on controversial political or legal issues," which was appropriate after White and "pledges or promises," which, in Bopp's view, were not. Candidates were then asked whether they "believe that there is no provision in our current Indiana constitution which is intended to protect a right to an abortion;" whether they "believe that there is no provision of our current Indiana Constitution which is intended to protect a right to assisted suicide;" and whether they "believe that a person should be able to sue another because he or she was born alive with a disability rather than aborted."

Candidates cannot be required to complete questionnaires such as those circulated by Bopp. In the post-White environment, however, those who resist may be accused of hiding behind invalidated ethics restrictions and feel political pressure to take positions on controversial legal issues they are likely to decide as judges. As a 2002 editorial in the Idaho Statesman pointed out, a "no-holds barred judicial campaign" could result in "wild pledges on anything from gun control to abortion" which might "box in a winning candidate" and "force a good judge to issue a bad ruling just to make good on an election promise."[83] Moreover, to the extent that candidates become increasingly embroiled in disputes over their positions on issues likely to come before them as judges, the recent wave of attack politics that dominates many independent advertising campaigns may soon reach advertising sponsored by the candidates as well.

---

[82]*ABA Commission on the 21st Century Judiciary, supra* note 62, at 119.
[83]*Justice Should Be Blind: Must It Be Silent As Well?*, IDAHO STATESMAN, September 19, 2002.

g. Relationships between courts and legislatures have often been problematic.

The effects of trends contributing to politicized high courts have not been confined to judicial elections. The political branches of government have an interest in the cases those courts decide because the political branches represent the people affected by court decisions and because some of the cases those courts decide have a direct impact on the political branches. Legislatures typically control court budgets, judicial pay increases, court jurisdiction, judicial impeachment, and the means to propose amendments to, if not actually amend, state constitutions. Governors are the most visible and powerful political figures in their states, who—apart from their central role in judicial selection—are uniquely positioned to influence public debates on the role of the courts in the administration of justice. Insofar as these political branch actors use the weapons at their disposal to retaliate against courts for making unpopular rulings and to encourage them to be more attentive to the will of the majority when deciding cases in the future, the net effect is to politicize the judiciary and, in some cases, threaten its institutional integrity and independence.

Commission consultants have cataloged a number of recent episodes in which altercations between the political branches and their respective judiciaries have culminated in threats to the judiciary's budget or jurisdiction or in other proposals to exert greater control over the judiciary as an institution. This is not to imply that such episodes are new to our national experience. Nor is it to suggest that they are universal; Moyer, for example, testified that in Ohio, there was no evidence of the legislature retaliating against the courts. Nor is it our intention to characterize each of the interbranch altercations described below as independence threatening or otherwise inappropriate. Rather, the goal is simply to document recent legislative efforts to affect the courts in ways that may have further politicized the judiciary.

Attempts to cut the judiciary's budget

In his testimony before the Commission, Roger Hartley observed that there is a "great potential for court budgets to be threatened or even reduced in response to unpopular decisions" and that budgets have in fact "been used as a sword against courts."[84] There have been a number of instances reported by Commission witnesses, consultants, and in the press, in which the judiciary's budget was threatened in retaliation for unpopular decisions:

---

[84]*ABA Commission on the 21st Century Judiciary*, Portland, Or. 115-116 (Nov. 1, 2002) (testimony of Roger Hartley, Professor, University of Arizona School of Public Administration and Policy).

• Prior to oral arguments in a case involving Florida's Death Penalty Reform Act, the chair of the Florida House council in charge of court appropriations sent a note to members of the Florida Supreme Court stating that "your decisions continue to be a mockery to the victims and their families." The note identified him as chairman of appropriations and was interpreted by one newspaper as a budgetary threat.[85]

• The president of the Maryland Senate threatened to cut the budget of the state's highest court because of a constitutional decision. This occurred after the legislature had voted for two years running to withhold millions of dollars from the state budget for Baltimore's courts until court reforms requested by Baltimore's mayor were implemented.[86]

• Professor Aviam Soifer has described an episode in Massachusetts in which the legislature "used its budgetary power to slash funding crucial to the judiciary's infrastructure" in retaliation for the court upholding the clean elections law.[87]

• Lawyer Andru Volinsky, who testified before the Commission, noted that in New Hampshire "the court's budgets had pretty much been accepted by the legislature" until the court decided an unpopular school-funding case, at which point they began to receive cutbacks higher than state agencies. Volinsky surmised that "there's some animus there that motivates that,"[88] a point bolstered by the statements of the New Hampshire governor, who had proposed cutting court funding in response to the court's school-funding decision.[89]

• In North Carolina, Democratic legislators prepared a budget plan that sought to eliminate the judicial district of a judge who had ruled against the Democrats in a redistricting case. A Democratic senator acknowledged that the cuts were not unrelated to the judge's decision.[90]

• A recent survey of state court administrators and some legislative and executive budget officers found that over 36 percent of court administrators (15 respondents) and 28.9 percent of legislative budget officers (13 respondents) believed that their legislatures had threatened

---

[85]Lisa Getter & Mitchell Landsberg, *Decision 2000/America Waits*, LOS ANGELES TIMES, November 16, 2000, at A21.

[86]Matthew Mosk, *Legislative Antagonism to Courts Intensifying*, THE WASHINGTON POST, March 27, 2000, at B01.

[87]Aviam Soifer, *Legislators Seek to Undermine State's Separation of Powers*, BOSTON HERALD, October 13, 2002.

[88]*ABA Commission on the 21st Century Judiciary*, Phila., Pa. 136 (Sept. 27, 2002) (testimony of Andru Volinsky, Lawyer).

[89]*As Shaheen Plans are Foiled, Some Judges Fall Out of Favor*, BOSTON GLOBE, May 2, 1999.

[90]Scott Mooneyham, *State Budget Keeps Judiciary Cuts*, THE RALEIGH NEWS & OBSERVER, June 20, 2002.

(directly or indirectly) to reduce the judiciary's budget to "influence or protest court rulings or policies." Eleven court administrators and eight legislative budget officers responded that the legislature had actually reduced the judiciary's budget at least once for those reasons.[91]

• Cutting the judiciary's budget is not always perceived as specific retaliation for court policies or decisions. When Massachusetts acting Governor Jane Swift proposed to cut $37 million from state court budgets, a Boston Globe editorial observed that Massachusetts state courts are "kicked around like a football at the State House, whose leadership likes to show judges how limited their power is."[92]

Attempts to curb court jurisdiction

Several state court systems have confronted efforts to curb their jurisdiction in reaction to unpopular decisions. Van Tassel reports the following:

• After Florida's Supreme Court stayed the implementation of the Death Penalty Reform Act, the governor and legislature threatened to shift rule-making authority from the supreme court to the legislature.

• In both Ohio and New Hampshire, decisions invalidating the states' school financing schemes met with attempts to remove school-funding jurisdiction from the courts and give the legislature sole authority to determine what constitutes a "thorough and efficient education" under the state constitution.[93]

• In New Hampshire, the state legislature proposed a constitutional amendment that would dramatically reduce the state supreme court's power to make rules governing state courts.[94]

• New York Governor George Pataki attacked the state's high court for its strict interpretation of the exclusionary rule. He then proposed legislation that would deprive the court of authority to decide cases on unlawfully seized evidence under the state constitution.[95]

---

[91]Douglas & Hartley, *The Politics of Court Budgeting in the States: Is Judicial Independence Threatened by the Budgetary Process?* 63 Public Administration Rev. 441, Table 7 (July/August 2003).

[92]Adrian Walker, *A Matter of Justice*, Boston Globe, July 25, 2002.

[93]Catherine Candisky, *Two Senators Propose to Amend State Constitution in School Funding Debate*, Columbus Dispatch, March 4, 1999; Shirley Elder, *Supreme Court Controversies Have Staying Power*, Boston Globe, June 24, 2001; Randy Ludlow, *School Call: Skip Courts — Lawmakers Want Funding Control*, Cincinnati Post, March 4, 1999.

[94]*Removing Trump Card: Judicial Reform Not Up to Judges*, Manchester Union Leader, April 30, 2001.

[95]*The Governor's Attack on the Judges*, The New York Times, Feb 3, 1996, at A-14.

Attempts to remove judges from office

Van Tassel describes several incidents in which legislators have sought to remove judges or justices for making unpopular decisions:

> • After the Vermont Supreme Court ruled Vermont's system of funding schools unconstitutional, opponents sought removal of the justices of that court. Vermont's system gives the legislature the power over reappointment to the courts. Former Senator John McClaughry led the charge against the court, arguing that the court's reasoning in the school - funding case was enough "to fire [Justices] Dooley, Johnson and Morse."[96]

> • In New Hampshire, Chief Justice David Brock faced down an attempted ouster by bill of address in 1999, only to be impeached in 2000. Although the charges had to do with lax enforcement of the court's recusal rules, the removal attempts apparently had their roots in the court's school-funding ruling. Justice Brock was acquitted on the impeachment charges but amassed an estimated $1 million legal bill.[97]

> • In another school-funding case, a Wyoming senator threatened to begin impeachment proceedings against the state's supreme court justices for their decision in that case.[98]

Constitutional amendments to constrain the courts' constitutional interpretations

In several states, legislators have introduced constitutional amendments designed to constrain the courts' power to interpret the constitution.

> • Bell reports on a proposed constitutional amendment in Texas that would prevent the Texas courts from interpreting the protections of the Texas constitution more broadly than its federal counterpart.

> • Two members of the New Jersey State Assembly proposed an amendment to the state constitution that would deny the state supreme court's final authority to rule legislative actions unconstitutional. The proposed amendment would allow a two-thirds majority of both houses of the state legislature to override any state supreme court decision.[99]

---

[96]Ross Sneyd, *Senators Seek to Open Retention Process*, ASSOCIATED PRESS, Feb. 10, 1999.

[97]Shirley Elder, *Supreme Court Controversies Have Staying Power*, BOSTON GLOBE, June 24, 2001.

[98]*Senator Ready to Impeach Judges*, CASPER (WYOMING) STAR-TRIBUNE, June 9, 2001.

[99]Associated Press, *Lawmakers Want to Curtail New Jersey's Supreme Court's Power*, TRENTON TIMES, Dec. 12, 2000.

Van Tassel's report includes two other examples:

> • In Florida, a "forced linkage" amendment required state search-and-seizure provisions to be "construed in conformity with the 4th amendment to the United States Constitution, as interpreted by the United States Supreme Court." Political scientist Barry Latzer noted: "Before forced linkage, Florida Supreme Court cases rejected U.S. Supreme Court interpretations in favor of broader rights 80 percent of the time; after forced linkage the rejection rate dipped to 18 percent."[100]

> • In 1997, Washington state legislators sought a constitutional amendment that would give final authority to the legislature on issues of constitutional interpretation.

The general sufficiency of judicial budgets and salaries

There is little evidence to date that legislatures have actually withheld pay increases for judges in retaliation for unpopular decisions. This is not to say, however, that the issue of judicial salaries is immune from political branch manipulation. For example, when the Illinois Judges Association contemplated a suit challenging the constitutionality of the legislature's decision to deny state officials—including judges—an annual cost-of-living pay increase, one Illinois legislator warned that that "would not be a wise move on their part" because "those folks in the General Assembly will tend to remember that."[101]

When it comes to judicial salaries, however, the more pressing concern is that the strength of the judiciary as an institution depends on its ability to attract judges who embody the principles articulated in Part I of this report. As Professor Richard Creswell explained with respect to the Georgia courts, "Having an excellent system of administering justice . . . depends on having excellent personnel." That, in turn, requires judges to be:

> sufficiently supported with legal research tools, law assistants, clerical staff, educational opportunities, reasonable performance expectations, and compensation and benefits packages to make Georgia's judgeships successfully competitive with the many other attractive opportunities available to excellent lawyers.[102]

When judicial salaries are low or routine cost-of-living adjustments are not made, it makes judicial office less attractive to qualified candidates and incumbents alike. The *Los Angeles Lawyer*, for example, reported on "a serious brain drain going on in our courts," in

---

[100]Barry Latzer, "California's Constitutional Counter-revolution," in CONSTITUIONAL POLITICS IN THE STATES: CONTEMPORARY CONTROVERSIES AND HISTORICAL PATTERNS, 168 (Alan Tarr, ed. 1996).

[101]*Some Judges Mull Lawsuit Over Pay Freeze*, THE HERALD NEWS, July 15, 2002.

[102]Richard Creswell, *Georgia Courts in the 21ˢᵗ Century: The Report of the Supreme Court of Georgia Blue Ribbon Commission on the Judiciary*, 53 MERCER L. REV. 1, 33 (2001).

which "we are losing many of our most experienced jurists" to alternative dispute resolution firms or private practice. "The dominant reason," the article reported, was that "they cannot afford to continue to serve as judges."[103]

With regard to budgets, there are some indications, noted above, that legislators and governors have sought to manipulate the courts' nonremunerative resources for political purposes. Regardless of whether or how often these manipulations occur, however, an essential point remains that the health and well being of the twenty-first century judiciary depends on it being adequately funded. In times of fiscal austerity, state judiciaries—which typically lack the political and lobbying clout of the executive branch and its agencies—often find it very difficult to secure adequate funding,[104] and this carries the potential for interbranch confrontation. For example, in Kansas, the supreme court recently resorted to implementing a "stopgap emergency" surcharge on court filings to compensate for a shortfall in the legislature's appropriation.[105] Charging that the court had strayed from its proper boundaries in taking such a measure, Kansas Rep. Tony Powell warned: "I do not think the Supreme Court wants a showdown with the legislature."[106] In Delaware, the chief justice appointed a court resources task force to study ways to stretch the state court budget. "The judiciary has compelling budget needs that must be met," the chief justice told the general assembly, and "we should not put at risk the performance of the judiciary, which is a uniquely valuable Delaware asset."[107]

B. The Lower Courts

Although considerable attention has been devoted to the issues of judicial independence and accountability in the last several years, the vast majority of that attention has been focused on state appellate courts and high courts in particular. This is to some extent understandable, insofar as the high courts are obvious targets of campaigns to curb courts and judges. They are highly visible, fewer in number, and their decisions have generated the most controversy by virtue of being the final word on what the law is in their respective jurisdictions, which has led to more competitive and expensive campaigns for high court seats.

There are, however, compelling reasons to devote more attention to understudied issues affecting the trial courts. In the year 2000,

---

[103] *The Case for Raising Judicial Salaries*, LOS ANGELES LAWYER, Feb. 2001.

[104] *ABA Commission on the 21st Century Judiciary, supra note 84, at 118-19 (discussing the courts' unique disadvantages in securing adequate funding from legislatures).

[105] *The Price of Justice*, 1 No. 18 A.B.A. J. E-REPORT 6 (May 10, 2002).

[106] John Hanna, *Supreme Court's Budget Order Alters Balance of Power in Government*, ASSOCIATED PRESS, March 17, 2002.

[107] *Fresh Thinking on Funding Outside Resources are Among Options a Task Force will Consider to Help Support Delaware Courts*, 1 No. 4 A.B.A. J. E-REPORT 6 (February 1, 2002).

there were 290,000 appeals filed in the nation's appellate courts, staffed by 1,300 judges and justices.[108] In that same year, there were 92 million new cases filed before more than 29,000 trial judges and quasi-judicial officers, staffing over 16,000 courts of limited and general jurisdiction.[109] In short, our system of justice in the United States is administered largely by the lower courts. To the extent that the public's perceptions of the judicial system matter—and the sixth principle articulated in Part I of this report tells us why they should—those perceptions may be formed in no small part on the basis of personal experiences with the trial courts as litigants, witnesses, and jurors.

Another reason to devote more attention to the trial courts is that many of the problems discussed above with reference to the high courts afflict the trial courts as well. A limited number of examples should suffice:

> • Trial judges, like high court justices, are put at risk of losing their seats on account of unpopular decisions rendered in isolated cases. One highly publicized example was the retention election of Illinois Judge Daniel Locallo, who generated significant opposition on the basis of a sentence he imposed in a single case.[110] And Bell reported to the Commission on Los Angeles Judge Joyce Karlin, who faced demands for her recall in the wake of a sentencing decision in a racially charged case.

> • On a related front, corporate and insurance defense counsel and their clients have expressed with increasing vehemence concern that a limited number of state trial courts are unduly plaintiff-friendly in tort-related cases. In support of their position, they point to data that Tobias and Spalding have summarized in their report to the Commission. Tobias and Spalding report, for example, that in Jefferson County, Mississippi, "there had never been a punitive damage verdict that surpassed $9 million prior to 1995. Since then, there have been at least 19, totaling more than $2 billion."[111] In response to defense-side arguments that judges in these courts are exhibiting a lack of independence and impartiality, pro-plaintiff groups have accused the accusers. A spokesperson for Americans for Insurance Reform recently alleged that by attacking these judges during an election cycle, "these corporations, particularly insurance companies, are so fanatical about their crusade for corporate immunity that

---

[108]Ostrum & Kauder, *supra* note 18, at 77.

[109]*Id.*, at 11.

[110]R. Bruce Dold, *Judges Up for Election Walking a Delicate Tightrope*, Chicago Tribune, Oct. 23, 1998, at N27.

[111]Tobias & Spalding, *supra* note 36, at 3.

they are now undermining one of the most sacred pre-cepts of our democracy, judicial independence."[112]

• Problems associated with raising money in judicial campaigns are hardly limited to high courts. A recent survey of over 2,400 judges found that 45 percent of lower court judges felt under pressure to raise money for their campaigns during election years, as compared to 36 percent of high court justices.[113]

• Trial judges appear no less concerned than their counterparts in the high courts about the real and perceived relationship between campaign contributions and judicial decisions. Forty-five percent of trial judges expressed the view that campaign contributions influenced judicial decisions to at least some degree (4 percent said "a great deal," 21 percent said "some" and 20 percent said "just a little," as compared to 36 percent who reported "none"). An identical percentage of high court respondents thought likewise, although more thought that contributions exerted a greater degree of influence. That same survey revealed that 58 percent of trial judges—as compared to 55 percent of high court justices—supported the proposition that "judges should be prohibited from presiding over and ruling in cases when one of the sides has given money to their campaign."[114]

• The concern that judicial campaigns have become increasingly politicized is shared by trial judges. Asked whether "the conduct and tone of judicial campaigns has gotten better or worse over the past 5 years," 54 percent of lower court judges thought it had gotten much or somewhat worse, as compared to only 8 percent who thought it was better. Those results mirrored the views of high court justices, 54 percent of whom thought it had gotten worse (although as compared to trial judges, a higher proportion of high court justices thought it was "much" worse), and 7 percent of whom thought it had gotten better.[115]

• Concern for the state of voter knowledge and apathy may, if anything, be even more acute among trial judges, whose campaigns typically receive less attention and where voter turnout can be lower than the high court's. Eighty-two percent of trial judges were concerned (59 percent "concerned a lot" and 23 percent "concerned a little") that "in some states, as few as 13 percent of people vote in judicial elections." And 87 percent of trial judges were concerned (61 percent "concerned a lot" and 26 percent

---

[112]Americans for Insurance Reform, *Consumer Coalition Calls on State Officials to Investigate Corporate Efforts to Intimidate and Oust Judges*, October 2, 2002 (press release) *available at* http://www.insurance-reform.org/pr/AIRJudge.pdf
[113]Justice at Stake Campaign, *supra* note 27.
[114]*Id.*
[115]*Id.*

"concerned a little") that "because voters have little information about judicial candidates, judges are often selected for reasons other than their qualifications."

• Uncertainty surrounding the impact of *Republican Party of Minnesota v. White* on judicial codes of ethics applies with equal force to the trial courts. For example, a New York trial judge recently won an action in federal district court relying on *White* in support of the proposition that an ongoing disciplinary proceeding investigating his campaign-related conduct violates his First Amendment rights.[116]

Over and above the fact that the trial courts are experiencing many of the same problems as the high courts, there are a number of trends especially relevant to the trial courts that make separate study particularly important.

I. Increases in Trial Court Caseload Over Time

The reports of Commission consultants discuss some of the factors contributing to the generally accepted point that lower court caseloads have increased more or less steadily over time. On the civil side of the docket, Tobias and Spalding refer to the so-called "litigation explosion," variously blamed on increased case filings in the areas of medical malpractice, products liability, and insurance coverage. Without disputing that until very recently the rate of civil filings generally has followed a longstanding upward trajectory, it is worth noting that tort filings specifically have bucked this trend, declining by 10 percent between 1991 and 2000.[117] On the criminal side, Bell discusses escalating public fear of crime in the 1980s and 1990s that precipitated political branch "wars" on crime in the state and federal systems. And in her report, Professor Barbara Babb discusses major developments in child protection, child custody, juvenile delinquency, marital dissolution, and family violence that have contributed to a recent surge of interest in those areas, which together account for more than 35 percent of the civil-case filings in the nation's state courts.[118]

These developments and others have contributed to increases in lower court case filings that have exceeded the rate of population growth over the course of the past generation. NCSC has reported that between 1977 and 1981, civil filings increased by 23 percent and criminal filings increased by 29 percent. Between 1984 and 2000, civil filings increased by 30 percent, criminal filings by 46 percent,

---

[116]Spargo v. New York State Commn. On Judicial Conduct, 244 F.Supp.2d 72 (NDNY 2003), *appeal docketed,* No. 03-7250(L) (2d Cir., Sept. 29, 2003); see Andrew Tilghman, *Ethics Probe Targets Judge,* TIMES-UNION (Oct. 19, 2002) at A1.

[117]Ostrum & Kauder, *supra* note 18, at 26.

[118]Barbara Babb, *Fashioning an Interdisciplinary Framework for Court Reform in Family Law: Application of an Ecological and Therapeutic Perspective,* 72 IND. L. J. 775 (1997).

juvenile filings by 66 percent, and domestic relations filings by 79 percent. In the last two or three years, however, there are signs that this pattern of steady growth is leveling off—at least temporarily. The center reported that in 1999 and 2000, juvenile, criminal, and civil filings declined for two consecutive years.[119]

The inexorable rise in lower court caseloads is relevant for two reasons. First, it creates the need for larger budgets and additional salaries that can contribute to friction between the judiciary and the political branches over issues of resource allocation. Second, as discussed below, caseload burdens—coupled with the changing nature of the litigants themselves—have contributed to the emergence of coping strategies that have changed the role of lower court judges in ways that arguably contribute to politicizing the judicial function.

2. Changes in the Nature of Litigants

In addition to there simply being more litigants in courts across the country than there used to be, there have been changes in the nature of the litigants themselves. Two changes are worthy of special mention here. First, more litigants are proceeding *pro se*. Second, people of color represent an increasingly significant percentage of the population and the litigant pool. As described below, these developments portend to change the role of the trial judge in ways that may affect the political climate in which the courts function.

a. *The trend toward* pro se *litigation and its impact on the role of the trial judge*

In its 2001 annual report on *Trends in the State Courts*, NCSC reports that "the courts have experienced an increase in the number of litigants that are representing themselves."[120] In his testimony before the Commission, David Tevelin, the director of the State Justice Institute, explained this development in terms of a wider cultural phenomenon:

> More and more people will be coming to court without
> lawyers and not just because they can't afford to pay them.
> They are coming because they live in a culture that makes
> self-reliance a virtue that is easier to achieve than ever before.
> Without anyone's help, Americans pump their own gas, run
> businesses out of their homes, and thanks to the Internet,
> they do everything from diagnose their own medical [symp-
> toms] to record their own albums to sell anything imaginable
> that happens to be lying around the household. Why
> shouldn't they think they can represent themselves in court?[121]

---

[119]Ostrum & Kauder, *supra* note 18, at 10.

[120]NATIONAL CENTER FOR STATE COURTS, TRENDS IN THE STATE COURTS 30 (2001).

[121]*ABA Commission on the 21st Century Judiciary*, Phila., Pa. 212 (Sept. 27, 2002) (testimony of David Tevelin, Director, State Justice Institute).

In response, court systems have begun to develop an array of mechanisms to assist *pro se* litigants. Included among these mechanisms are self-help centers to provide *pro se* litigants with reference materials, one-on-one assistance with court staff or volunteers, court-sponsored legal advice by "facilitators," improved Internet access to court information, and collaborative approaches to assisting *pro se* litigants that include the legal and community services organizations and the local bar.

The relevance of this development to the mission of this Commission is subtle but potentially profound. As Tevelin emphasized in his testimony, the move toward accommodating *pro se* litigants along with the advent of problem-solving courts (discussed in greater detail below):

> encourage greater participation by judges [in] broad-based efforts to improve the justice system, if not society in general, greater involvement with members of the public, and a more prominent public role of the bench.[122]

Insofar as judges are shedding the mantle of aloof neutrality and becoming more actively involved in helping litigants to help themselves, it may represent a significant shift in the role of the trial judge. The issue is whether this is a troubling trend that needs to be addressed or a positive one that ought to be encouraged.

b. *Diversification of America and public confidence in the courts*

Perhaps the most critical demographic change to affect the twenty-first century judiciary will be the changing racial and ethnic make-up of the American public. The U.S. Census Bureau has projected that the non-Hispanic white population will be declining steadily from 74 percent in 1995, to 72 percent in 2000, to 64 percent in 2020, and to 53 percent in 2050. During the same time period, the Hispanic population is projected to increase at a rate of more than 2 percent per year, while the black population is projected to double in size.

The implications of such demographic shifts are many and complex, but one demands particular attention in the present context. Principle 6 of this report states: "Judges and the judiciary must have the confidence of the public." Yet among people of color in this country—African Americans in particular—such confidence is dramatically lower than among the population as a whole. A 2001 survey conducted by the Justice at Stake Campaign revealed that 85 percent of African Americans believe that "there are two systems of justice—one for the rich and powerful, and one for everyone else." Also,

---

[122] *Id.* at 214.

while a majority of whites (62 percent) believe that judges are fair and impartial, a majority of African Americans (55 percent) believe that judges are not fair and impartial. Moreover, only 43 percent of African Americans, as opposed to 67 percent of whites, believe that judges are committed to the public interest.[123] In a 1999 national survey conducted for NCSC, while 34 percent of non-Hispanic whites "strongly agreed" that "[j]udges are generally honest and fair in deciding cases," the percentage declined to 29 percent for Hispanics, and 18 percent for African Americans. Almost 70 percent of African Americans believed that the courts treated blacks worse than they treated whites and Hispanics, and 40 percent of whites and Hispanics agreed.[124]

Nor are these perceptions confined to the lay public. In a survey conducted by the *ABA Journal* and the *National Bar Association Magazine*, 52 percent of African American lawyers polled believe that "very much" racial bias exists in the justice system; and 55 percent of white lawyers believe "some" racial bias exists.[125]

These numbers demand sincere and immediate attention for at least two reasons. First, to the extent that the justice system actually disfavors African Americans or other people of color, it is sharply at odds with the principle of even-handed justice upon which the health and legitimacy of the system depends. Second, if minority populations' lack of confidence in the judiciary is left unaddressed, then the overall level of public confidence in the judiciary will correspondingly diminish as these populations grow to occupy a larger and larger proportion of the demographic whole. This both explains and justifies the need for a diverse judicial system as the seventh principle for the twenty-first century judiciary, as discussed in Section I of this Report.

Among the indicators of bias toward minorities in the justice system, observers commonly point to racially unrepresentative juries, disparate arrest, sentencing, and incarceration rates, tolerance of police misconduct, inferior access to competent counsel, and unequal treatment at bail and probation proceedings.[126] All of these perceptions exist against a backdrop of disproportionately low numbers of people of color serving in official capacities in the justice system relative to their numbers in the population at large. In Georgia, for example, African Americans make up 26 percent of the state

---

[123] Justice at Stake Campaign, *supra* note 27.

[124] NATIONAL CENTER FOR STATE COURTS, *supra* note 74.

[125] Terry Carter, *Divided Justice*, A.B.A. J., Feb. 1999, at 43.

[126] *See* Stephen B. Bright, *Can Judicial Independence Be Attained in the South? Overcoming Elections, and Misperceptions about the Role of the Judiciary*, 14 GA. ST. U. L. REV. 817, 828-32 (1998).

population, yet only 6 percent of state court judges.[127] Bryan Stevenson, executive director of the Equal Justice Initiative of Alabama, told the Commission that 73 percent of felony defendants in Alabama are people of color, and when they appear at trial:

> They face a white judge. They face a white prosecutor. We have elected district attorneys. There are no black district attorneys in Alabama. And less than 2 percent of the State Bar is African American. So, frequently, they are the only person of color in the court. [And] we're a state that has unlimited peremptory strikes . . . . [W]e still have cases where the majority of black counties, African American defendants are tried by all-white juries that involved 24 or 26 peremptory strikes being used.[128]

Mr. Stevenson notes that "there are no black judges on any of our appellate courts. . . . There are no people of color on the Alabama Supreme Court, the Alabama Court of Civil Appeals, and the Alabama Court of Criminal Appeals."[129] Further, given that all judicial offices in Alabama are elected offices, he points out that any effort to increase diversity through minority-voting initiatives or electoral reform confronts some very sobering facts and statistics.

> [W]e also have disenfranchisement laws. In Alabama, you permanently lose the right to vote based on a criminal conviction. Right now 31 percent of the black male population have permanently lost the right to vote. The projection is that by the year 2005 that number could be as high as 40 percent, which would actually get us at about the same level we were in the 1960s before the Voting Rights Act. And, of course, as these trends continue, the kind of political reforms many of us even thought possible become less and less viable.[130]

It appears clear that minority representation in the justice system has direct implications for the perceived legitimacy of judicial decisions. John Bonifaz, executive director of the National Voting Rights Institute, commenting to the ABA Commission on Public Financing of Judicial Campaigns with regard to racial diversity of California courts, noted:

---

[127] *The Percentage of Georgia Judges who are Black Remains Small*, SAVANNAH MORNING NEWS, May 19, 2002. Moreover, this is not confined to southern states. In Maryland, for example, where African-Americans have made notable progress in securing judgeships, of the state's 261 judges, two are Hispanic and none are Asian. Manuel Roig-Franzia, *Asian, Hispanic Judges Rare*, WASHINGTON POST, March 3, 2002.

[128] *ABA Commission on the 21st Century Judiciary*, Austin, Tex. 51 (Nov. 22, 2002) (testimony of Bryan Stevenson, Executive Director, Equal Justice Initiative of Alabama). A former president of the Hispanic National Bar Association notes that judges "are feared, not respected, by minorities who appear in lily-white forums." Mike Martinez, *Why Doesn't Utah Have More Hispanic Judges?*, DESERET NEWS, December 3, 2001.

[129] *ABA Commission on the 21st Century Judiciary, supra* note 128, at 28.

[130] *Id.* at 52.

[T]he Los Angeles County court system doesn't reflect the population as a whole. And when it comes to matters of racial justice, particularly when it comes to matters with the criminal justice system and disproportionate numbers of African Americans and Latinos in our prison system, the question of appearing to be fair was a real one.[131]

In a similar vein, Lisa Chang, president of the National Asian Pacific American Bar Association, testified before the Commission that:

if we see that we have Asian Pacific American judges, that we are part of the system, and we can communicate with that system and participate in the system, it will go a long way towards addressing . . . perceived differences in terms of sentencing or treatment in the courts. I think people will be willing to accept the legitimacy of the court if they see that they are actually participating in it in a meaningful way.[132]

In her testimony before the Commission, Suzanne Townsend, president of the National Native American Bar Association, agreed that diversifying not only the judiciary, but the legal profession as a whole, would do much to reverse the ongoing erosion of public trust and confidence in the justice system. She pointed out, however, that the trends are moving in the wrong direction:

Ever fewer minority students are choosing law as a career. The entry into the profession has slowed considerably since 1995. And in 1999, for the first time since 1985, minority entry into law school actually declined. The scarcity of minority lawyers has a direct effect on the makeup of the judiciary as does the scarcity of minority lawyers who are partners at large law firms, which in most states serve as farm teams for the state bench.[133]

Where experienced minority lawyers are relatively scarce, it becomes increasingly important that legislatures and governors in states using merit selection systems make conscious efforts not to overlook the qualified minority candidates who are available for judi-

---

[131] *ABA Commission on Public Financing of Judicial Campaigns*, Austin, Tex. 162-63 (Nov. 17, 2000) (testimony of John Bonifaz, Executive Director, National Voting Rights Institute).

[132] *ABA Commission on the 21st Century Judiciary*, Phila., Pa. 104-05 (Sept. 27, 2002) (testimony of Lisa Chang, President, National Asian Pacific American Bar Association).

[133] *ABA Commission on the 21st Century Judiciary*, Portland, Or. 43-44 (Nov. 1, 2002) (testimony of Suzanne Townsend, President, National Native American Bar Association).

cial posts, as this can exacerbate public perceptions of exclusion.[134] It is also clear that these governors must be alert to the racial make-up of the judicial nominating commissions through which the candidates they select must first pass. Historically, state judicial nominating commissions have been overwhelmingly white and predominantly male; and despite some progress in the 1990s, they remain largely so.[135]

In the context of increasingly politicized state judicial elections, questions about the level of the minority presence on the bench take on particular relevance. Minority groups rely on an independent judiciary to protect their legal rights by upholding the rule of law even when it is unpopular with the majority. As the judiciary becomes more subject to majoritarian political pressures, the continuing ability of the courts to maintain the level of independence necessary to protect the outnumbered is a matter of understandable concern. As Malcom Robinson, president of the National Bar Association, told the Commission:

> The judiciary, as we see it, is there to interpret the Constitution and [to] protect the minority from overreaching by the majority. [As] we go into the twenty-first century, there are certain things we have observed. One is that the independence of the judiciary is being seriously eroded. The body politic appears to be losing confidence in the judiciary. There seems to be a disconnect between the judiciary and the body politic. . . . The fact is that the body politic is made up of very diverse populations in terms of race, gender, and other areas. And that type of diversity is not reflected significantly on the judiciary.[136]

In her testimony before the ABA Commission on Separation of Powers and Judicial Independence, Constance Rice, western regional counsel for the NAACP Legal Defense and Educational Fund, emphasized that the judiciary derives its legitimacy and thus its power to persuade "through the consent of the public and because the public has faith in that judiciary." She added, however:

---

[134]When Massachusetts Acting Governor Jane Swift appointed only 4 minority judges in 25 opportunities, Robert V. Ward, dean of Southern New England School of Law, observed: "A total of about 15 percent is not likely to cause anyone to label the governor a champion of diversity. Fifteen percent is hardly a profile of courage." Robert V. Ward, *Swift's Legacy Could Be Her Judges*, BOSTON GLOBE, Aug. 23, 2002. This applies in the context of gender as well. For example, when Colorado Governor Bill Owens was presented with three candidates (two male and one female) for an El Paso County judgeship, he chose to interview only the two male candidates. State Representative Jennifer Vierga called Owens's decision "absolutely atrocious," and noted that she found it "disrespectful that the governor chose to not interview the one female in the group." Lynn Bartels, *Group Claims Spurning Indicative of Governor's Pattern of Favoring Men*, ROCKY MOUNTAIN NEWS, June 6, 2002.
[135]*See* Malia Reddick, *Merit Selection: A Review of the Social Scientific Literature*, 106 DICK. L. REV. 729, 730-32 (2002).
[136]*ABA Commission on the 21st Century Judiciary*, Austin, Tex. 101-03 (Nov. 22, 2002) (testimony of Malcolm Robinson, President, National Bar Association).

> [T]here are parts of the community that I work in [where] I cannot speak with any credibility about the credibility of the judicial system. I'm talking mainly about class. It is poor African Americans, poor whites, poor Latinos, poor Asian Pacific Americans, poor people of every race who are considered part of the underclass.
>
> I can no longer go to that sector of the public and speak credibly about the integrity, the fairness, or the lack of bias in our judicial system. I simply can't. [T]here are sectors of the public I can not discuss the judicial system with anymore and convince them that they should have faith with it, that they should view it as impartial, that they should give it the credence and the support that the public has to give it in order for the judiciary to work. We have lost poor people.[137]

As Rice's testimony implies, in an era of heavily financed judicial elections, the system's ability to protect the interests of the outspent is likewise deserving of scrutiny. Lisa Chang notes that "[a] lot of the Asian Pacific American community is not affluent, and . . . is not familiar with and used to the idea of making political contributions."[138] Judge Patricio Moya Serna, then chief justice of the Supreme Court of New Mexico, told the Commission that without significant changes in the way judicial elections are financed, "it's going to be exclusion, exclusion, exclusion, because minorities cannot compete. They cannot get millions of dollars."[139]

In his testimony before the ABA Commission on Public Financing of Judicial Campaigns, John Bonifaz pointed to data from Wisconsin relating to the intersection of minority status and wealth in the context of judicial elections. He reported that .0003 percent of the electorate in supreme court races supplied 18.5 percent of total contributions and that 4.1 percent of contributors, representing less than 2 percent of the voters in supreme court elections, provided over half of all donations to those races. In addition, when contributions were traced to the zip codes of the contributors, he found that ten wealthy, largely white Wisconsin zip codes supplied 43.3 percent of all contributions as compared to the ten Wisconsin zip codes where people of color are in the majority, which contributed only 1.8 percent. He concluded that "there's a real disparity here between those who have access to the money and their ability to participate in this process and those who don't, and the impact is felt most severely on communities of color."[140]

---

[137] *ABA Commission on Separation of Powers and Judicial Independence*, S.F., Cal. 244–45, 248–49 (Feb. 21, 1997) (testimony of Constance Rice, Western Regional Counsel, NAACP Legal Defense and Educational Fund).

[138] *ABA Commission on the 21st Century Judiciary, supra* note 132, at 94.

[139] *ABA Commission on the 21st Century Judiciary*, Portland, Or. 32 (Nov. 1, 2002) (testimony of Patricio M. Serna, Chief Justice, Supreme Court of New Mexico).

[140] *ABA Commission on Public Financing of Judicial Campaigns, supra* note 131, at 166–68.

Stephen Bright offered the Commission the following summation of the relationship between the modern justice system and communities with insubstantial financial resources:

> We're going to come to a reckoning here very shortly where we are going to have to either sandblast "Equal Justice Under Law" off the Supreme Court building or we're going to have to do something about access to justice for people who don't have any money.

> Poor people, more than anybody, need access to the courts . . . because they don't have a PAC, they don't have a representative, they don't have a congressman, they don't have anybody else. And unfortunately, I think the courts are farther away from those people, both state and federal, than they've been in a long time.[141]

In short, while the combined effects of increasing politicization and soaring levels of special-interest financing on state judicial elections are points of concern for the American public in general, they are of particular concern for people of color and low-income people of all backgrounds and may exacerbate their sense of estrangement from the courts. In addition, the continued lack of gender diversity at many levels of the justice system threatens the public's confidence in the courts. Any concerted effort to ensure and earn public confidence in the twenty-first century judiciary will be critically incomplete if it does not allocate substantial and sincere attention to these sectors of the American public that are increasing both in their numbers and in their sense of disenchantment with the justice system.

3. Changes in the Role of Courts

Certain changes in the role of courts over time are well-documented. The term "trial judge" is increasingly becoming a contradiction in terms as fewer cases go to trial in state or federal courts.[142] The time, expense and unpredictability of trials have made negotiated or judge-brokered settlements and alternative dispute resolution mechanisms increasingly attractive in a wide range of contexts. One effect of this development has been to create an alternative dispute resolution market for judges, which as discussed above in connection with the importance of adequate judicial salaries, can serve as a "brain drain" for jurists who leave the bench to become mediators or arbitrators. Another effect is to change the role of the judge from someone who dispassionately tries cases to someone who rolls up her sleeves and helps the parties to resolve their dispute by means short of trial.

---

[141] *ABA Commission on the 21st Century Judiciary*, Austin, Tex. 177, 179 (Nov. 22, 2002) (testimony of Stephen Bright, Director, Southern Center for Human Rights).
[142] Hope Viner Samborn, *The Vanishing Trial*, A.B.A. J. October 2002, at 24.

Another less widely appreciated sign of the changing role of the trial judge has been the nationwide move toward problem-solving courts. The nation's first problem-solving court opened in Dade County, Florida, in 1989.[143] In response to chronic drug-related criminal recidivism and overcrowded correctional facilities, the county court began sentencing drug-addicted offenders to long-term, judicially supervised drug treatment in lieu of incarceration. The success of that court attracted national attention and is credited with setting off what New York Chief Judge Judith S. Kaye has called "the quiet revolution called problem-solving justice."[144] The idea has been extended beyond drug courts to encompass dozens of specialized areas of concern, including mental illness, domestic violence, as well as numerous "quality-of-life" crimes such as prostitution and shoplifting.

While no single definition fits all problem-solving courts, in his testimony before the Commission, Greg Berman, director of the Center for Court Innovation, identified the following three essential features of the problem-solving court idea:

> 1) *Intensive judicial monitoring.* Even after sentencing, problem-solving courts tend to require offenders to return to court regularly to report on their progress with drug or mental health treatment, job training, community restitution, and other components of their sentence not involving incarceration.
>
> 2) *Aggressive professional outreach.* Problem-solving courts reach beyond the courthouse walls to engage social scientists and social service providers to create a more symbiotic relationship between these off-site providers and the courts.
>
> 3) *Community engagement.* Problem-solving courts reach out to, not only professional service providers, but also to community leaders, community groups, and to citizens to encourage them to become involved participants in the justice system.[145]

Clearly, problem-solving courts represent a marked departure from the traditional roles of both state courts and state court judges. They have arisen in response to equally dramatic changes, as described by Kaye:

> Unquestionably, the first modern-day reality that you have to look at is the numbers of cases in the state courts, which are

---

[143]Symposium, *The Changing Face of Justice: The Evolution of Problem Solving*, 29 FORDHAM URB. L. J. 1790, 1805 (2002).

[144]Judith S. Kaye, *Problem-Solving Courts: Keynote Address*, 29 FORDHAM URB. L.J. 1925, 1928 (2002).

[145]*ABA Commission on the 21st Century Judiciary*, Phila., Pa. 179-80 (Sept. 27, 2002) (testimony of Greg Berman, Director, Center for Court Innovation).

huge. Then there is the nature of the cases—there are not only more of them, but they've changed. We've witnessed the breakdown of the family and of other traditional safety nets. We're seeing many, many more substance abuse cases . . . huge numbers of domestic violence cases . . . [and] quality-of-life crimes. And it's not just the subject of the cases that's different. We get a lot of repeat business. We're recycling the same people through the system.[146]

As this description implies, there is more behind the movement toward problem-solving courts than just the courts trying to find nontraditional ways to cope with what Berman called the "incredible explosion in state court caseloads." In a sense, the movement is non-traditional in two directions: the courts are reaching out, trying to influence what comes into the court from the community (i.e., the debilitating caseload); but the community is also reaching in, trying to influence what comes from the court back out into the community (i.e., the procession of unreformed, repeat offenders with intact drug addictions or other features that render them ill-equipped to play a healthy role in the community.)

Although a body of reliable data has yet to emerge, this more col-laborative, holistic approach to justice has shown promising results. There are now more than 1,500 problem-solving courts across the country, and many report remarkable reductions in low-level crime and improved compliance by offenders sentenced to community restitution or substance-abuse treatment programs. Drug courts have achieved consistent reductions in recidivism and drug use among participants, as well as significant reductions in overall criminal jus-tice costs.[147]

Perhaps most promising is that, as Berman observes, "these problem-solving courts have shown some signs that they are able to chip away at the decline in public trust and confidence" in the justice system. Berman notes, for example, that only 9 percent of communi-ty members polled had positive views of the justice system before the establishment of the Red Hook Community Justice Center, a prob-lem-solving court in Brooklyn. After the court had been established, this number rose to 70 percent. According to Aubrey Fox of the Center for Court Innovation, public-opinion surveys about prob-lem-solving courts show that "the people who are most supportive of these measures are exactly the same groups, blacks and Latinos, who report being dissatisfied with the operation of the courts."[148]

At the same time, there is concern that, positive results notwith-standing, the very idea of courts and judges "reaching out" and social

---

[146]Judith S. Kaye *quoted in* Greg Berman, *What is a Traditional Judge Anyway? Problem-solving in the State Courts*, 84 JUDICATURE 78, 80 (2000).

[147]Greg Berman & John Feinblatt, *Problem-solving Courts: A Brief Primer*, 23 LAW & POLICY 9, 9-10 (2001).

[148]Aubrey Fox, *What the Data Shows [sic]*, 29 FORDHAM URB. L. J. 1827, 1843 (2002).

workers or treatment professionals "reaching in" represents a challenge to the core principles of judicial independence and impartiality. Even supporters, such as Tevelin, acknowledged that "the responsibilities of being a judge in the state courts of the twenty-first century differ from the traditional responsibilities," noting that "judges are being called upon—fairly or unfairly, wisely or unwisely—to become involved in a variety of collaborative, off-the-bench type activities." Tevelin describes risks inherent in such an approach:

> I think the more courts get pulled into the role of social service agencies, the role of collaborator—and [as] I've said, there's many good aspects to that—the more likely it may be that people will try to continue to politicize the judiciary, try to exercise more executive and legislative control, try to make judges less traditional and more like other politicians.[149]

Problem-solving courts have shown considerable potential to address some of the most intractable problems state courts face—clogged dockets, strained budgets, recidivism, and perhaps most importantly, a lack of public confidence in the justice system, especially within communities of color. It is therefore understandable that problem-solving courts have demonstrated themselves to be more than a fad. According to Berman:

> There's just too many of them now to be dismissed in that way, and I think the real question is . . . what's the fit? . . . Is the goal here to continue to replicate these things or is the goal to somehow embed the ideas of problem-solving courts in every courtroom throughout a state system or throughout the country?"[150]

As encouraging as some of the early experiences with problem-solving courts have been, however, there is no denying the tension between the role of judge as engaged problem-solver, and the more traditional model of judge as detached referee. As problem-solving courts continue their ascendancy, coming to terms with this tension may be increasingly important.

---

[149] *ABA Commission on the 21st Century Judiciary, supra note 121, at 221.*
[150] *ABA Commission on the 21st Century Judiciary, supra note 145, at 183, 186.*

Conclusions *and* Recommendations

SECTION 3

Conclusions and Recommendations

As the preceding section of this report reveals, our survey of the issues confronting the twenty-first century judiciary has been wide ranging. It is possible, however, to organize those issues—and the Commission's corresponding conclusions and recommendations—into three broad categories: those that relate to preserving the judiciary's institutional legitimacy; those that relate to improving judicial selection; and those that relate to promoting an independent judicial branch that works effectively with the political branches of government. It is to those conclusions and recommendations that we now turn.

A. Preserving the Judiciary's Institutional Legitimacy

In *The Federalist Papers*, Alexander Hamilton remarked that "the judiciary, from the nature of its functions, will always be the least dangerous to the political rights of the Constitution; because it will be least in capacity to annoy or injure them."[151] Unlike the political branches, the judiciary possesses neither the sword nor the purse. The courts are dependent on Congress for their funds and on the president to execute their orders, which ensures that the judiciary cannot act without the acquiescence of the political branches and the people they represent. The continuing ability of the courts to function then depends upon public acceptance of their institutional legitimacy; without it, the courts can and will be ignored or obliterated.

All issues addressed in this report are, in a very real way, relevant to promoting public acceptance of the courts—including those of judicial selection and the judiciary's relationship with the political branches, which we reserve for discussion in later sections. There are, however, a number of issues that we regard as especially vital to the judiciary's institutional legitimacy, which warrant separate treatment here.

1. Judicial Qualifications, Training, and Evaluation

The Commission recommends that states establish credible, neutral, nonpartisan, and diverse deliberative bodies to assess the qualifications of all judicial aspirants so as to limit the candidate pool to those who are well-qualified.

The issue of ensuring a qualified judiciary is typically linked to judicial selection. That makes obvious sense. The point at which to determine whether a lawyer possesses the qualifications necessary to be a judge is at the point when he or she is selected. For that reason, the conclusions and recommendations here will be relied upon later in our discussion of judicial selection. The Commission believes,

---

[151] THE FEDERALIST NO. 78 (Alexander Hamilton).

however, that the importance of a well-qualified judiciary transcends the issue of selection to such an extent as to warrant separate treatment here. There is more at stake here than simply promoting judicial competence. The continuing legitimacy of our judicial institutions requires that a process be in place to reassure the public that the judges who interpret our laws, rule on our civil claims, resolve disputes affecting our families, and sentence our citizens are capable and highly qualified.

It is quite common for states in which judges are initially appointed to rely on judicial selection commissions to evaluate the qualifications of candidates the governor appoints. In some states, such as California, the Commission evaluates candidates the governor has previously identified. In other states, such as Missouri, the Commission creates a pool of qualified candidates from which the governor's appointees are drawn.

In 2000, the ABA adopted standards for state judicial selection that expanded commission-based systems for the evaluation of judicial aspirants to include candidates in contested elections. In its report, the Commission on State Judicial Selection Standards offered the following explanation:

> The evaluation of a judicial aspirant's qualifications by a neutral, non-partisan, credible, deliberative body is a key element of traditional appointment systems. By incorporating this crucial element into an election system, as well as bolstering the process in appointment systems, the standards strive to provide a fundamental shift in the selection process, without advocating an institutional change in state judicial selection methods. The creation of credible, deliberative, nonpartisan bodies to evaluate the qualifications of all judicial aspirants—regardless of whether that person stands for election, is nominated through the appointment process, or reaches the bench through the interim appointment process— serves to assure the public that those judicial aspirants have met a threshold set of qualifications.

We agree with the Commission on State Judicial Selection. This is not to imply that judges who have been selected in states with contested elections that have no commission-based evaluation system are, on average, less qualified than their counterparts in states where such systems are in place. Rather, our point is simply that a commission-based evaluation system can make a valuable contribution toward promoting public trust and confidence in the courts by reassuring the public that no judges—regardless of how they are selected—will be allowed to serve unless they possess the qualifications necessary to be good judges.[152]

This recommendation should not be construed as an endorsement of all commission-based, judicial evaluation programs currently in place. In some jurisdictions, concerns have been raised that the selection commission's evaluations of judicial candidates are unduly influenced by the appointing authority. In others, critics assert that evaluations are influenced too much by politics in general.[153] If such concerns are well-founded, the selection commission is neither nonpartisan nor neutral, will not be perceived by the public as credible, and will fail in its essential purpose. Just as judicial independence is needed to ensure an impartial judge, so too an independent selection commission is needed to ensure impartial evaluation of judicial aspirants.

The Commission likewise believes that judicial selection commissions should be constituted with an eye toward achieving diversity within the judicial system, which, as discussed in Part I of this Report, is the seventh of eight enduring principles that ought to guide the twenty-first century judiciary. As elaborated upon below in its discussion of recommendations related to diversifying the judicial system, the Commission believes that diversification of judicial selection commissions is instrumental to achieving greater diversity of the judiciary itself.

> **The Commission recommends that the judicial branch take primary responsibility for providing continuing judicial education, that continuing judicial education be required for all judges, and that state appropriations be sufficient to provide adequate funding for continuing judicial education programs.**

Just as a process for assessing judicial qualifications can promote public confidence in the judiciary by assuring that all judges are capable and qualified, so too, continuing judicial education programs can promote public confidence by assuring that judges keep abreast of new developments relevant to the work they do. This objective can only be met if all judges participate in continuing judi-

---

[152]For example, despite controversy surrounding an appointment to the state supreme court, New Jersey Governor McGreevey was praised for first sending the appointment to the state bar association for review, a practice that had been discontinued by his predecessor, Governor Whitman. *Bar Code*, Philadelphia Inquirer, July 16, 2002.

[153]For example, a Rhode Island editorial asserted that the state judicial nominating commission rejected a highly qualified candidate, Superior Court Judge Michael Silverstein, for a seat on the state supreme court solely because of his lack of political connections. *The High Court Here*, Providence Journal, Dec. 12, 2000. More pointedly, a Nebraska editorialist derides the state's judicial nominating commissions for corrupting the state's merit selection system. He asserts that the commissions have changed the nomination process from "a legitimate evaluation of merit" to "a clandestine, political crapshoot," whereby the candidate of the commission's choice is deliberately grouped "with individuals the commissioners believe will be unacceptable to the governor." J. Kirk Brown, *Judicial Commissions Fail People of Nebraska*, Omaha World-Herald, Sept. 7, 2000.

cial education programs and have an obligation to do so. The Commission is aware of an ongoing controversy surrounding whether and to what extent it is appropriate for judges to attend privately funded judicial education programs in which program sponsors reimburse attendees their expenses. Without taking a position on that controversy, the Commission believes that state court systems have a critical role to play in the continuing education of their own judges. The courts themselves are often best situated to monitor their own judges' familiarity with recent developments and to develop programs to address deficiencies. [154] For that reason, the Commission recommends that the judicial branch take primary responsibility for providing judicial education services to the judges of the state and that the states adequately fund such programs. The New York State Judicial Institute and the National Judicial College are but two examples of how judicial education can be provided.

The Commission recommends that Congress fully fund the State Justice Institute.

Although our report focuses on state court systems, the issue of promoting judicial education as a means to ensure judicial competence and public confidence in the courts is one with obvious national implications. Over the course of the past two decades, our federal government has returned a range of issues of nationwide importance to state control. With respect to the perennially pressing problem of crime, the federal government has continued to play a significant role but has also devoted considerable resources to expanding the states' capacity to police their communities and prosecute lawbreakers. The success of these ventures depends in no small part on the state courts, which must process the influx of cases these developments generate. In this regard, preparing state judges to undertake the responsibilities that Congress is counting on them to perform capably and conscientiously should fairly be characterized as a national priority.

The State Justice Institute (SJI) has funded judicial education programs around the country and has served as an information clearinghouse for court systems interested in replicating programs that others have tried.[155] The Commission concludes that Congress should continue to fund the important work of SJI. Although the Commission's focus here has been on the role that SJI plays in promoting judicial education, the institute's larger mission to fund projects designed to improve state court operations generally should be of

---

[154] Arizona Supreme Court Justice Charles Jones is now "using his supervisory powers over lower courts to increase training requirements for justices of the peace and Municipal Court judges." This, according to the *Arizona Republic*, is "the least the public should expect." This Commission agrees. *Training Reform in JP Courts Welcome*, ARIZONA REPUBLIC, June 30, 2002.

[155] *ABA Commission on the 21st Century Judiciary, supra* note 121, at 202, 209.

considerable importance to our federal government at a time when we depend increasingly on states to further our national priorities. The Commission therefore recommends that SJI be fully funded for reasons including, but not limited to, the important role it plays in furthering judicial education.

The Commission recommends that the states fully fund NCSC.

NCSC is the single most important source of information and analysis on state court operations in the United States. The Commission has depended heavily on NCSC reports, questionnaires, data, and the assistance of its personnel in the preparation of this report. Anyone who does serious research or writing on the state courts relies upon information that the center provides. Even more important, perhaps, anyone who is concerned about the role of the courts in the twenty-first century and is committed to improving their performance depends on NCSC data, research, and analysis for guidance. Much of the funding for the center comes from the states themselves. The Commission therefore recommends that states fully fund NCSC. As many states confront fiscal crises across the country and legislatures look for ways to trim state budgets, the Commission seeks to emphasize the enormous contribution that the center makes relative to the modest contribution of dollars needed to underwrite its operations.

The Commission recommends that states develop judicial evaluation programs to assess the performance of all sitting judges.

Many states employ some form of judicial performance evaluation. In most states, evaluations are conducted by state bars; in six states, official, state-sponsored evaluations are conducted as part of the retention election process. In the latter jurisdictions, retention evaluation commissions, comprised of lawyers, judges, and non-lawyers, evaluate judges on the basis of information gathered from litigants, witnesses, jurors, and lawyers. The factors subject to official state-sponsored evaluation vary from state to state but typically include such matters as an incumbent's integrity, communications skills, judicial temperament, administrative performance, fairness, preparation, and attentiveness. The judge's knowledge and understanding of the law may likewise be evaluated on the basis of information gathered from members of the bar. Of course, there is no reason why these more comprehensive criteria cannot be used even in states that rely on state bars for evaluations. The Iowa State Bar Association recently revised its ratings system for retention elections from one that simply surveyed whether attorneys thought a judge should be retained or not to one where attorneys rate judges on twelve factors including knowledge of the law, objectivity, and clarity of writing.[156]

As with judicial qualifications, discussion of judicial evaluation programs is often linked to judicial selection. The virtues of judicial performance evaluations are, however, multifaceted. To be sure, voters in retention elections can gather valuable information about incumbent judges from such evaluations, and there is some support for the proposition that judicial performance evaluations exert a positive impact on voter turnout in judicial retention elections.[157] In the Commission's view, however, performance evaluations can be extremely useful regardless of how judges are initially selected or whether they are subject to reselection processes.

Irrespective of whether judges stand for election at any stage in their careers, judicial performance evaluations can be an important accountability-promoting measure. Judges are public servants whose salaries are paid and operating budgets are funded by taxpayers, who are entitled to know whether the public officials they support are doing their jobs satisfactorily. Even if the judges under review are not subject to reselection, publicizing performance evaluations can be rewarding or chastening (depending on the results) for the affected judge and furnish an excellent opportunity for judicial self-improvement. A commendable example in this regard is South Carolina Chief Justice Jean Toal, who requested the state bar to issue an early report on her performance—three years before she would face re-election. "[T]he chief ought to set the tone," she stated. "I'm a big proponent of this rating. I think it keeps us on our toes."[158] As Toal implies, the routine availability of regular feedback on all judges within a court system will serve the long-term interest of reassuring the public that judges are not immune from scrutiny.

The Commission concludes that bar-sponsored surveys alone are insufficient to achieve the above-stated objectives. If the public is to have confidence in the judicial evaluation process, it is important that nonlawyers participate both as information providers and as evaluators. Accordingly, the Commission recommends that states create judicial performance evaluation commissions modeled after the retention evaluation commissions already in place in six states, with one important difference—the primary purpose served by the commissions recommended here is to evaluate and facilitate the improvement of judicial performance and not merely to assist in judicial reselection.

---

[156] *Sizing Up State Judges*, DES MOINES REGISTER, October 4, 2000.

[157] Seth Andersen, *Judicial Retention Evaluation Programs*, 34 Loy. L.A. L. Rev. 1375, 1379 (2001).

[158] Cindi Ross Scoppe, *Evaluations Show Toal, Other Judges Doing a Pretty Good Job*, THE STATE, January 2, 2001.

2. Judicial Ethics and Discipline

Judicial accountability is absolutely essential to preserving public trust and confidence in our courts. Judges are entrusted to uphold the law independently and impartially. When they violate that trust, it is vital that processes be in place to correct the problem. As discussed below, in conjunction with its recommendations on judicial selection, the Commission does not believe that judicial elections are a desirable means to promote accountability because of their potential to undermine judicial independence, impartiality, and the rule of law. There are, however, other means to promote accountability that the Commission supports and seeks to enhance.

The Commission recommends that the ABA undertake a comprehensive review of the *Model Code of Judicial Conduct.*

Codes of judicial conduct serve a critical role in promoting judicial accountability by creating a body of rules designed to ensure that judges comport themselves in ways consistent with their duty to uphold the law impartially. If adequately publicized, moreover, codes of conduct can reassure the public that there are established ethical constraints on judicial conduct.

Existing codes of judicial conduct have served the state judiciaries well over time, but recent events called to the Commission's attention over the course of four hearings lead it to conclude that the time has come for the ABA to undertake a comprehensive review of its *Model Code of Judicial Conduct*. First, and perhaps most obviously, the United States Supreme Court's decision in *Republican Party of Minnesota v. White* requires a rethinking of the code as it pertains to judicial campaign conduct. Easily a dozen witnesses who testified before the Commission alluded to the uncertain impact that *White* will have on rules regulating campaign speech in judicial elections. How far can and should the code go in continuing to regulate candidates who take positions, appear to commit themselves, or make explicit promises with respect to issues they are likely to decide as judges? To the extent that the code may not prohibit candidates from making particular kinds of statements during judicial campaigns, may it still require those candidates to recuse themselves later in cases to which their prior comments relate? During the life of the Commission, at least two federal court cases have been decided that relied on the Supreme Court's decision in *White* to strike down other state ethics restrictions on judicial campaign speech and have only added to the state of uncertainty.[159]

---

[159]*See* Weaver v. Bonner, 309 F.3d 1312 (11th Cir. 2002); Spargo v. New York State Commn. on Judicial Conduct, 244 F. Supp.2d 72 (N.D.N.Y. 2003), *appeal docketed*, No. 03-7250(L) (2d Cir., Sept. 29, 2003); *see also*, Adam Liptak, *Judges and Politics Mix: U.S. Ruling breaks Down a Wall*, New York Times, Feb. 24, 2003 (reporting on case involving New York trial judge Thomas Spargo).

Second, the changing role of trial judges, described in the background section of this report, may justify some rethinking of the code as it applies to them. The traditional image of a judge, which the code seeks to preserve, is that of a disinterested referee. An emerging trend that several witnesses brought to the Commission's attention, however, calls upon judges to roll up their sleeves and serve as engaged problem solvers on a disparate array of issues ranging from crime, juvenile delinquency, and drug and alcohol dependency to divorce and child support. As will be discussed at greater length below, the Commission encourages the growth and development of problem-solving courts as a means to enhance public confidence in our judicial systems, but the *Model Code of Judicial Conduct* may require revision to accommodate such changes.

Third, and more generally, the last comprehensive revision of the *Model Code of Judicial Conduct* occurred in 1990, prior to the acceleration of events leading to a heightened level of interest in and concern over issues of judicial independence and accountability around the country. Revisiting the code in light of those developments is well advised.

The Commission recommends that codes of judicial conduct be actively enforced.

It all but goes without saying that to be effective, codes of judicial conduct must be enforced. All states have disciplinary systems in place, but the aggressiveness with which their respective codes of conduct are enforced can vary dramatically. In North Carolina, an editorial notes that "more than 100 times, the agency that investigates elected judges accused of misconduct has told judges that they have committed a violation of judicial ethics and warned them not to do it again—all in secret." As a result, "voters will go to the polls without complete information. . . . By state law, the [agency's job] is to investigate complaints, dismiss unfounded ones, and recommend . . . censure or remov[al] [of] judges for misbehavior. The law says nothing about private admonitions."[160]

Texas presents a good example of successful reform. The Texas Commission on Judicial Conduct is comprised of eleven members—five judges, two practicing lawyers, and four nonlawyers. ABA Commission member and Texas Rep. Pete Gallego described the Texas Commission on Judicial Conduct as "a backwater agency that did nothing to anybody for a long time" until it encountered "problems with the legislature in terms of criticism," at which point Margaret Reaves was appointed as the new executive director.

---

[160]Matthew Eisley, *Voters in Dark about Judges' Ethical Records*, RALEIGH NEWS & OBSERVER, Oct. 14, 2002.

In her testimony before the Commission,[161] Reaves described how the Texas commission revitalized itself. First and foremost, it took steps to "create more public awareness," by "giving the sanctions to the press and notifying them of what was going on," putting relevant information on the commission's web page, and by "letting people know they had the right to file complaints, that the complaints they filed would be investigated fully and fairly . . . and that they would be notified of the results." With respect to the notice complainants received when their complaints were dismissed, the Texas commission moved from a perfunctory form notice to a personalized letter explaining why. And the entire staff began to travel the state, meeting with judges in judicial education programs to discuss the ethical rules and their enforcement.

The effects of Reaves' efforts are measurable. In the year before her arrival, the Texas commission received a total of 743 complaints against the state's 3,500 judicial officers; in her first year, that number increased to over 1,200. During her tenure, the number of requests for reconsideration of complaints the Commission dismissed declined to 43, down from 133 in the year prior to her arrival. Texas Chief Justice Thomas R. Phillips, a member of the ABA Commission on the Twenty-first Century Judiciary, commended the Texas Commission on Judicial Conduct for hiring "Margaret without any consultation with us . . . they're totally independent—as they ought to be" and for "making the public aware that they exist as an outlet" without creating an adversarial relationship with the judiciary.[162]

In the Commission's view, the experience of the Texas Commission on Judicial Conduct should serve as a model for other states. If judicial discipline is to promote the legitimacy of our courts in the public eye:

> • the disciplinary body should include non-lawyer members;
>
> • the public should be made aware of the disciplinary process;
>
> • discipline should be imposed when it is deserved;
>
> • the public should be made aware when sanctions are imposed;
>
> • complainants should be furnished with an explanation when sanctions are not imposed.

---

[161] *ABA Commission on the 21st Century Judiciary*, Austin, Tex. 229-47, (Nov. 22, 2002) (testimony of Margaret Reaves, Executive Director, Texas Commission on Judicial Conduct).
[162] *Id.* at 246-47.

3. Diversification of the Justice System

This Commission is convinced that increasing the diversity of the judicial branch is more than an attractive goal for the twenty-first century judiciary. It is a necessity. Within fifty years, fully half of all Americans will be a member of a racial or ethnic minority. Meanwhile, recent surveys reveal an alarming erosion of trust and confidence in the justice system among people of color. Specifically, surveys reveal persistent attitudes that people of color are not treated fairly by courts and that—because of factors such as language barriers, racial bias, and the increasing influence of money in judicial elections—their access to justice is inferior to that of non-Hispanic whites.

Moreover, the lack of racial or ethnic diversity among legal professionals exacerbates these perceptions. Particularly important in this regard is the relative lack of minority judges in state judiciaries, a figure that now stands at approximately 8 percent, while people of color comprise nearly 30 percent of the national population. The Commission is convinced that continued failure to meaningfully diversify the courts will work to the detriment of the twenty-first century judiciary's overall health, quality, and level of public support. Diversification of the judicial branch should therefore be regarded as an urgent priority.

> **The Commission recommends that members of the legal profession expand their use of training and recruitment programs to encourage minority lawyers to join their firms, to include them fully in firm life, and to prepare them for pursuing careers on the bench following their years in practice.** [163]

Diversity among the ranks of legal professionals is critical not only to the perception of inclusiveness but also to its reality. It is imperative that the legal profession aggressively assumes a leadership role and approaches diversification with conscious, persistent, and zealous commitment.

To be sure, minority lawyers should be actively recruited to join established firms, but that is only the beginning. For generations, firms have made it their business to train, mentor, and acculturate new recruits for the purpose of grooming them for partnership and beyond—including careers on the bench. The practicing bar needs to appreciate, however, that for young minority lawyers—who may perceive themselves (and be perceived) as outsiders thrust into an unfamiliar environment—special efforts need to be taken to communicate the message that firm training and mentoring processes are there for the benefit of all firm lawyers, including them. For that reason,

---

[163] The American Bar Association House of Delegates adopted a principle addressing diversity in broader terms. (See Appendix A for policy adopted by the ABA.)

Commission advisor Bernard F. Ashe has written that lawyers "must reach out to make the workplace a comfortable environment for success. This means adjusting attitudes, culture and language in the workplace. It also means mentoring to facilitate a feeling of inclusion. . . . Lawyers must play a role in creating an atmosphere for improvement in the tensions of the workplace."[164]

> **The Commission recommends that states with commissions that evaluate the qualifications of judicial aspirants strive to diversify those commissions and sensitize them to the need to assess qualifications more flexibly and inclusively.**

Some Commission witnesses expressed the concern that for judicial aspirants of color, appointive systems can be a closed door; they do not know where to begin, who to contact, or how to initiate the process. To a significant extent, this problem is addressed by the preceding recommendation. If minority lawyers, to no less an extent than their majority counterparts, come to enjoy the benefits of training, mentoring, and inclusion in the life and politics of the profession, they will be equipped with the tools they need to secure judicial office, regardless of the method by which judges are selected. In states that appoint their judges with the assistance of nominating commissions, however, additional steps can be taken to promote diversification of the bench more actively.

Social science research studying whether appointive or elective systems of judicial selection produce a more diverse judiciary has yielded inconclusive results.[165] As elaborated upon below, the Commission concludes that the enduring principles of a sound judiciary are best served if judges are appointed. The Commission notes, however, that several witnesses criticized the commission-based appointive model for judicial selection on the grounds that it is not as well-suited to promote a diverse bench. As one writer has recently explained:

> Proponents of a diverse bench argue that merit selection prevents women and people of color from reaching the bench by entrenching a system dominated "by state and local bar associations whose members overwhelmingly are white, male Protestant, conservative 'establishment' attorneys." Some empirical studies of the relationship between judicial diversity on state courts and judicial selection methods validate this assertion. At the same time, several studies find no correlation between selection method and diversity, and others show a positive correlation between merit selection and the diversity of the bench.[166]

---

[164]Bernard F. Ashe, *Racial Progress in the New Millennium—A Different Shade: Mentoring and Outreach, Not Buzzwords,* 11 Experience 2, 21 (Winter 2001).

[165]See Malia Reddick, *supra* note 135, at 740-42.

[166]*Id.* at 740-41.

The varying results of studies comparing the relative ability of elective and appointive systems to promote racial and gender diversity may be attributable, at least in part, to differences among states with appointive systems in their relative commitment to diverse selection commissions and a diverse bench. The above-quoted author reports a recent study finding that "[i]n the five states for which data was [sic] available, there was some evidence that diverse commissions attracted more diverse applicants and selected more diverse nominees."[167]

The message is clear. States with appointive systems that are serious about the need to diversify the bench—and every state should be—can begin by taking steps to make certain that the commissions that evaluate the qualifications of judicial aspirants include more than the "usual suspects." If special efforts are made to reach out to women and people of color to serve on such commissions, it will send a powerful signal to people of color and women within the legal community and the public at large that the door to judicial office is open to them.

Integral to communicating the message that judicial office is available to minority lawyers is the nominating commission's appreciation for the need to assess the qualifications of all judicial aspirants with sensitivity. Some seemingly neutral indicia of a meritorious candidate may inadvertently exclude minority lawyers who lack such indicia for reasons that have little bearing on their qualifications for judicial office. Thus, for example, Deborah Goldberg, deputy director of the Brennan Center, reported to the Commission on a nominating commission that had evaluated applicant credentials with reference to their securities litigation experience—a practice area traditionally dominated by white males.[168] Our point is not to suggest that nomination commissions should abandon traditional criteria for evaluating candidate qualifications; our point is simply that traditional criteria can be freighted with traditional biases that nomination commissions should avoid by examining candidate qualifications with greater flexibility and sensitivity.

> **The Commission recommends that lawyers and judges participate in an aggressive outreach effort to encourage minority enrollment in colleges and law schools.**

Diversity efforts within the bench and bar can only be so successful without a qualified pool of diverse law school graduates. African American and Hispanic lawyers comprise only 4 percent and 3 percent respectively of lawyers in the United States—far below their representation in the general population. The percentage of minority lawyers who occupy leadership positions within the profession is

---

[167] *Id.* at 731-32.

[168] *ABA Commission on the 21st Century Judiciary*, Raleigh, N.C. (March 14, 2003) (panel presentation by Deborah Goldberg, Director, Democracy Program, Brennan Center for Justice).

lower still.[169] As Serna told this Commission: "We're looking at an institutional problem. . . . We're going to have to increase the pool of people of color in law schools. There has been a retrenching of recruitment of people of color in law schools throughout the country, and we've got to reverse that trend."[170] Indeed, the increase in minority law school enrollment, "which had been steady since 1985, ended in 1995. In the past five years, minority enrollment has increased only 0.4 percent—the smallest five-year increase in 20 years."[171]

The state of the law regarding race-conscious admissions policies is currently before the U.S. Supreme Court. Although that decision may affect the manner in which state institutions are permitted to improve minority enrollment, it should have no bearing on their continuing commitment to do everything within their constitutional power to create a student body that reflects the diversity of the society that college and law school graduates serve. Regardless of the Supreme Court's decision, then, law schools should aggressively improve minority outreach and recruitment efforts at colleges and universities around the country, including, but not limited to, those that are traditionally black.

Legal professionals themselves, however, should reach even deeper. As Serna observed, "We have to go even to high schools, because there's a disproportionate dropout rate amongst minorities."[172] Visits by judges and lawyers to high schools, youth centers, and other places where the public congregates are critical to increase the personal interaction with people of color that can create opportunities for encouraging students to pursue college degrees and legal careers.

The Commission recommends active promotion of a representative work force and diverse court appointments.

Lawyers and judges are not the only faces of the judicial branch. The rationales of actual and apparent inclusiveness that underlie the need for diversity among lawyers and judges apply equally to other court employees, who often are an individual's first point of interaction with the judicial system. Courts should adopt formalized recruitment, hiring, and promotion policies and practices to ensure that the pool of qualified applicants for court employment is as broad and diverse as possible. NCSC recommends "placing ads in foreign-language newspapers, accessing minority databases, approaching minority colleges, and contacting minority professional associations," as important outreach efforts in this regard.[173]

---

[169]Elizabeth Chambliss, *Miles to Go 2000: Progress of People of Color in the Legal Profession,* American Bar Association Commission on Racial and Ethnic Diversity in the Profession (2002) at 1, 9.

[170]*ABA Commission on the 21st Century Judiciary, supra* note 139, at 25-26.

[171]Chambliss, *supra* note 169, at 1.

[172]*ABA Commission on the 21st Century Judiciary, supra* note 139, at 26.

[173]National Center for State Courts, *Race and Ethnic Bias Trends in 2002: Diversity in the Courts,* (2002) *available at* http://www.ncsconline.org/WC/Publications/KIS_RacEth_Trends02_Pub.pdf.

The Commission recommends that courts act aggressively to ensure that language barriers do not limit access to the justice system.

Implicit in the promise of equal justice under law is the "ability of the courts to understand those who come before them and to be understood in return."[174] This can and should be made a practical reality. Courts should enact measures to minimize language barriers so that non-English speaking citizens are not deterred from pursuing their legal rights in American courts. These measures include making all relevant court information – e.g., general information, court forms, signage—available in non-English languages commonly spoken in the community. The National Conference of Special Court Judges sponsored an ABA booklet titled Translations of Commonly Used Court Phrases[175] to be used by judges, court employees, and litigants in the absence of an interpreter. The booklet contains translations of dozens of basic court phrases in thirty languages.

While such measures are indispensable, they cannot displace the need for adequate interpreter services. Interpreters are necessary not only in sufficient numbers to meet the need in a given court setting, but interpreters should also receive appropriate training in cultural and racial diversity. Moreover, judges and other court personnel should be trained to identify the not-always-obvious circumstances under which an interpreter is necessary.

The Commission recommends that courts have in place formal policies and processes for handling allegations of bias.

People of color are not fully confident that they will always be treated in an unbiased manner by the courts. If this lost trust is to be restored, it is critical that allegations of bias be vigorously addressed when they arise. Courts should establish formal mechanisms for the investigation, evaluation, and resolution of allegations of specific incidents of bias. These mechanisms should include simple and accessible procedures for litigants and other interested persons to report such allegations in a manner that promotes confidence that they will be addressed promptly and objectively.

The Commission encourages sharing of information regarding diversity among the courts in a state and among the states.

Diversity is a system-wide goal that will require system-wide solutions. Accordingly, the Commission strongly recommends that state courts assume a leadership role in establishing both intra- and inter-

---

[174]ROBERT K. PIRRAGLIA, AMERICAN BAR ASSOCIATION JUDICIAL DIVISION, *Foreword to* TRANSLATIONS OF COMMONLY USED COURT PHRASES (1998).
[175]*Id.*

state data collection and information-sharing networks to ensure that the best practices and innovative strategies developed on local levels are made available both statewide and nationwide. Such networks would also provide critical information in the effort to identify often-overlooked inequities in the system. NCSC has taken an important step toward this goal by maintaining an online clearing-house of state task-force materials with up-to-date information about diversity strategies, best practices, and other information resources being developed within each state.[176] Yet as the Conference of State Court Administrators has noted, and this Commission strongly agrees, "States would benefit from a structured method of sharing their respective programs with each other, and one way to do this would be by designating a contact person in each state's court administration through whom NCSC could obtain and share information regularly."[177]

The Commission recommends that measures be adopted to improve and expand jury pool representation.

Among people of color recently surveyed, 77 percent believed that "[j]uries are the most important part of our judicial system."[178] Therefore, this is a critical point at which minority confidence in the system is determined. Meaningful steps should be taken to ensure that every jury pool represents a fair cross section of the community from which it is drawn. Such steps include expanding source lists and reducing exemptions to increase the number of residents available for the pool. Also, obstacles common to low-income people often lessen their participation on juries. "Reducing the length and frequency of service, raising compensation, even providing child care, all make it easier for individuals to serve without unduly interfering with work and family obligations."[179]

4. Improving Court-Community Relationships

The Commission recommends that courts take steps to promote public understanding of and confidence in the courts among jurors, witnesses, and litigants.

Public perceptions of the courts are undoubtedly influenced by what people read in the papers, hear on the radio, see on the evening news or in campaign advertising, and learn in school. In addition, however, their views can be profoundly shaped by direct contact with the judicial system as jurors, witnesses, or litigants, or indirectly

---

[176]National Center for State Courts, *Racial and Ethnic Bias: Clearinghouse of State Task Force Materials,* (last modified January 6, 2003) *available at* http://www.ncsconline.org/.
[177]National Center for State Courts, Conference of State Court Administrators, *White Paper on State Court's Responsibility to Address Issues of Racial and Ethnic Fairness,* at 6 (2001).
[178]AMERICAN BAR ASSOCIATION, *supra* note 72, at Table 6.
[179]National Center for State Courts, Conference of State Court Administrators, *supra* note 177, at 4.

when a friend or family member serves in those capacities. These points of contact should be capitalized upon, and a number of courts are already doing so. Jury service, for example, creates a unique opportunity for court personnel and the judges themselves to provide the public with information on the operation of the courts, the importance of juries, and the relevance of judicial independence and accountability to the role courts play in American government. It likewise creates a duty on judges and court personnel to treat jurors with fairness and respect because jury service will be the only point of interaction with the justice system for many people.

> **The Commission recommends that courts engage and collaborate with the communities of which they are a part by hosting trips to courthouses and by judges and court administrators speaking in schools and other community settings.**

The preceding recommendation addresses ways to promote public confidence among those who find themselves obliged to go to court as witnesses, jurors, or litigants. As to those who are not obligated to come to the courthouse, however, the Commission believes that courts and judges should explore additional ways to strengthen their ties to the community and improve their relationship with the public they serve. Judges and court personnel should be encouraged to become involved with civic organizations and primary and secondary schools, speak at school and organization events as a way to educate the public on the role of the courts, encourage students from communities of color to pursue legal careers, and build bridges between judges and the community. Courts should encourage courthouse visits from schools and other groups and open channels of communication with community leaders. The ABA Judicial Division Judges Network is an example of judges reaching out to their communities. As problem-solving justice becomes increasingly pervasive, the importance of these outreach efforts will only become greater.

> **The Commission encourages the continuation of problem-solving courts as a means to promote public confidence in the courts.**

The ABA is already on record in support of problem-solving courts as an innovative means to achieve promising results in the areas of crime, substance abuse, juvenile delinquency, and family law. Our Commission, however, has not been created for the purpose of developing strategies to improve the enforcement of substantive law. We have been asked to explore ways in which a politicized judiciary may be made less so, and to that end, the Commission concludes that problem-solving courts should be encouraged as a means to enhance public trust and confidence in the courts. As elaborated upon in the background section of this report, the introduction of problem-solving courts into communities with deep-seated skepticism of their local court systems has yielded promising gains in public approval. By making judges more visible and active "problem solvers" in their communities, such courts have the potential to reduce public alienation from the courts—particularly in communities of color where such alienation is a commonplace.

Problem-solving courts are no panacea, and the Commission's recommendation encouraging their proliferation should not be read in isolation. To the extent that problem-solving courts call upon judges to further modify their traditional roles as detached referees, it raises questions as to how far problem-solving judges may go before running afoul of their ethical obligations. For that reason (among others), the Commission has recommended that the Model Code of Judicial Conduct be re-examined. This recommendation must likewise be read in tandem with earlier recommendations regarding diversification of the bench. If courts are to become accepted as community problem solvers, it may be all the more important that the judges in those courts reflect the diversity of the communities they serve. Finally, the Commission's earlier recommendations regarding judicial training and education are uniquely relevant here. To the extent that judges are being asked to serve a very different role than before, the importance of adequate training and education to make the transition smoothly is obvious.

B. Improving Judicial Selection

Some of the most serious problems confronting our judicial systems today relate to judicial selection and reselection. As discussed at length in the background section of this report, judicial election campaigns at all levels are increasingly focused on isolated issues of intense political interest. The issue de jour varies by jurisdiction and campaign. Sometimes it is products liability, insurance, or medical malpractice litigation; sometimes it is crime; sometimes it is school funding, abortion, or capital punishment. But the message sent to the electorate is the same in each case; sitting judges should lose their jobs if they make a ruling of law in a particular case that a popular majority thinks is wrong. In the Commission's view, that message is antithetical to principles of judicial independence, impartiality, and the rule of law.

These increasingly shrill single-issue messages have been communicated in campaign advertising often run not by the candidates themselves but by independent organizations. The candidates then are left with no choice but to defend themselves by raising more and more money from contributors, from lawyers, and from other groups interested in the outcomes of cases judges decide. That, in turn, has undermined public confidence in the courts by making judges appear increasingly dependent on their contributors, making judicial office increasingly available only to candidates with wealth or with wealthy contributors, and making judges look and act like stereotypical "politicians."

To complicate matters even further, judicial elections are likely to become an increasingly problematic means of judicial selection in the aftermath of the United States Supreme Court's decision in *Republican Party of Minnesota v. White*. Scholars are bound to disagree as to the breadth of the *White* decision and the extent to which the First Amendment freedom-of-speech provisions prevent state high courts from imposing ethical limits on the campaign speech of judicial candidates. Although we now know that states may not simply prohibit candidates from announcing their views on controversial issues that could come before them as judges, uncertainties remain as to whether, for example, the states retain regulatory authority over candidates who make statements that appear to commit them to deciding particular issues in particular ways.

Additional litigation may be needed to resolve such uncertainties, but it is clear from the testimony we received from supporters and critics of the Supreme Court's ruling that the White case is likely to politicize judicial elections as never before. Judicial candidates will be competing for votes on the basis of their positions on issues they will later decide as judges. When voters ask for the candidates' views on politically explosive issues of the day, the candidates must either answer, or decline and hazard a negative reaction from the electorate at the ballot box. And the risk that judges will be selected not because they are best qualified to impartially uphold the law but because they will best represent their "constituents" views from the bench becomes increasingly real.

Underlying the majority's opinion in *White* is a relatively simple and straightforward message: A state that opts to select its judges by election may not, consistent with the First Amendment, deny judicial candidates the opportunity to discuss what the election is about, and the election is in no small part about the issues those candidates will decide as judges. If a state is concerned that judicial candidates will compromise their impartiality when they take positions on issues that may come before them later as judges, it has an obvious solution, as emphasized by Justice Sandra Day O'Connor in her concurring opinion. It may select judges by means other than election.

In the Commission's view, states *should* be concerned about the impact of judicial elections on judicial impartiality and the rule of law. Moreover, as judicial campaigns become further politicized in the aftermath of *White*, the need to act on those concerns and rethink the future of judicial elections may be increasingly acute.

Notwithstanding widespread dissatisfaction with the judicial selection process in many states, judicial selection reform is among the most contentious subjects that the Commission has been directed to address for at least two reasons. First, nowhere is the tension between judicial independence and judicial accountability more palpable than in the context of judicial selection. It is one thing to acknowledge the need for selection systems to preserve and promote independence *and* accountability—a point with which few would disagree—and quite another to determine what selection system strikes the optimal balance between the two, where consensus is highly elusive. Disagreement over the relative merits of appointive versus elective systems of judicial selection thus persists with no sign of abating. Professor Paul Carrington and Adam Long report on a state chief justice who "not long ago declared that there is no method of selecting and retaining judges that is worth a damn. He was not the first to express that wisdom."[180] Although we might not go quite that far, it is fairly said that there is no perfect selection system.

Second, nowhere is the challenge of balancing the philosophically preferable and the politically possible more daunting than in the context of judicial selection. On the one hand, if we recommend that states adopt our preferred selection system without regard to whether there is any realistic hope of those states eventually following our lead, we will have squandered a unique opportunity to improve judicial selection in the United States. On the other hand, if we simply decline to think outside the box created by the political realities that exist in 2003 and confine our recommendations to those that legislatures are willing to implement tomorrow, we will have issued a timid report that ignores our charge to assess and address the needs of the state judiciaries for the coming century.

To overcome these difficulties, the Commission has decided to sequence its judicial selection recommendations. We will begin by presenting our primary conclusions and recommendations to implement the selection system that we regard as optimal in the long term, recognizing that one size does not fit all and that our preferred system of selection may not be as well-suited as other alternatives for adoption in some states. We will then present additional recommendations to improve other selection systems in states that are unprepared to adopt our primary recommendations.[181]

---

[180]Paul Carrington and Adam Long, *The Independence and Democratic Accountability of the Supreme Court of Ohio*, 30 CAP. U. L. REV. 455, 471 (2002).

[181]The Commission was unanimous in its view that our recommendations should be sequenced so as to better meet different needs of different states with flexibility. And the Commission was virtually unanimous that the sequence we present here was optimal.

1. The Preferred System of Judicial Selection

• **The Commission recommends, as the preferred system of state court judicial selection, a commission-based appointive system with the following components:**

• **The Commission recommends that the governor appoint judges from a pool of judicial aspirants whose qualifications have been reviewed and approved by a credible, neutral, nonpartisan, diverse deliberative body or commission.**

• **The Commission recommends that judicial appointees serve a single, lengthy term of at least 15 years or until a specified age and not be subject to a reselection process.**[182] **Judges so appointed should be entitled to retirement benefits upon completion of judicial service.**

• **The Commission recommends that judges not otherwise subject to reselection, nonetheless, remain subject to regular judicial performance evaluations and disciplinary processes that include removal for misconduct.**

The American Bar Association has long supported appointive-based or so-called "merit selection" systems for the selection of state judges, and in the Commission's view, rightly so, for several reasons. First, the administration of justice should not turn on the outcome of popularity contests. If we accept the enduring principles identified in the first section of this report, then a good judge is a competent and conscientious lawyer with a judicial temperament who is independent enough to uphold the law impartially without regard to whether the results will be politically popular with voters. Second, initial appointment reduces the corrosive influence of money in judicial selection by sparing candidates the need to solicit contributions from individuals and organizations with an interest in the cases the candidates will decide as judges. Some argue that in appointive systems, campaign contributions are simply redirected from judicial candidates to the appointing governors, but that is an important difference because it is the money that flows directly from contributors to judicial candidates that gives rise to a perception of dependence. Third, the escalating cost of running judicial campaigns operates to exclude from the pool of viable candidates those of limited financial means who lack access to contributors with significant financial resources. The potential impact of this development on efforts to diversify the bench is especially troublesome. Fourth, the prospect of

---

[182]The American Bar Association House of Delegates adopted a recommendation stating, "Judicial appointees should serve until a specified age." (See Appendix A for policy adopted by the ABA.)

soliciting contributions from special interests and being publicly pressured to take positions on issues they must later decide as judges threatens to discourage many capable and qualified people from seeking judicial office. For these and other reasons upon which the ABA has relied in the past, the Commission believes that judges should initially be selected by appointment.

Consistent with an earlier recommendation in this Report, the Commission likewise recommends that an independent deliberative body evaluate the qualifications of all judicial aspirants and that candidates eligible for nomination to judicial office be limited to those who have been approved by such a body. In grounding its support for appointive judiciaries on the principle that the viability of a would-be judge's candidacy should not turn on her or his political popularity, the Commission does not mean to suggest that appointive systems are apolitical. Any method of judicial selection will inevitably be political because judges decide issues of intense social, cultural, economic, and political interest to the public and the other branches of government. In this inherently political environment, however, the requirement that independent commissions review the qualifications of and approve all would-be judges provides a safety net to assure that all nominees possess the baseline capabilities, credentials, and temperament needed to be excellent judges.

Despite the occasional tendency to regard "politics" as a bad word, at its root, politics refers to the process by which citizens govern themselves. In that regard, it is not only inevitable but also perhaps even desirable that judicial selection have a "political" aspect to ensure that would-be judges are acceptable to the people they serve. Because judges, by virtue of their need to remain independent and impartial, serve a role in government that is fundamentally different from that of other public officials, the Commission has recommended against the use of elections as a means to ensure public acceptability.

The Commission did, however, consider another possibility: legislative confirmation of gubernatorial appointments. Requiring that judges be approved by an independent commission and *both* political branches of government could conceivably increase public confidence in the judges at the point of initial selection and serve as a form of prospective accountability that reduces the need for resort to more problematic reselection processes later. A majority of the Commission ultimately decided, however, not to recommend legislative confirmation as a component of its preferred selection system. The protracted and combative confirmation process in the federal system, coupled with the highly politicized relationship between governors and legislators in many states, has led the Commission not to recommend such an approach.

The last of the Commission's recommendations with respect to the selection system it regards as optimal is that states not employ reselection processes. Discussions of judicial selection often overlook a distinction that the Commission regards as absolutely critical, between initial selection and reselection. When nonincumbents run for judicial office in contested elections, the threat that elections pose to their future independence and impartiality—though extant—is limited. Granted, nonincumbent candidates can be made to appear beholden either to their contributors, to positions they took on the campaign trail, or more generally to the electoral majority responsible for selecting them. But unlike incumbent judges, first-time judicial office seekers are not at risk of being removed from office because they made rulings of law that did not sit well with voters.

A similar point can be made with respect to judges initially selected by appointment. The process by which those candidates are first chosen may be partisan and political, and some judges may feel a lingering allegiance to whoever appointed them. But they are not put in danger of losing jobs they currently hold on account of judicial decisions made in those positions.

In the Commission's view, the worst selection-related judicial independence problems arise in the context of judicial reselection. It is then that judges who have declared popular laws unconstitutional, rejected constitutional challenges to unpopular laws, upheld the claims of unpopular litigants, or rejected the claims of popular litigants are subject to loss of tenure as a consequence. And it is then that judges may feel the greatest pressure to do what is politically popular rather than what the law requires. Public confidence in the courts is, in turn, undermined to the extent that judicial decisions made in the shadow of upcoming elections are perceived—rightly or wrongly—as motivated by fear of defeat.

The problems with reselection may be most common in contested reelection campaigns but are at risk of occurring in any reselection process—electoral or otherwise. Thus, for example, the issue arises in states that delegate the task of judicial reselection to legislatures, whose enactments judges are to interpret and, if unconstitutional, invalidate. For that reason, the Commission recommends against resort to reselection processes.

While the Commission recommends that judges be appointed to the bench without the possibility of subsequent reappointment, reelection, or retention election, the Commission has remained flexible as to the optimal length of a judge's term of office. Most states that appoint judges without the possibility of subsequent reselection cap judicial terms at a specified age. States could also set judicial terms at a fixed number of years. In either case, however, it is important that states take pains to preserve judicial retirement benefits because judicial office will lose its appeal to the best and brightest lawyers if judges are obligated to conclude judicial service before their retirement benefits vest.

If states opt for a single term, it is important that the term be of considerable length—at least fifteen or more years—for several reasons. First, there are obvious advantages that flow from experience on the bench that will be lost if judges are confined to short terms of office. Second, the most qualified candidates for judge will often be lawyers with very successful private practices that they may be reluctant to abandon if they are obligated to return to practice after only a few years on the bench. Third, to the extent that lawyers view judicial service as the culmination of their legal careers and not simply as a temporary detour from private practice, short terms may discourage younger lawyers from seeking judicial office. Fourth, insofar as judges are obligated to reenter the job market at the conclusion of their judicial service, their independence from prospective employers who appear before them as lawyers and litigants in the waning years of their judicial terms may become a concern.

In earlier recommendations, the Commission urged that systems of judicial discipline be actively enforced and that regular and comprehensive judicial evaluation programs be instituted. These recommendations are critically important to ensuring accountability in a system that does not rely on reselection processes. All states have procedures for judicial removal, typically including but not limited to those subsumed by the disciplinary process.

The Commission believes that judges must be removable for cause to preserve the institutional legitimacy of the courts. It is beyond the scope of this report to describe in detail the nature and extent of "for cause" removal. By way of general guidance, however, the Commission points to the enduring principles discussed in the first part of this report. An overriding goal of our system of justice is to uphold the rule of law. Judges should never be subject to removal for upholding the law as they construe it to be written, even when they are in error, for then the judge's decision-making independence—so essential to safeguarding the rule of law in the long run—will be undermined. On the other hand, we do not want judges who are so independent that they are utterly unaccountable to the rule of law they have sworn to uphold. Thus, judges who disregard the rule of law altogether by taking bribes or committing other crimes that undermine public confidence in the courts should be removed. One could reach a similar conclusion with respect to judges who, despite the best efforts of nominating commissions to weed out unqualified candidates, manifest an utter lack of the competence, character, or temperament requisite to upholding the law impartially.

2. Alternative Recommendations on Systems of Judicial Selection

The Commission opposes the use of judicial elections as a means of initial selection and reselection for the reasons discussed above. Over the long term, as elections become ever "noisier, nastier and costlier," to borrow the phrase of a noted scholar,[183] the Commission believes that this view will win widespread acceptance. Over the short term, however, the Commission acknowledges that support for judicial elections remains entrenched in many states. It is to those states that the Commission now directs its attention, with recommendations aimed at ameliorating some of the deleterious effects of elections on the enduring principles of a good judicial system.

> **For states that cannot abandon reselection processes altogether, the Commission recommends that judges be subject to reappointment by a credible, neutral, nonpartisan, diverse deliberative body.**

States reluctant to relinquish control over judicial reselection can reduce the risk that judges will lose their tenure for reasons detrimental to judicial independence and impartiality by delegating the task of reappointing judges to the same commissions that are to assist in the process of initial selection. A commission-based reselection process, such as that used in Hawaii, may be better suited than contested or retention elections to evaluating judicial performance with reference to incumbents' competence, diligence, character, and temperament—and without regard to the popularity of the judges' rulings.

> **For states that cannot abandon judicial elections altogether, the Commission recommends that elections be employed only at the point of initial selection.**

It bears emphasis that the Commission's greatest concern with respect to judicial elections is their potential to undermine judicial independence, impartiality, and the rule of law by threatening judges with loss of tenure if their prior rulings are disagreeable to a majority of the electorate. As far as elections are concerned, however, that concern is relevant only when they are employed to reselect judges. At the point of initial selection, judicial candidates may worry, at least after the *White* decision, that they may not win judicial office in the first place unless they express politically popular views on issues likely to come before them later. But they are not put at risk of losing their jobs because they honored their oaths of office by upholding the law in the teeth of public opposition.

---

[183]Roy Schotland *quoted in* Thomas Phillips, *When Money Talks, the Judiciary Must Balk*, THE WASHINGTON POST, April 14, 2002, at B2.

Accordingly, the Commission recommends that if elections are used as a means of judicial selection, they be employed solely for the purpose of initial selection and not reselection. Once elected, candidates should be permitted to serve until a specified age or for a single, lengthy term.

Consistent with the Commission's earlier recommendation, candidates favored for judicial office should be limited to those whose qualifications have been approved by an independent, deliberative body. It may be noted that when making the case for appointed judiciaries, the Commission did not contend, as many proponents of appointed judiciaries have in the past, that judges who are appointed will, on average, be better qualified than their elected counterparts. Empirical research contradicts such a conclusion. Moreover, lingering doubts can, in the Commission's view, be extinguished if the qualifications of every judicial aspirant—elected or appointed—are evaluated and approved.

If such a system is implemented, subjecting sitting judges to elections may still be necessary in the limited sense that when a governor fills mid-term vacancies with new appointees, those appointees may later need to run for election to be eligible to sit for a full term. In the Commission's view, however, if a judge must be subjected to election, it is preferable for it occur in the initial stage of the judge's tenure when the risk that the election will become a referendum on the popularity of the judge's past rulings is less likely to occur.

For states that retain judicial elections as a means of reselection, the Commission recommends that judges stand for retention election rather than run in contested elections.

The American Bar Association has long supported so-called "merit selection" systems in which judges are appointed by governors from a pool of candidates whose qualifications are approved by a merit-selection commission. Typically, merit selection systems require appointed judges to stand for retention elections after a term of years. The Commission's preferred method of judicial selection embraces all aspects of traditional merit selection systems, except the retention election feature. Because the Commission is troubled by the impact of reselection on judicial independence, impartiality, and the rule of law, it has serious reservations about any reselection process. If elections are unavoidable, the Commission regards it as preferable that they be employed at the point of initial selection for reasons discussed above.

In criticizing retention elections, the Commission does not intend to undermine the efforts of those who are seeking to implement traditional merit selection systems in states that employ contested elections as means of judicial selection and reselection. Quite the contrary, we are following the lead of a merit-selection system proponent who admonished the Commission to "take the high ground" and not "compromise [its] principles," before testifying that in merit selection proposals, the "principal goal" of the retention election is itself a "compromise" designed to overcome the "political reality" of entrenched support for judicial elections.[184]

If, however, a state is unwilling to abandon elections at the point of reselection, the Commission believes that retention elections are preferable to contested elections. In retention elections, judges run against their records rather than against opposing candidates, which means that incumbents are at risk of losing their seats only if voters deem their records unacceptable. Because voters have no way of knowing whether the judge that the governor would appoint to replace the ousted incumbent would be preferable, dissatisfaction must run relatively high before a serious campaign to remove a judge will emerge. In contested elections, on the other hand, an incumbent's record will be challenged whenever there is an opponent who wants the incumbent's job, and the incumbent will lose whenever the opposing candidate convinces the electorate that he is preferable. The political pressure brought to bear on a sitting judge who must decide a controversial case in the months leading up to an election is therefore likely to be correspondingly higher. It is unsurprising, then, that most—though not all—of the meanest, and priciest, and most troubling judicial campaigns have been in contested elections rather than retention elections. Accordingly, if states insist on some form of election to reselect judges, the Commission concludes that retention elections are preferable to contested elections.

> **For states that retain contested judicial elections as a means to select or reselect judges, the Commission recommends that all such elections be nonpartisan and conducted in a nonpartisan manner.**

To the extent that states retain their allegiance to contested elections as a means of judicial selection—at the point of initial selection or reselection—the Commission recommends that all such elections be nonpartisan. As a general matter, judges are responsible for upholding the law without regard to whether they are Democrats, Republicans, Libertarians, or independents. Without disputing that a judge's political philosophy can exert some influence over a judge's thinking on some questions of law, partisan elections make party affiliation the single most salient feature of a judge's candidacy by including it as the only information about the candidates on the bal-

---

[184] *ABA Commission on the 21st Century Judiciary*, Phila., Pa. 74-75 (Sept. 27, 2002) (testimony of Clifford Haines, Chair, Pennsylvanians for Modern Courts). Mr. Haines added that a secondary justification for retention elections was to remove an appointee who "turns out to be a disaster"—a problem the Commission regards as better remedied through improved methods of judicial evaluation, discipline and removal.

lot itself. Some states go even further by enabling voters to pull a single-party lever for all candidates in all branches of government, including judges. The net effect is to further blur, if not obliterate, the distinction between judges and other elected officials in the public's mind by conveying the impression that the decision making of judges, like that of legislators and governors, is driven by allegiance to party, rather than to law. It is therefore unsurprising that many of the most extreme examples of independence-threatening election-related behavior have occurred in states that select their judges in either openly partisan elections or elections that are nonpartisan in name only.

Contested elections—be they used to elect a judge initially or to reelect a judge for another term—should therefore be conducted in a nonpartisan manner. Political parties should not be responsible for nominating judicial candidates, and the judicial candidates' partisan affiliation should not appear on ballots in either primary or general elections. States with true nonpartisan elections, such as those in Wisconsin, must therefore be distinguished from states such as Michigan, where the political parties nominate candidates to run in ostensibly nonpartisan general elections, which in fact have been very partisan indeed. In the recent past, states such as North Carolina and Arkansas have moved toward nonpartisan systems—a trend that should be encouraged.

> **For states that continue to employ judicial elections as a means of judicial reselection, the Commission recommends that judicial terms be as long as possible.**

The Commission agrees with the first National Summit on Improving Judicial Selection, which concluded that states in which judges serve for relatively short terms would do well to make judicial terms longer. [185] Regardless of whether states employ partisan, non-partisan, or retention elections as means to reselect sitting judges, the risk that sitting judges will lose their tenure on account of unpopular rulings or allow apprehension of the electorate to color their decision making, is necessarily reduced if elections are made less frequent by lengthening judicial terms. In this regard, we share the view of Morris Overstreet, a former chief justice of the Texas Court of Criminal Appeals, when he testified before the Commission, "if you don't have to go back and face the voters, you don't have to worry about how they're going to retaliate or if they're going to retaliate." That led him to propose judicial terms of ten to fifteen years, which would "reduce even the thought of having to be

---

[185] *Call to Action: Statement of the National Summit on Improving Judicial Selection*, 34 Loy. L.A. L. Rev. 1353 (2001).

reelected or reappointed" and "produce some independence" as a result.[186]

For states that use elections to select or reselect judges, the Commission recommends that states provide the electorate with voter guides on the candidate(s).

In his testimony before the Commission, Joseph Tomain urged the Commission to recommend voter guides as a useful means to better inform the electorate in judicial elections.[187] At our Portland, Oregon, hearing, Gerry Alexander, Chief Justice of the Washington Supreme Court, furnished the Commission with examples of voters' pamphlets used in that state.

When Professor Roy Schotland testified before the ABA Commission on Public Financing of Judicial Campaigns, he made a special point of endorsing the use of voter guides in states that elect their judges. As Schotland described them, "voter pamphlets, which have pictures and little descriptions of each candidate for each office, have been in place and enormously popular in the four West Coast states for almost a century." He noted that the effectiveness of voter guides was reflected in exit polling data, which shows that "voters regard [voter pamphlets] as their favorite source of information." Because voter pamphlet programs are comparatively inexpensive and have been successfully implemented in several states, Schotland concluded that exporting such programs to other jurisdictions would be quite feasible.[188]

The ABA Commission on Public Financing of Judicial Campaigns recommended the proliferation of voter guides for states that use judicial elections, and we concur. To the extent that elections are employed to select or reselect judges, voters should be supplied with more information rather than less. We therefore share the views of the state chief justices who, in their call to action following a summit meeting on judicial selection, concluded:

> State and local governments should prepare and disseminate judicial candidate voter guides by print and electronic means to all registered voters before any judicial election at no cost to judicial candidates. Congress should provide a free mailing frank to any voters' guide sponsored by a state or local government.[189]

---

[186]*ABA Commission on the 21st Century Judiciary*, Austin, Tex. 77-78 (Nov. 22, 2002) (testimony of Morris Overstreet, former Chief Justice, Texas Court of Criminal Appeals).

[187]*ABA Commission on the 21st Century Judiciary, supra* note 47, at 168.

[188]*ABA Commission on Public Financing of Judicial Campaigns*, Wash., D.C. 113-16 (Jan. 27, 2001) (testimony of Roy Schotland, Professor, Georgetown University Law Center).

[189]*Call to Action: State of the National Summit on Improving Judicial Selection, supra* note 185, at 1357.

For states that use elections to select or reselect judges, the Commission recommends that state bars or other appropriate entities initiate a dialogue among affected interests in an effort to deescalate the contributions "arms race" in judicial campaigns.

In states where judicial campaigns have focused on issues relating to products liability, tort reform, or medical malpractice, dissatisfaction with the process is widespread. Individuals and organizations sympathetic to the interests of defendants in civil litigation dislike spending enormous sums of money on judicial elections and worry about its impact on impartial justice. As Gottschalk testified before the Commission:

> We are reaping what we sow. Why should the public believe our courts will dispassionately and fairly dispense justice based on the unique facts and pertinent laws of each particular case when each political party, each candidate, and each candidate's supporter are telling the public in each election that the candidates have perceived notions and bias[es] which will dictate how they will rule in many of the cases that come before them? We know these ads are unfair, one-sided, exaggerated, and often downright disgusting.[190]

Trial lawyers and others with pro-plaintiff leanings are equally troubled by the impact of money on judicial elections. Robert Peck, a Commission advisor and counsel to the American Trial Lawyers Association, echoed Gottschalk's concerns, adding that "we are equally anxious to look for a way out of this."[191] The problem, from the perspective of both sides, is a reluctance to "disarm" unilaterally, for fear that doing so will give the other side unfair advantage.

We agree with Gottschalk, that "one of the outcomes of this Commission might be to get much more focused on getting leaders together in a way to talk about bilateral steps that could be taken there."[192] It may be that the differences separating the warring factions on the civil justice issue are simply too great to bridge. But there is clearly common ground, in that significant segments of both the business and trial-lawyer communities acknowledge that too much money is being spent on a dubious cause that has yielded disastrous results. The Commission therefore encourages state bars or other appropriate bodies to initiate talks between the affected interests in jurisdictions where campaign costs have soared for the purpose of exploring whether agreement to suspend the judicial campaign contributions "arms race" is feasible.

---

[190]*ABA Commission on the 21st Century Judiciary, supra* note 46, at 196.

[191]*ABA Commission on the 21st Century Judiciary,* Austin, Tex. 226 (statement of Robert Peck).

[192]*ABA Commission on the 21st Century Judiciary, supra* note 46, at 222.

For states that use elections to select or reselect judges, the Commission recommends that state bars or other appropriate entities reach out to candidates and affected interests in an effort to establish voluntary guidelines on judicial campaign conduct.

The U.S. Supreme Court's decision in *White* has created considerable uncertainty as to the First Amendment limits on the power of state high courts to regulate candidates' campaign-related speech. Such uncertainties, however, impose no constraints on voluntary action. In the preceding recommendation, the Commission has urged that state bars or other appropriate entities initiate a dialogue between the business community and the trial bar in an effort to escape the cycle of escalating campaign spending that a growing number of states have begun to experience. Even if participants in the process are reluctant to "disarm," it may be possible to reach voluntary agreement on campaign practices that can better protect the interests of promoting judicial independence and accountability. In his testimony before the Commission, Archer described his efforts to initiate a dialogue with those involved in the recent judicial elections in Michigan to the end of securing voluntary compliance with a set of campaign conduct guidelines designed to avoid problems encountered in the previous election cycle.[193] The Commission believes that this approach holds promise and recommends that state bar leaders initiate comparable dialogues in their respective states. The goal should be to convince all affected interests—the candidates, trial lawyers, business interests, political parties, and others—that a truly independent and impartial judiciary is in the best interest of all concerned, and compliance with voluntary campaign guidelines is the best means to that end.

The Constitution Project has developed "Higher Ground Standards of Conduct for Judicial Candidates," which may provide state bar leaders with a starting point in their discussions.[194] They include some provisions that are already a part of many codes of judicial conduct but elevate their profile if candidates subscribe to them publicly. They declare, for example, that candidates should not make promises about how they will decide issues that may come before them; that they should only solicit or accept funds through their campaign committees; that they should promptly disclose the sources of contributions they receive; that they should not make misleading statements themselves; that they should take responsibility for the information their own campaigns disseminate in advertising or otherwise; and that they should condemn misleading statements and advertising disseminated by others on their behalf.

---

[193] *ABA Commission on the 21st Century Judiciary, supra* note 66, at 19-23.

[194] *See* Constitution Project, *The Higher Ground: Standards of Conduct for Judicial Candidates, available at* http://www.constitutionproject.org/ci/standards.pdf.

Archer's statement of principles, included in Appendix B, provides another source of information. It seeks to limit signatories from representing that a judicial candidate has engaged in criminal conduct, racial or ethnic bias, immoral conduct, or professional misconduct in the absence of an official ruling by a regulatory or judicial body.

For states that do not abandon contested elections at the point of initial selection or reselection, the Commission recommends that states create systems of public financing for appellate court elections.

For states that elect their judges in contested elections, the potential advantages of underwriting judicial campaigns with public funds are clear. The more money judges receive from public sources, the less they will have to raise from private groups and individuals who are interested in the outcomes of cases the judges decide, which will reduce the potential for campaign contributions to influence judicial behavior and address the public perception that such influence occurs. Indeed, the case for public financing of judicial elections may be more compelling than it is for the legislative or executive branch races, notwithstanding the fact that almost all public-funding programs have confined themselves to political branch contests. Governors and legislators are supposed to be influenced by their constituents' point of view. In judicial races, on the other hand, where "constituent" and other external influence over a judge's independent decision making is inappropriate, the desirability of insulating judges from the influence of—and the appearance of influence of—private campaign contributions is correspondingly greater. Therefore, the Commission supports ABA policy as recommended by the Commission on Public Financing of Judicial Campaigns, which states that jurisdictions selecting judges in contested elections should finance those elections with public monies.[195]

For states that retain contested judicial elections and do not adopt systems of public financing, the Commission recommends that states impose limits on contributions to judicial campaigns.

In states that continue to finance elections through private contributions, the perception that judges are influenced by their contributors is exacerbated to the extent that contributions are permitted in amounts large enough to foster such perceptions. The ABA has recently amended the Model Rules of Judicial Conduct to require that a judge recuse himself in cases where a lawyer or litigant has contributed to the judge's campaign in excess of a specified amount. In addition, however, the states should impose caps on contributions to

---

[195] *See* American Bar Association, *supra note 63*, at 7.

judicial campaigns and establish maximum contributions at a level that will reduce the appearance that judges are dependant on or beholden to any one individual, interest group, law firm, or corporation.

C. Promoting an Independent Judicial Branch that Works Effectively with the Political Branches of Government

Up to this point, the Commission's concern with judicial independence has focused on the decision-making independence of individual judges—their capacity to decide cases according to law without inappropriate interference from voters, contributors, interest groups, political opponents, the media, or public officials. As described earlier in the course of enumerating the enduring principles of a sound judiciary, however, there is a second form of judicial independence that relates to the capacity of the judiciary to preserve itself as a separate and coequal branch of state government. Without some measure of "institutional independence," state judiciaries would be so completely beholden to the political branches for their survival as to eviscerate their capacity to keep the political branches in check through the exercise of judicial review. Accordingly, state constitutions establish their judiciaries as separate branches of government, and many go further than their federal counterpart by making the separation of powers among the branches explicit or by delegating to the judicial branch specified powers of self-governance.

At the same time, state judiciaries are by no means completely independent. Most significantly for our purposes, state constitutions typically give legislatures the power to authorize—or not—the expenditure of funds for judicial budgets and salary increases, which can serve as a powerful check on the judiciary's institutional autonomy. When exercised responsibly, the legislature's power of the purse constitutes an appropriate and essential check to ensure that the judiciary is operating efficiently and effectively. Recently, however, states around the country have experienced budgetary deficits that often exert a disproportionate impact on judicial systems. As the ABA Journal recently reported, "A state budget crisis is gripping the justice system, forcing many states to close courts and prisons, release some inmates early, stop prosecuting certain nonviolent crimes, and slash indigent defense funding."[196]

In some cases, discussed in the background section of the report, the legislature has cut the judiciary's budget in ways that at least appear to be retaliatory. More often, budget cuts are not the product of legislative indifference or animus but of a need for state-wide fiscal austerity. Even then, however, state judiciaries are often ill equipped to lobby legislatures for their fair share of the shrinking

---

[196]David Hudson Jr., *Courts' Cash Crunch*, 2 No. 3 A.B.A. J. E-Report 1 (January 24, 2003).

fiscal pie and lose ground relative to other priorities the legislature regards as more pressing.

Although the Commission discusses the issue of the judiciary's continuing independence as a branch last and devotes less space to its recommendations here than in the preceding two sections, it would be a mistake to infer that the Commission regards the issue here as less important. The fiscal health of many states has taken a sharp decline in the immediate past, which has created crisis conditions for court budgets in a number of states. Those conditions demand immediate attention. They are, however, currently being attended to by other organizations or other entities within the ABA. For that reason, we have elected not to develop our recommendations here in as much detail and focus our efforts on lending support to other ongoing efforts by calling public attention to them.

The Commission recommends the establishment of standards for minimum funding of judicial systems.

State courts must be adequately funded. The fair and impartial administration of justice is a priority of the highest order. Protecting and preserving that system requires adequate funding for judgeships, staff, facilities, and jury trials. The cost of running state court systems represents a small percentage of the states' overall operating budgets, averaging only 1.5 percent across the country. For these reasons, the Commission believes that states should develop and adhere to minimum standards for state court funding.

Minimum funding standards can help to guard against retaliatory budget cuts that, in the Commission's view, are simply indefensible. In times of fiscal belt tightening, minimum funding standards can likewise assist legislatures in assessing whether and how deeply the judiciary's budget can be cut without impairing the courts' capacity to render fair and impartial justice. "Minimum funding standards" as that phrase is used here, does not mean setting minimum dollar amounts for state appropriations to the judicial branch. Rather, it means isolating the core functions that a judiciary and the judicial system must perform and the critical services it must provide for the benefit of lawmakers confronting hard choices when crafting state budgets. In times of fiscal austerity, all branches of government must make sacrifices; minimum funding standards can assist judges and legislators in establishing the floor below which state budgets must not go if the judicial system's core mission is to be preserved.

The Commission notes that some research and writing has been devoted to the issue of adequate court funding.[197] To date, how-

---

[197] *See generally,* Institute for Court Management, *Courts and the Public Interest: A Call for Sustainable Resources* (May 2002).

ever, no comprehensive effort has been undertaken to explore minimum funding standards that the Commission recommends here.

> **The Commission recommends that the judiciary's budget
> be segregated from that of the political branches and that it
> be presented to the legislature for approval with a mini-
> mum of nontransferable, line itemization.**

The state judiciary is not an administrative agency in the
executive branch but an independent branch of government and
needs to be treated as such. In the federal system, the judiciary's
annual budget request was controlled by the Department of Justice
until 1939, when the attorney general successfully lobbied Congress
to have the judiciary present its own budget requests through a newly
created Administrative Office of U.S. Courts. Not all states, however,
have followed the federal government's lead.[198] If the judiciary is an
independent branch of government, its budget should be assessed
independently of the executive branch. The Commission urges states
to abandon the antiquated practice of folding the judiciary's budget
request into that of the executive branch and giving the executive
branch power to adjust the judiciary's appropriations request before
it is acted upon by state legislature.

In a similar vein, the legislature has a duty to minimize waste
in state government and take pains to assure itself that appropriations
are spent wisely, but at some point, careful oversight can degenerate
into micromanagement of a coequal branch of government. In
Massachusetts, for example, the judiciary's budget is funded in more
than 100 separate line items, in which the courts have no capacity to
transfer funds from one item to another.[199] The net effect is to invite
micromanagement, or worse—retaliatory budget cuts of particular
line items, as discussed in Part II of this report. To the extent that
states preserve line itemization as a means to preserve the judiciary's
financial accountability, the burden on courts can be reduced if they
are authorized to transfer funds among approved line items.

---

[198] *See generally,* James W. Douglas and Roger E. Hartley, *State Court Budgeting and Judicial
Independence: Clues from Oklahoma and Virginia,* 33 ADMIN. & SOCIETY 54, 67 (March 2001).
("Unlike Oklahoma, the judiciary in Virginia does not submit its budget request directly to the
legislature. Instead, after putting together the budget request, the Chief Justice submits the budget to
the governor's Department of Planning and Budget. Here, the governor's staff has the power to review
and alter the request prior to sending it on to the legislature as part of the governor's executive budget
document.")
[199] *ABA Commission on the 21st Century Judiciary,* Portland, Or. 148-49 (Nov. 1, 2002) (remarks of
Margaret Marshall, Chief Justice, Supreme Judicial Court of Massachusetts and member of the ABA
Commission on the 21st Century Judiciary).

The Commission recommends that states create independent commissions to establish judicial salaries.

If the judiciary is to be capable, qualified, and independent, it is imperative that judges be adequately compensated. Judges should be selected from the ranks of our most talented private practitioners, government lawyers, and academicians. While it may be true that some financial sacrifice is a price many fine women and men are prepared to pay when they ascend the bench, there is a point below which salaries may not fall without discouraging the best and the brightest from seeking judicial office. As recent events described in Part II of this report reveal, however, in many places judicial salaries are not even keeping pace with inflation, let alone staying competitive with the market for the services of qualified lawyers. State judge pay ranges often fall below that of many state and local officials; in California, for example, trial judges are paid less than many county sheriffs and district attorneys.

The process by which salaries are set is likewise important to the independence and impartiality of the judiciary. Judicial independence can only be harmed by the annual spectacle of judges going, hat in hand, to beg their legislatures for much needed salary increases and cost-of-living adjustments.

The Commission heard testimony concerning the experience in the state of Washington with a salary commission that sets the pay levels for judges independent of the political branches.[200] Washington is not the only state to employ a salary commission of this kind. Some twenty states currently employ salary commissions of some kind, of which nine have the power to issue binding recommendations unless affirmatively disapproved.[201]

The Commission regards this as a very promising avenue to explore. The ABA Standing Committee on Judicial Independence is currently developing a detailed salary commission proposal, and the Commission supports the standing committee in its efforts.

The Commission recommends that states create opportunities for regular meetings among representatives from all three branches of government to promote inter-branch communication as a means to avoid unnecessary confrontations on such issues as court funding, judicial salaries, and structural reform of courts.

Often the conflicts that arise between courts and legislatures over judicial budgets, salaries, and their priority relative to other

---

[200]*ABA Commission on the 21st Century Judiciary*, Portland, Or. 169-72 (Nov. 1, 2002) (testimony of Gerry Alexander, Chief Justice, Supreme Court of Washington).

[201] Janice Fernette & Mary Pat Berkenbaugh, *Judicial Compensation Commissions*, National Center for State Courts (1994), *available at* http://www.ncsconline.org.

state needs is the product not of political animus but of a communications failure. Although courts speak to legislatures in their opinions, and legislatures speak to courts in the statutes they enact, opportunities for less formal interaction are often quite limited. The necessary separation and independence of legislative and judicial functions do not require isolation. To the contrary, there is much to be gained by creating mechanisms to foster comity and interbranch communication that can defuse crises before they occur.

The Commission therefore recommends that states create opportunities for regular meetings among representatives from the three branches of government, to discuss issues of mutual concern. Such meetings can take a variety of forms: states may constitute tri-branch commissions to improve court operations; one branch of government may host periodic conclaves; state law schools may host periodic conferences; and individual judges may simply reach out to their local legislators. The ABA Standing Committee on Judicial Independence is seeking to establish a model for this kind of inter-branch activity, and the Commission encourages these efforts.

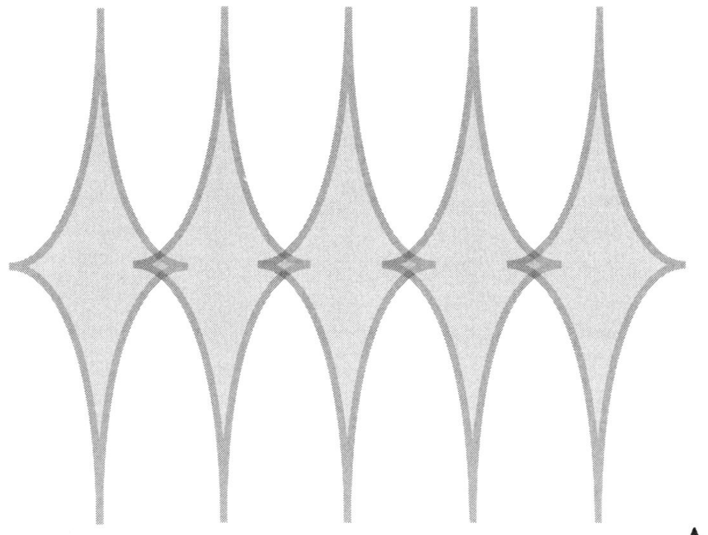

APPENDIX A

AMERICAN BAR ASSOCIATION
COMMISSION ON THE 21ST CENTURY JUDICIARY
JUDICIAL DIVISION
SECTION OF FAMILY LAW
STANDING COMMITTEE ON FEDERAL JUDICIAL IMPROVEMENTS
STANDING COMMITTEE ON JUDICIAL INDEPENDENCE
COALITION FOR JUSTICE
SECTION OF LITIGATION

REPORT TO THE HOUSE OF DELEGATES
RECOMMENDATION

RESOLVED, That the American Bar Association adopts the Principles and Conclusions of the Commission on the 21st Century Judiciary, dated August 2003, to ensure judicial independence, accountability and efficiency.

FURTHER RESOLVED, That the American Bar Association urges all state, local and territorial bar associations to ensure the integrity of state and territorial judiciaries by promoting the implementation of the Principles and Conclusions of the Commission on the 21st Century Judiciary.

American Bar Association
Commission on the 21st Century Judiciary

Principles and Conclusions
August 2003

I.　　**Enduring Principles**

A. Judges should uphold the law.
B. Judges should be independent.
C. Judges should be impartial.
D. Judges should possess the appropriate temperament and character.
E. Judges should possess the appropriate capabilities and credentials.
F. Judges and the Judiciary should have the confidence of the public.
G. The judicial system should be diverse and reflective of the society it serves.
H. Judges should be constrained to perform their duties in a manner that justifies public faith and confidence in the courts.

II.　　**Preserving the Judiciary's Institutional Legitimacy**

A. Judicial Qualifications, Training and Evaluation

States should establish credible, neutral, non-partisan and diverse deliberative bodies to assess the qualifications of all judicial aspirants so as to limit the candidate pool to those who are well qualified.

The judicial branch should take primary responsibility for providing continuing judicial education, that continuing judicial education should be required for all judges, and that state appropriations should be sufficient to provide adequate funding for continuing judicial education programs.

Congress should fully fund the State Justice Institute.

States should fully fund the National Center for State Courts.

States should develop judicial evaluation programs to assess the performance of all sitting judges.

B. Judicial Ethics and Discipline

The American Bar Association should undertake a comprehensive review of the Model Code of Judicial Conduct.

The codes of judicial conduct should be actively enforced.

C. Diversification of the Justice System

Members of the legal profession should expand their use of training and recruitment programs to encourage lawyers who reflect diversity to join their firms, they should include them fully in firm life, and they should prepare them for pursuing careers on the bench following their years in practice.

Courts should promote a representative work force and diverse court appointments.

Courts should act aggressively to ensure that language barriers do not limit access to the justice system.

Courts should have in place formal policies and processes for handling allegations of bias.

Information regarding diversity should be shared among the courts in a state and among the states.

Measures should be adopted to improve and expand jury pool representation.

D. Improving Court-Community Relationships

Courts should take steps to promote public understanding of and confidence in the courts among jurors, witnesses and litigants.

Courts should engage and collaborate with the communities of which they are a part, by hosting trips to courthouses and by judges and court administrators speaking in schools and other community settings.

The continuation of problem-solving courts as a means to promote public confidence in the courts.

III. Improving Judicial Selection

A. The preferred system of state court judicial selection is a commission-based appointive system, with the following components:

The governor should appoint judges from a pool of judicial aspirants whose qualifications have been reviewed and approved by a credible, neutral, non-partisan, diverse deliberative body or commission.

Judicial appointees should serve until a specified age. Judges so appointed should not be subject to reselection processes, and should be entitled to retirement benefits upon completion of judicial service.

Judges should not otherwise be subject to reselection, nonetheless remain subject to regular judicial performance evaluations and disciplinary processes that include removal for misconduct.

B. Alternative Recommendations on Systems of Judicial Selection

For states that cannot abandon the judicial reselection process altogether, judges should be subject to reappointment by a credible, neutral, non-partisan, diverse deliberative body.

For states that cannot abandon judicial elections altogether, elections should be employed only at the point of initial selection.

For states that retain judicial elections as a means of reselection, judges should stand for retention election, rather than run in contested elections.

For states that retain contested judicial elections as a means to select or reselect judges, all such elections should be non-partisan and conducted in a non-partisan manner.

For states that continue to employ judicial elections as a means of judicial reselection, judicial terms should be as long as possible.

For states that use elections to select or reselect judges, states should provide the electorate with voter guides on the candidate(s).

For states that use elections to select or reselect judges, state bars or other appropriate entities should initiate a dialogue among affected interests, in an effort to deescalate the contributions arms race in judicial campaigns.

For states that use elections to select or reselect judges, state bars or other appropriate entities should reach out to candidates and affected interests, in an effort to establish voluntary guidelines on judicial campaign conduct.

For states that do not abandon contested elections at the point of initial selection or reselection, states should create systems of public financing for appellate court elections.

For states that retain contested judicial elections and do not adopt systems of public financing, states should impose limits on contributions to judicial candidates.

IV. Promoting an Independent Judicial Branch that Works Effectively with the Political Branches of Government

Standards for minimum funding of judicial systems should be established.

The judiciary's budget should be segregated from that of the political branches, and it should be presented to the legislature for approval with a minimum of non-transferable line itemization.

States should create independent commissions to establish judicial salaries.

States should create opportunities for regular meetings among representatives from all three branches of government to promote inter-branch communication as a means to avoid unnecessary confrontations on such issues as court funding, judicial salaries, and structural reform of courts.

Report

The judicial systems of the United States at the beginning of the 21st Century remain unparalleled in their capacity to deliver fair and impartial justice, but these systems are in great jeopardy. Our state courts play a critical role in preserving American freedom and democracy. Almost 100 million cases are resolved peacefully and with relatively little fanfare by some 30,000 state judges each year. Increased political involvement in the judiciary, diminished public trust and confidence in the justice system, and uncertain resources supporting the courts, however, place burdens on the judiciary's capacity to continue to provide fair and impartial justice. Indeed, the escalating partisanship and corrosive effects of excessive money in judicial campaigns, coupled with changes in society at large and the courts themselves, have served to create an environment that places our system of justice, administered by independent and impartial judges, at risk.

Background

The American Bar Association (ABA) has long been dedicated to preserving judicial independence and ensuring that justice is administered impartially throughout the federal and state courts, at all levels. As the national representative of the legal profession, the ABA remains keenly aware of the challenges facing the judicial systems and works to preserve judicial independence and impartiality. Uniquely situated to respond to threats to our justice systems, the ABA has a responsibility not only to respond to immediate challenges but also to look to the future and develop programs and initiatives to strengthen judicial administration as well as the public's trust and confidence in the judiciary.

Over the past decade, ABA leadership has exercised this important responsibility by initiating a variety of programs to support the judiciary. In 1996, the Committee on Separation of Powers and Judicial Independence issued a seminal report on the state of the judicial system. This report guided much of the recent work of the Association in the area of judicial independence. In 1997, the Special Committee on Judicial Independence was created to respond to unwarranted criticism of judges, promote public trust and confidence in, and understanding of, the role of the state judiciaries, and to develop programs throughout the states to preserve judicial independence. The Special Committee, which became a Standing Committee in 1999, undertook a number of important programmatic activities and, under the leadership of Alfred P. Carlton, Jr., secured over $1,000,000 in outside funding to develop model programs. These programs include a model response to criticism of judges, standards on state judicial selection, and a model for public financing of judicial campaigns. Each of these initiatives marked the first time such topics were addressed on a national level and each has been adopted in the states, to various degrees.

In addition to the work of the Standing Committee, Philip Anderson, during his year as President of the ABA, organized three national programs on judicial independence, which culminated in a national conference on public trust and confidence in the judiciary. This conference provided an opportunity for extensive public outreach and collaboration, and set an agenda for the bar to focus on the public's perception of the role of the judiciary.

The Commission on the 21st Century Judiciary

Continuing with the important work done during his tenure as Chair of the Standing Committee on Judicial Independence, and with a keen appreciation for a changing landscape of how state judges are selected, retained, provided independence, and made accountable, President Carlton, as ABA President-Elect, undertook a year long planning process to devise a strategy to address these challenges faced by state judiciaries. As a leading spokesperson for judicial independence, he recognized the need for the organized bar to think strategically and comprehensively about the myriad problems facing state judiciaries, many of which have arisen just in the last decade.

Upon becoming President of the ABA last August, Carlton convened the Commission on the 21st Century Judiciary to study, report and make recommendations with regard to various aspects of state judicial systems to ensure fairness, impartiality and accountability in the judiciary. President Carlton directed the Commission to provide a framework for addressing and alleviating the extent to which our courts have been excessively politicized. Further, the Commission was directed to explore ways to improve judicial selection and articulate principles to promote an independent and accountable judiciary. The Commission was charged with reaching out to the widest possible audience in developing recommendations for defusing the partisan battle over the courts and thereby preserving the principles that ensure judicial independence and accountability.

Abner Mikva, former U.S. Representative, White House Counsel, and Chief Judge of the US Court of Appeals for the District of Columbia Circuit, and William S. Sessions, former director of the FBI and U.S. District Judge, serve as honorary co-chairs of the Commission. Edward W. Madeira, Jr. of Philadelphia, who has long been active in judicial independence issues, chairs the Commission, and Charles Gardner Geyh, an Indiana University School of Law Professor, serves as reporter to the Commission. In addition, Commission members include Chief Justice Margaret Marshall of Massachusetts; Chief Justice Thomas Phillips of Texas; Barbara Roberts, former governor of Oregon; Stephen Zack of Florida; Thomas Ross of North Carolina, a former judge and state court administrator; Julius Chambers of North Carolina; Ric Duques, the chair of the board of First Data Corp. of Florida; George Frazza, former general counsel of Johnson & Johnson of New York; Representative Pete Gallego of the Texas House of Representatives; and Patricia Hynes of New York. Jose Feliciano serves as the ABA Board of Governors liaison to the Commission. The work of the Commission was funded by generous grants from the Open Society Institute, The Joyce Foundation and the Z. Smith Reynolds Foundation, with additional support from Lexis-Nexis.

Recognizing the need for a wide representation of viewpoints, and in the spirit of collaboration that has so strengthened the work of the Association, an advisory committee was formed with representatives from a number of national organizations and ABA entities. The members of the advisory committee represented the ABA Section of Litigation, the ABA Judicial Division, the ABA Tort Trial and Insurance Practice Section, the ABA Section of Legal Education, the ABA Standing Committee on Strategic Communications, the ABA Section Officers Conference, the US Chamber of Commerce Institute for Legal Reform, the League of Women Voters of the United States, the Defense Research Institute, the American Trial Lawyers Association, the American College of Trial Lawyers, corporate counsel, and the Hispanic National Bar Association.

The Commission held public hearings in Detroit, Michigan; Philadelphia, Pennsylvania; Portland, Oregon; and Austin, Texas. At the hearings, experts on problem-solving courts, judicial compensation, court system funding, juvenile courts, death penalty litigation, and judicial selection were joined by leaders of national bar associations of color, state chief justices, and legal and political science scholars in providing testimony on critical issues contributing to excessive political pressures on the judiciary. Over thirty experts testified at these hearings and provided the Commission with great insights into the challenges facing state judiciaries across the country. These hearings, as well as a plethora of written materials and testimony, guided the work of the commission in developing a series of recommendations for improvements in processes that impact both judicial independence and judicial accountability. By holding hearings in four regions of the country, the Commission recognized the wide disparity in challenges facing the judiciary, and expert testimony corroborated the belief that while some problems might occur in each state and locality, they manifest themselves and impact the states in very different ways. This perspective guided the Commission as it crafted its recommendations and fueled the Commission's thinking that there is no simple solution to any of these issues. Responses must be tailored to the unique challenges of each locale, and the ABA, as a national organization, must provide enough alternatives to make the recommendations useful. Thus, the recommendations crafted by the Commission are comprehensive, and tailored to provide options and choices for different states.

Following the hearings, the Commission held a colloquium in Raleigh, North Carolina, where over 150 judges, lawyers, members of the public, legal and political science scholars vetted the preliminary recommendations of the Commission. During the colloquium, participants engaged in an interactive dialogue on issues such as the changing role of the judge in American society; the role of the public in selecting and retaining judges; and the appropriate balance between judicial independence and accountability to the public. Using the colloquium as an opportunity for public participation allowed the Commission to garner additional input from across the country, making the completed product, a set of eight enduring principles and thirty-one recommendations, relevant, comprehensive, and adaptable.

In accomplishing its goals, the Commission developed a set of enduring principles that underscore the importance of an independent, impartial judiciary to uphold the rule of law in a constitutional, democratic republic and to maintain the trust and confidence of the public. In addition, recent developments among the states that have politicized the judiciary in ways that challenge some of those enduring principles were developed. Finally, a series of recommendations were made to serve as a framework for the ABA and the states to begin to address and counteract developments that have politicized the courts unnecessarily.

Enduring Principles

The Commission enumerates eight enduring principles that should be central components to each state's understanding of the role of the judiciary as a co-equal branch of government. The essential elements to promoting judicial independence, accountability and impartiality recognize that judges should uphold the rule of law and should be impartial and independent. Judges should possess the appropriate temperament and character, as well as appropriate capabilities and credentials. Judges should have the confidence of the public and the justice system should be diverse and reflect the society it serves. Finally, judges should be constrained to perform their duties in a manner that justifies public faith and confidence in the courts.

Challenges to State Judiciaries

The Commission identifies a number of factors and trends that have led to the politicization of state courts. These include the proliferation of controversial cases generally; the rediscovery of state constitutions to litigate constitutional rights and responsibilities; the increases in caseload; the interposition of intermediate appellate courts between trial courts and courts of last resort; the spread of the two-party system; and the emergence of single-issue groups, coupled with the emergence of a skeptical and conflicted public. In addition, changes in the nature of litigants, including a trend towards pro se litigation and its impact on the role of the trial judge, and the diversification of America and its impact on the public's confidence in the courts, as well as changes in the role of the courts, including the rise of problem-solving courts, were recognized.

These factors and trends contribute to increased politicization of the courts, where the fair and impartial administration of justice is at risk. Specifically, the Commission is concerned about state high court election campaigns that increasingly are focused on isolated issues of intense political interest coupled with the rising cost of judicial elections and the impact that expensive campaigns have on the public's perception that judges are influenced by their contributors. Further, the Commission is troubled by the recognition that some of the most politicized and misleading campaign related speech comes in the form of "issue advertising" developed by outside groups. These issue ads and the expensive campaigns are all the more troubling with the recognition that the public is insufficiently familiar with judicial candidates, judicial qualifications and the judicial system. Additionally, a cause of concern is the considerable uncertainty surrounding the constitutionality of ethical limits on judicial campaign speech brought about by the recent decision of the Supreme Court of the United States in Republican Party of Minnesota v. White. 536 US 765 (2002). Finally, relationships between courts and legislatures often have been problematic, manifested by attempts to cut the judiciary's budget, attempts to curb court jurisdiction, attempts to remove judges from office, and proposals for constitutional amendments to constrain the courts' constitutional interpretations.

The identification of these various trends is a crucial component to the work of the Commission. Previously, attempts to address factors impacting judicial independence have focused on one set of issues or one particular threat, i.e., judicial selection issues, the high cost of judicial elections, jury service, diversity in the profession and on the bench, or court funding, to name just a few. The Commission is looking from the perspective of the judiciary itself, trying to identify factors that impact the administration of justice in this new century. Taking a comprehensive view of the challenges facing the judiciary provides a fresh perspective. By identifying factors and trends, the Commission not only broadens the scope of its efforts, but recognizes that most trends are interrelated and solutions must also be interrelated. The comprehensive review of trends affecting the judiciary allows the Commission to deepen its understanding of threats to judicial independence and the administration of justice, and also allows the Commission to add depth to its recommendations, acknowledging the interrelated nature of these challenges and the critical need to craft state-specific solutions that take into account all aspects of judicial administration.

Commission Recommendations

The Commission offers thirty-one different recommendations designed to address the myriad challenges threatening state courts in the 21st Century. The recommendations can be grouped into three main categories.

A. Preserving the Judiciary's Institutional Legitimacy

The first set of recommendations is designed to preserve the judiciary's institutional legitimacy by improving judicial qualifications, training and evaluation. These recommendations recognize the vital role played by a variety of organizations dedicated to the preservation of an independent, accountable and impartial judiciary, such as the State Justice Institute and the National Center for State Courts. Additionally, these recommendations acknowledge that credible review of candidate qualifications before selection, and continuing judicial education after a candidate becomes a judge, ensures that state judiciaries are comprised of well qualified, highly trained individuals. To that end, the Commission recommends that states establish credible, neutral, non-partisan and diverse deliberative bodies to assess the qualifications of all judicial aspirants so as to limit the candidate pool to those who are well qualified. Additionally, these recommendations recognize that the judicial branch should take primary responsibility for providing continuing judicial education and that not only should such judicial education be required of all judges but states should provide adequate funding to support these educational programs.

The next recommendations, focusing on judicial ethics and discipline, suggest a comprehensive review of the ABA Model Code of Judicial Conduct. Additionally, the Commission recommends that the codes of judicial conduct in the states should be actively enforced.

The Commission strongly recommends that increasing diversity of the judicial branch is more than an attractive goal for the 21st century judiciary; it is a necessity. Within fifty years, fully half of all Americans will be persons of color. But recent surveys reveal an alarming erosion of trust and confidence in the justice system among people of color. These surveys reveal that people of color do not believe that they are treated fairly by courts, and that because of factors such as language barriers, racial bias, and the increasing influence of money in judicial elections, their access to justice is inferior to that of non-Hispanic whites. Moreover, the lack of racial or ethnic diversity among legal professionals exacerbates these perceptions. Particularly important in this regard is the relative lack of minority judges in state judiciaries, a figure that is estimated at approximately 8%, while people of color comprise nearly 30% of the national population. The Commission is convinced that the continued failure to meaningfully diversify the courts will work to the detriment of the 21st Century judiciary's overall health, quality, and level of public support.

These recommendations recognize the critical importance of a diverse bench, with formal policies for addressing bias in the system, to ensuring public trust and confidence in the judiciary. Specific recommendations include expanding the use of training and recruitment programs to encourage minority lawyers to join firms; providing for the active promotion of a representative work force and diverse court appointments; creating formal policies and processes for handling allegations of bias; sharing information regarding diversity among courts both intra-state and inter-state; and adopting methods to eliminate language barriers and improve and expand jury pool representation.

Other recommendations address improving court-community relationships by furthering the use of problem-solving courts as well as encouraging greater outreach to the public. The Commission recommends a number of methods to improve outreach, including collaborating with members of the community by hosting trips to courthouses and by judges and court administrators speaking in schools and community settings. Additionally, steps should be taken to promote public understanding of and confidence in the courts among jurors, witnesses and litigants.

B.   Improving Judicial Selection

Some of the most serious problems confronting our judicial systems today relate to judicial selection and reselection. Judicial election campaigns at all levels are increasingly focused on isolated issues of intense political interest. In the Commission's view, states should be concerned about the impact of judicial elections on judicial impartiality and the rule of law. Notwithstanding increasing concern about the judicial selection process in many states, judicial selection improvement is among the most contentious subjects that the Commission has been directed to address. Nowhere is the tension between judicial independence and judicial accountability more palpable than in the context of judicial selection. Although there is general consensus that selection systems should preserve and promote independence and accountability, determining how to strike that balance in a judicial selection system is subject to intense debate. Additionally, nowhere is the challenge of balancing the theoretical with the practical more daunting than in the context of judicial selection. To overcome these difficulties, the Commission has presented its judicial selection recommendations by identifying a preferred system of judicial selection and then making alternative recommendations.

The Commission believes that the preferred system of state court judicial selection is a commission-based appointive system with components that include gubernatorial appointment from a pool of judicial aspirants whose qualifications have been reviewed and approved by a credible, neutral, non-partisan, diverse deliberative body. Additionally, judicial appointees should serve a single term of at least 15 years or until a specified age, should not otherwise be subject to reselection and should be provided appropriate retirement benefits upon completion of judicial service.

The Commission opposes the use of judicial elections as a means of initial selection and reselection, concluding that judicial elections are antithetical to a republican form of government. The Commission acknowledges, though, that support for judicial elections remains entrenched in many states. With that in mind, the Commission offers a series of alternative judicial selection recommendations aimed at ameliorating some of the deleterious effects of elections on the enduring principles of a good judicial system. In reviewing the reselection process, states should use a credible, neutral, non-partisan, diverse deliberative body to handle judicial reappointment, and, if a state retains elections for reselection, then the elections be retention elections instead of contested elections. For states that retain elections as the method of judicial selection, the elections should be non-partisan, public financing should be provided for appellate level elections, voter guides should be provided to the electorate, judicial terms should be as long as possible, states should impose limits on contributions to judicial candidates if public financing is not employed, state bars or other appropriate entities should work to initiate a dialogue among affected interests to deescalate the contributions arms race in judicial campaigns, and state bars or other interested entities should establish voluntary guidelines on campaign conduct.

C. Promoting an Independent Judicial Branch that Works Effectively with the Political Branches of Government

The Commission finally makes recommendations that relate to the capacity of the judiciary to preserve itself as a separate and co-equal branch of state government. Without some measure of institutional independence, state judiciaries would be so beholden to the political branches for their survival as to eviscerate their capacity to keep the political branches in check through the exercise of judicial review. While state constitutions often make the separation of powers among the branches explicit or delegate to the judicial branch specified powers of self-governance, state judiciaries are by no means completely independent. Most importantly, state constitutions typically give legislatures the power to authorize, or not authorize, the expenditure of funds for judicial budgets and salary increases. When exercised responsibly, the legislature's power of the purse constitutes an appropriate and essential check, but recently, states around the country have experienced budgetary deficits that often exert a disproportionate impact on judicial systems. It is this fiscal crisis, and the tenuous balance of power between the co-equal branches of government, that underlies this set of recommendations.

The Commission recommends that standards for minimum funding of judicial systems should be established. This does not mean setting minimum dollar amounts for state appropriations to the judicial branch. Rather, it means isolating the core functions that a judiciary must perform and the critical services it must provide, for the benefit of lawmakers confronting hard choices when crafting state budgets. Minimum funding standards can assist judges and legislators in establishing the floor below which state budgets must not go if the judiciary's constitutional obligations are to be preserved. In addition, the Commission recommends that the judiciary's budget should be segregated from that of the political branches and it should be presented to the legislature for approval with a minimum of non-transferable line itemization. The state judiciary is not an administrative agency in the executive branch, but an independent branch of government and needs to be treated as such. States are urged to abandon the antiquated practice of folding the judiciary's budget requests into the executive branch and giving the executive branch power to adjust the judiciary's appropriations requests before they are accepted by state legislatures. Further, the Commission recognizes that if the judiciary is to be capable, qualified and independent, it is imperative that judges be adequately compensated. Thus, the Commission recommends the creation of independent commissions to establish judicial salaries. Finally, the states should create opportunities for regular meetings among representatives from all three branches of government to promote inter-branch communication as a means to avoid unnecessary confrontations and provide for better understanding and more appropriate collaboration on such issues as court funding, judicial salaries, and structural reform of courts.

Conclusion

As an institution unique to American government, an independent judicial branch guarantees every citizen access to a branch of government designed to protect the rights and liberties afforded by federal and state constitutions. Fundamental to this unique role of the courts is the necessity for the judiciary to be distinct from the other two branches of government, functioning independently to ensure an effective role in our republican form of government. The differences unique to the judiciary, manifested in ethical restrictions on judges, judicial selection methods, and the nature of the judicial process, are vital aspects of maintaining balance among the branches of government.

Over time, however, the role of the judiciary has undergone a transformation, particularly in relation to the other branches. Judicial elections are a prime example of this erosion of separation in the nature and role of the branches of government. Recent judicial election cycles have seen a dramatic shift in the cost, tone and tenor of judicial campaigns. States have registered increases in judicial campaign expenditures that range from 100% to 350%. The involvement of third party interest groups and the shift in the tone and tenor of judicial campaigns, manifested by recent challenges to state codes of judicial ethics, have conspired to create an arena for judicial selection that jeopardizes the independence and impartiality of the judicial system and, more importantly, threatens to erode the public's trust and confidence in the system.

The changing nature of judicial campaigns and judicial selection is but one illustration of the shifting nature and role of the judiciary. Courts over the past decade have worked to confront issues of diversity on the bench and among court personnel. Judges have recognized the broadening role they can play in resolving disputes through problem-solving court models. These issues have allowed the courts to develop stronger ties to the community they serve while also becoming more representative of that community. The state courts handle an enormous volume of cases that literally touches the lives of most if not all Americans, indicating the importance of maintaining the judiciary as a branch of government capable of fulfilling its fundamental constitutional obligations in the separation of powers.

With the promulgation of a comprehensive set of recommendations, touching on aspects of the judicial system and considering a wide range of tensions and challenges, the Commission on the 21st Century Judiciary proposes a series of recommendations for change that will maintain independent, impartial state judiciaries, functioning as effective, co-equal branches of government, for generations to come. The American Bar Association has, for over a century, been a national leader in efforts to preserve judicial independence and impartiality. The ABA, with the guidance of these comprehensive recommendations, will provide myriad options for improving the administration of justice to state and local leaders throughout the country.

Respectfully submitted,
Edward W. Madeira, Jr., Chair
Commission on the 21st Century Judiciary
August 2003

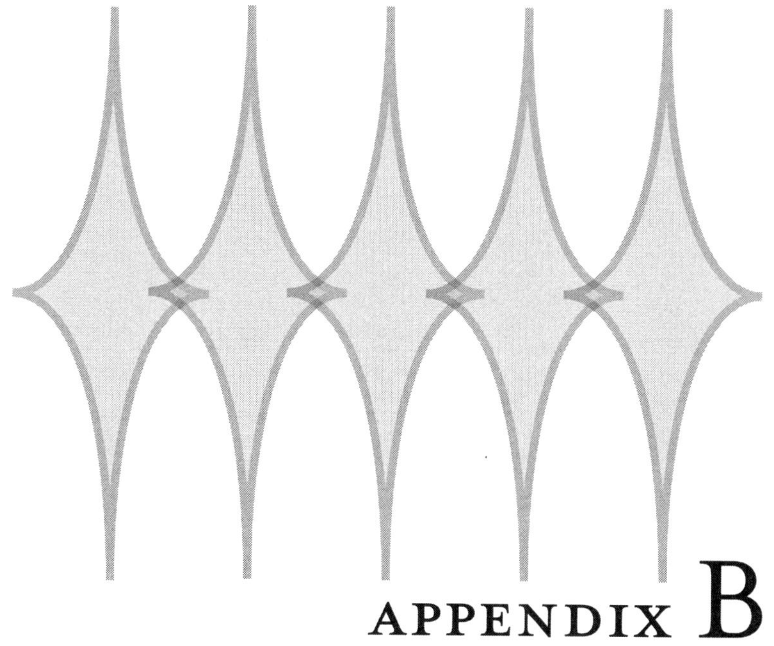

APPENDIX B

AMERICAN BAR ASSOCIATION COMMISSION ON THE 21st CENTURY JUDICIARY

ROSTER OF WITNESSES AND FACULTY COMMISSION HEARINGS AND NATIONAL COLLOQUIUM

The ABA Commission on the 21st Century Judiciary held four national hearings between August and November 2002, and a National Colloquium in March 2003. A wide variety of national experts on the judiciary, including scholars, lawyers, state chief justices, and public leaders, testified before the commission on a number of topics. Hearings were held at Wayne State University Law School in Detroit, Michigan; James A. Byrne U.S. Courthouse in Philadelphia, Pennsylvania; Portland State University College of Urban and Public Affairs in Portland, Oregon; and the Old Supreme Court Chambers of the Texas State Capitol in Austin, Texas. The four hearings generated a total of 1,032 pages of testimony.

The following people testified before the Commission at its four hearings:

Hon. Gerry Alexander, Chief Justice, Supreme Court of Washington
Hon. Dennis Archer, President-Elect, American Bar Association
Hon. Phyllis Beck, Pennsylvania Superior Court
Greg Berman, Director, Center for Court Innovation
James Bopp, Jr., Bopp, Coleson & Bostrom
Mark Brewer, Chair, Michigan Democratic Party
Stephen Bright, Director, Southern Center for Human Rights
Dr. Bill Burges, President, Burges & Burges
Lisa Chang, President, National Asian Pacific American Bar
    Association
Allan Gordon, Chancellor, Philadelphia Bar Association
Thomas Gottschalk, General Counsel, General Motors Corporation
Clifford Haines, Pennsylvanians for Modern Courts
Hon. Brenda Harbin-Forte, Alameda County Superior Court, former Dean, B.E. Witkin Judicial College of California (provided written testimony)
Guy Harrison, President, State Bar of Texas

Dr. Roger Hartley, University of Arizona School of Public Administration and Policy

J. Barlow Herget, political consultant, Raleigh, North Carolina

Hon. Dale Koch, Presiding Judge, Multnomah County Courts; member, Board of Trustees, National Council of Juvenile and Family Court Judges

Angel Lopez, President, Oregon Bar Association

Hon. Frederica Massiah-Jackson, President Judge, Philadelphia Court of Common Pleas

Hon. Thomas Moyer, Chief Justice, Supreme Court of Ohio

Robert Newell, President, Multnomah County Bar Association

Hon. Morris Overstreet, former Justice, Texas Court of Criminal Appeals

Margaret Reaves, Executive Director, Texas State Commission on Judicial Conduct

Malcolm Robinson, President, National Bar Association

Hon. Patricio Serna, Chief Justice, Supreme Court of New Mexico; President, National Consortium of Task Forces and Commissions on Racial and Ethnic Bias in the Courts

Bryan Stevenson, Executive Director, Equal Justice Initiative of A Alabama

David Tevelin, Director, State Justice Institute

Joseph Tomain, Dean, University of Cincinnati College of Law

Suzanne Townsend, President, National Native American Bar Association

Reginald Turner, President, Michigan Bar Association

Andru Volinsky, Stein, Volinsky & Callaghan, PA

In addition, the Commission sought written testimony from any interested party. The Commission received written statements from the following organizations:

ABA Death Penalty Moratorium Implementation Project

ABA Section of Individual Rights and Responsibilities, Death Penalty Committee

Campaign and Media Legal Center

Center for American Politics and Citizenship at the University of Maryland

California Center for Judicial Education and Research

Justice at Stake Campaign

Hennepin County (MN) Bar Association

State Bar of Wisconsin Committee on Politics and the Wisconsin Judiciary

The National Colloquium on the 21st Century Judiciary was held at the North Carolina Bar Center in Cary, North Carolina. In addition to members of the Commission and ABA President Alfred P. Carlton, Jr., the following people served as faculty at the colloquium:

Cynthia Canary, Director, Illinois Campaign for Political Reform
Paul Carrington, Professor, Duke University School of Law
Deborah Goldberg, Acting Director, Democracy Program, Brennan
    Center for Justice
Charles E.M. Kolb, President, Committee for Economic
    Development
Judith B. Moran, Consultant, Center for Families, Children and the
    Courts, University of Baltimore School of Law
Gene Nichol, Dean, University of North Carolina at Chapel Hill
    School of Law
Andrew Spalding, University of Nevada – Las Vegas
G. Alan Tarr, Professor and Director, Center for State
    Constitutional Studies, Rutgers University - Camden
Joseph Tomain, Dean, University of Cincinnati College of Law
Emily Field Van Tassel, Historian and Legal Scholar
Roger Warren, President, National Center for State Courts
Frances K. Zemans, Justice System Consultant; Former Executive
    Vice-President and Director, American Judicature Society

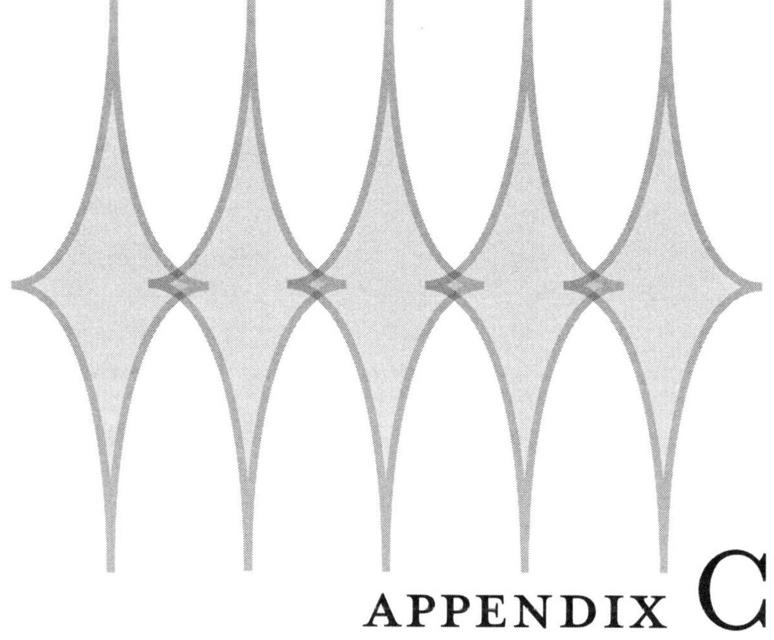

APPENDIX C

STATEMENT OF PRINCIPLES REGARDING MICHIGAN JUDICIAL CAMPAIGNS

Proposed by Dennis W. Archer
President-Elect, 2002-2003
American Bar Association

We, the undersigned, agree that judicial campaigns should be conducted in a manner that encourages public trust and confidence in the justice system. Accordingly, we agree that judicial campaigns, whether conducted on behalf of candidates for judicial office or by others interested in the election of particular judicial candidates, should adhere to the following practices:

(1) criminal conduct shall not be attributed to a judicial candidate (unless consistent with the ruling of an official regulatory or judicial body);

(2) racial or ethnic bias shall not be attributed to a judicial candidate (unless consistent with the ruling of an official regulatory or judicial body);

(3) immoral conduct shall not be attributed to a judicial candidate (unless consistent with the ruling of an official regulatory or judicial body);

(4) knowing misrepresentations about a judicial candidate are not appropriate subjects for an advertisement about the judicial candidate; and

(5) professional or judicial misconduct shall not be attributed to a judicial candidate directly or by inference (unless consistent with the ruling of an official regulatory or judicial body).

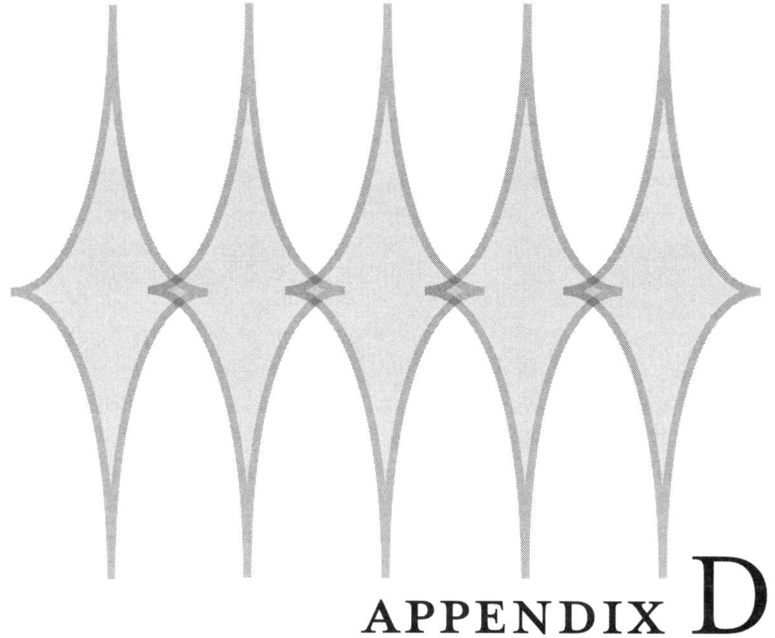

APPENDIX D

STATE JUDICIAL SELECTION AND JUDICIAL INDEPENDENCE

G. Alan Tarr[*]

"Judicial independence is not primarily a matter of judicial text."[1]

In 1986, groups opposing Chief Justice Rose Bird and two associate justices of the California Supreme Court spent roughly $5.5 million to defeat them. In 1994 and 1996, the winning candidates for seats on the Texas Supreme Court spent almost $9.2 million. In 2000, "businesses affiliated with the Ohio Chamber of Commerce spent millions on three soft-money ads for one Supreme Court race."[2] And the same year in Michigan, more than $3 million was spent in races to fill three supreme court positions.[3]

What is striking about this escalation in the cost and contentiousness of judicial elections is that it has not bee
n confined to states with partisan judicial elections. Texas selects its judges in partisan elections, but Ohio and Michigan dispense with party labels and conduct nominally nonpartisan elections, and California re-elects its judges in retention elections.[4] Thus interstate differences in the mode of judicial selection have not prevented the development of very similar political processes.

This white paper explores the causes of this apparent convergence and its implications for judicial independence. Initially, it examines differences between nominal and actual systems of judicial selection in the states. Next, it analyzes various political and legal develop-ments that have affected state judicial selection and thus judicial independence. Finally, it examines state-specific factors that have promoted judicial independence and offers conclusions about the implications of this analysis for securing the independence of state judiciaries.

Realism about State Judicial Selection

Scholars tend to categorize states by their systems of judicial selec-tion: partisan election, nonpartisan election, legislative election, gubernatorial appointment, or merit selection. Although these cate-gories provide a useful starting point, they do not fully capture the

[*] Chair, Department of Political Science, Rutgers University - Camden, and Director, Center for State Constitutional Studies.

[1] J. Mark Ramseyer, *The Puzzling (In)dependence of Courts: A Comparative Approach*, 23 J. LEGAL STUD. 721, 746 (1994).

[2] Emily Heller & Mark Ballard, *Hard-fought, big-money judicial races*, NATIONAL LAW JOURNAL, November 6, 2000, A1.

[3] Emily Heller, *Mixed Results for C of C*, NATIONAL LAW JOURNAL, November 20, 2000, A11.

[4] Information on systems of state judicial selection are found in BOOK OF THE STATES 2000-01, at 137-39, tbl. 4.4 (2000.

interstate and intrastate diversity in judicial selection. Identical methods of judicial selection may lead to quite dissimilar political dynamics, and dissimilar selection methods may yield similar political dynamics. Some examples may illustrate the dangers of over generalizing about selection systems and caution against the easy assumption that judicial independence can be secured merely by changing the mode of judicial selection.

First, nominal systems of judicial selection may mask the political realities of selection in the states. Ohio and Michigan offer prime examples. Both states conduct nonpartisan judicial elections, yet the elections have an intensely partisan character. The explanation is simple: although judicial candidates in Michigan and Ohio run without party labels, they are nominated in party primaries, their party affiliations are widely publicized, and the Republican and Democratic Parties mobilize on behalf of their candidates. Tennessee provides, if anything, an even more striking case; in that state, a politicization of judicial selection occurred despite a shift from partisan election to merit selection. In 1990, when the state still elected its state supreme court in partisan elections, all five justices ran unopposed. Yet after the state shifted to merit selection in 1994, judicial selection grew more contentious. Justice Penny White was opposed and defeated in a 1998 retention election, and Justice Lyle Reid, the next potential target of those who defeated Justice White, decided not to seek retention.[5] (This demonstrates that close elections may have effects beyond the mere occasional defeat of sitting judges.)

Second, even though a state retains the same mode of selection, changes in state law may fundamentally transform the system of judicial selection. Florida is a case in point. In 1996, Florida adopted a constitutional amendment that increased from three to six the number of nominees submitted to the governor by judicial nominating commissions, and it subsequently gave the governor a greater role in selecting the membership of judicial nominating commissions. These changes made it more likely that Florida governors would find ideologically compatible nominees on the lists submitted to them and would be able to choose judges on that basis. Thus, although the system might still be classified as a merit selection system, it has in fact shifted toward a system of political appointment.[6]

---

[5] Traciel V. Reid, *The Politicization of Judicial Retention Elections: The Defeat of Justices Lanphier and White*, RESEARCH ON JUDICIAL SELECTION 1999, 48 (2000).

[6] Charles H. Sheldon & Linda S. Maule, CHOOSING JUSTICE: THE RECRUITMENT OF STATE AND FEDERAL JUDGES 137 (1997), and Rebecca Mae Salokar & Kimberly A. Shaw, *The Impact of National Politics on State Courts: Florida After Election 2000*, 23 Just. Sys. J. 57 (2002).

Third, state law may create hybrid systems within a single state. For instance, some states have adopted different modes of selection for judges on various courts. South Dakota, Missouri, and Florida (among others) use merit selection to choose their appellate judges but elect their trial judges in nonpartisan elections. A number of states use more than one mechanism to fill positions on the same court, electing judges to full terms but authorizing the governor to fill midterm vacancies. In practice, their systems of judicial election have come to resemble appointive systems, at least with regard to judges' initial accession to the bench.[7] For example, although California nominally elects its trial judges in nonpartisan elections, 88 percent of the trial judges elevated to the bench during the 1970s were initially appointed to fill vacancies.[8] Nationally, it is estimated that in states with nonpartisan elections, two out of every three justices reach the state supreme court by appointment (although less than 40 percent of justices in states with partisan elections do so).[9] Some of these appointees never face a serious electoral challenge. Even if they do, they enjoy the substantial advantage of incumbency and fare just as well as do their colleagues who were initially elected to the bench.[10]

Fourth, although judicial elections seem to "imply constituencies, candidates, campaigns, organized support, opposition, and campaign funds,"[11] in fact judicial elections vary widely in their competitiveness. Many judicial elections, particularly at the trial-court level, are uncontested. According to one study, judges on the major trial courts of Ohio were opposed only 27 percent of the time, those on Michigan trial courts only 26 percent of the time, and those on California trial courts only 7 percent of the time.[12] These figures are particularly striking because all three states have strong interparty competition. Incumbent judges on state appellate courts likewise may face only token opposition or none at all. From 1980-1995, incum-

---

[7] Robert Boatright and Kevin Esterling have noted that 10 of the 21 states that authorize midterm appointments employ a nominating commission to guide midterm appointments. *See* Robert G. Boatright & Kevin M. Esterling, *Methodological Issues in the Study of Judicial Selection: A Critique of Empirical Research and Suggestions for Future Directions*, RESEARCH ON JUDICIAL SELECTION 1999, 80 (2000).

[8] John Paul Ryan, Allan Ashman, Bruce D. Sales, & Sandra Shane-Bubow, AMERICAN TRIAL JUDGES 122 (1980).

[9] Philip L. Dubois, FROM BALLOT TO BENCH 246-47 (1980). *See also* James Herndon, *Appointment as a Means of Initial Accession to Elective State Courts of Last Resort*, 38 N. DAKOTA L. REV. 60 (1962). This pattern holds true even within a single state—the shift from partisan to nonpartisan election in Nevada coincided with a shift to greater use of appointment as a means of initial access to the bench. *See* Michael W. Bowers, *The Impact of Judicial Selection Methods in Nevada: Some Empirical Observations*, 2 NEVADA PUB. AFF. REV. 6 (1990).

[10] Melinda Gann Hall, *State Supreme Courts in American Democracy: Probing the Myths of Judicial Reform*, 95 AM. POL. SCI. REV. 315, 324 (2001).

[11] Hans A. Linde, *The Judge as Political Candidate*, 40 CLEVELAND STATE L. REV. 1, 2 (1992).

[12] Lawrence Baum, AMERICAN COURTS 102 (2d ed. 1990).

bent justices on state supreme courts who were running in partisan elections were challenged only 61 percent of the time, and on average they received 72 percent of the vote. Nonpartisan elections were even less competitive: incumbent justices were challenged only 44 percent of the time, and on average they received 80 percent of the vote.[13]

Fifth, "a selection system is only as apolitical as the decision-makers in that system."[14] The states' experience with retention elections underscores that point. Retention elections were originally conceived of as a means to provide for public participation in the selection process while avoiding the intrusion of partisan politics. Proponents of retention elections assumed that eliminating party labels, campaigning, and combative personal confrontations between challengers and incumbents would enable voters to focus on the record and professional qualifications of sitting judges.[15] One may well question whether a judge's professional qualifications are what in fact influence voters in retention elections—one researcher found that more than half the voters in a Wyoming retention election admitted that they knew nothing at all about any of the candidates for retention.[16] Nonetheless, voters in retention elections have typically supported incumbents unless given a reason not to do so. From 1964-1998, only fifty-two of 4,588 judges running in retention elections were not retained.[17]

When political figures and interest groups have become involved in judicial retention elections, however, they have transformed those elections into races virtually indistinguishable from partisan contests. Interest groups active in retention elections have relied upon traditional methods of political campaigning—those seeking to unseat Justice David Lanphier of the Nebraska Supreme Court in 1996, for example, engaged in door-to-door campaigning, created phone banks, and sent mass mailings. And opposition groups in retention elections have constructed political coalitions that mirror the coalitions formed for other partisan political disputes. The groups that joined to defeat White in 1996, for instance, included the Tennessee Conservative Union, victims' rights organizations, law enforcement

---

[13] Hall, *supra* note 10, at 318, tables 2 & 3. An observer during the 1970s concluded that "of the total number of judicial elections held in the 50 states, closely contested, partisan `unjudicial' judicial elections probably constitute no more than 5 to 7 percent of the total." Henry R. Glick, *The Promise and Performance of the Missouri Plan: Judicial Selection in the Fifty States*, 32 U. Miami L. Rev. 509, 519 (1978).

[14] Boatright, *supra* note 7, at 82. Or as Stephen Bright has noted, "Retention elections have the same potential for intimidation and a chilling effect on judicial decisionmaking as direct election." *See* Stephen B. Bright, *Can Judicial Independence be Attained in the South? Overcoming History, Elections, and Misperceptions about the Role of the Judiciary*, 14 Ga. St. L. Rev. 817, 859 (1998).

[15] Kevin M. Esterling, *Judicial Accountability the Right Way*, 82 Judicature 206 (1999), and William K. Hall & Larry T. Aspin, *The Roll-off Effect in Judicial Retention Elections*, 24 Soc. Sci. J. 415, 418 (1987).

[16] Kenyon N. Griffin & Michael J. Horan, *Patterns of Voter Behavior in Judicial Retention Elections for Supreme Court Justices in Wyoming*, 67 Judicature 72 (1983).

[17] Larry T. Aspin, *Trends in Judicial Retention Elections, 1964-1998*, 83 Judicature 79 (1999).

groups, religious conservatives, and the state Republican Party.[18] The aim of these opposition groups is usually not merely to punish a particular justice but to send a message to other justices and thereby to affect the orientation and decisions of the court.

One should not conclude from these observations that the formal system of judicial selection in a state is altogether irrelevant. Judicial selection systems do make a difference, but they are only one among several factors affecting the politics of judicial selection (and hence the degree of judicial independence) within individual states. Moreover, the choice of a system of judicial selection is itself a crucial political decision, reflecting a state's broader orientation toward politics, law, and judicial independence.

The Broader Context of State Judicial Selection

Judicial selection does not occur in a political vacuum. The same factors that have influenced American politics and law in recent decades have also had an effect on judicial selection, whether it be by election or appointment. (Or, to paraphrase Justice Benjamin Cardozo, "the great tides and currents which engulf the rest of men [seeking public office] do not turn aside in their course and pass the judges by."[19]) This is important to keep in mind. As the character of American politics and law has changed, these changes have inevitably and inescapably affected state judicial selection, with consequences for efforts to secure judicial independence.

One of the most dramatic changes during the latter half of the twentieth century was the spread of two-party competition throughout the nation. Many states that at one time were dominated by a single party, particularly in the South and in New England, now regularly conduct highly competitive elections. This is important because, perhaps not surprisingly, a major factor affecting the level of partisan and group conflict in the selection of judges is the overall level of partisan and group competition within a state.[20] In states in which a single party predominates, conflict and competition in judicial elections—as in other elections—tend to be limited. But in states in which party competition is intense and in which parties establish clear ideological identities, that intensity tends to spill over into judicial elections. In Pennsylvania, for example, Republicans and Democrats vigorously compete for the governorship and for control of the state legislature, and they compete just as vigorously for control of the state's courts. From 1979-1997, there were elections for nine vacant seats on the

---

[18] Reid, *supra* note 5, at 54.

[19] Benjamin Cardozo, THE NATURE OF THE LEGAL PROCESS 168 (1921).

[20] Hall, *supra* note 10, at 318, tbls. 2 & 3.

Pennsylvania Supreme Court, all hotly contested races, with Republicans winning five seats and Democrats four.[21]

Politicization of judicial races is particularly likely when a state shifts from dominance by a single party to more balanced party competition. In such circumstances, the emerging political party seeks to capture control of all the institutions of state government, including the courts. Texas has long elected its judges in partisan elections, but prior to 1980 these elections tended to be uncontested, low-key affairs. Only with the rise of the Texas Republican Party did this situation change. The emergence of the Republicans as a viable political alternative encouraged vigorous party competition for all offices, including seats on the state bench. As a result, six incumbent justices of the Texas Supreme Court and numerous lower court judges were defeated in their re-election bids from 1980-1998.[22]

A shift in the partisan balance of power in a state can also increase the level of political conflict between a state legislature and state courts. The partisan and ideological composition of a state legislature can change quickly, given the relatively short terms that legislators serve. In contrast, judges—particularly appellate judges—tend to serve longer terms, so turnover on the bench is more gradual. As a result, when a major political shift occurs in a state, the state's judges may be perceived—whatever their mode of selection—as out of step with the state's newly reigning political forces. Thus, after they gained control of the state legislature in 1996 and the governorship in 1998, Republicans in Florida tended to view the Florida Supreme Court, even though selected by merit selection, as a "remnant of the heyday of Democratic dominance" in Florida.[23]

A second major development with implications for judicial independence is the increasing involvement of courts, particularly in recent decades, in addressing issues with far-reaching policy consequences. This judicial involvement may reflect, as some scholars argue, a worldwide movement toward expanding judicial power or judicial activism.[24] Alternatively, it may reflect factors native to the United States, such as the American penchant for judicializing political conflicts.[25] Whatever the causes, the shift is reflected in the dockets of state supreme courts. During the late nineteenth century, state

---

[21] James Eisenstein, *Financing Pennsylvania's Supreme Court Candidates*, 84 JUDICATURE 10, 12 (2000).

[22] Kyle Cheek & Anthony Champagne, *Money in Texas Supreme Court Elections, 1980-1998*, 84 JUDICATURE 20, 22 (2000).

[23] Salokar & Shaw, *supra* note 6, at 59-60.

[24] *See generally* THE GLOBAL EXPANSION OF JUDICIAL POWER (C. Neal Tate & Torbjorn Vallinder, eds.) (1995).

[25] *See generally* Robert A. Kagan, ADVERSARIAL LEGALISM: THE AMERICAN WAY OF LAW (2001).

supreme courts were struggling with overwhelming caseloads dominated by minor disputes and commercial cases. By the end of the
1960s, however, they had become "less concerned with the stabilization and protection of property rights, more concerned with the
individual and the downtrodden, and more willing to consider rulings that promote social change."[26] In part, this transformation
occurred because most states during the twentieth century created
intermediate appellate courts to handle routine cases. This shift to
discretionary review for state high courts freed them to concentrate
on shaping the law of the state—"the architecture of the system [told]
the judges of the top court to be creative."[27] The 1970s saw the rediscovery of state constitutions and the emergence of the new judicial
federalism—that is, reliance on state declarations of rights to provide
protections unavailable under the United States Constitution—thus
providing new opportunities for state appellate judges to be creative
and to shape the law of their states.[28] At the same time, social reform
groups—concerned about the shift in orientation of the U.S.
Supreme Court—began to look to state courts as a new arena in which
to pursue their goals.

As a consequence, many state courts have found themselves confronted with a variety of novel and controversial issues. As the use of the
constitutional initiative has increased, they have been forced to rule
on the constitutionality of various initiatives adopted by voters.
Needless to say, invalidation of such initiatives can activate a well-
organized group of initiative supporters against the "offending"
judges. State supreme courts have also issued rulings on such hot-
button issues as school finance, abortion, same-sex marriage, tort
reform, and taxing and spending limits (to name just a few). It is
hardly surprising that their rulings have excited controversy. Groups
intensely interested in those issues have sought to ensure that jurists
sympathetic to their views were on the bench or to defeat those justices who ruled contrary to their views by galvanizing public senti-
ment against "offending" jurists.[29] In addition, as Charles Sheldon
and Linda Maule have noted: "Interest groups have discovered that
contributions to court contests have a pay-off similar to contributions to legislative races."[30] Were the Alabama, Ohio, and Texas

---

[26] Robert A. Kagan et al., *The Business of State Supreme Courts, 1870-1970*, 30 STAN. L. REV. 121, 155 (1977).

[27] Paul D. Carrington, Daniel J. Meador, & Maurice Rosenberg, JUSTICE ON APPEAL 150 (1976).

[28] G. Alan Tarr, *The New Judicial Federalism in Perspective*, 72 NOTRE DAME L. REV.1097 (1997).

[29] Moreover, once advocates for one side on an issue become involved in the judicial selection process, that involvement will activate those on the other side, escalating the political conflict over selection. This seems to have occurred in the tort law area, where the plaintiffs' bar enjoyed an initial success, leading to the activation of business groups. Indeed, a recent article suggested that "contested judicial elections have appeared to degenerate in a growing number of states into an auction for control of the civil justice system." *See* John L. Dodd & Christopher Murray, *The Case for Judicial Appointments*, 13, available at http://www.fed-soc.org/Publications/White%20Papers/judicialappointments.htm

[30] Sheldon & Maule, *supra* note 6, at 76.

Supreme Courts to cease dealing with torts and tort reform, one suspects that the plaintiffs' bar and business groups would no longer offer huge campaign contributions to candidates for seats on those courts. But as long as those courts and others continue to address legal issues that are simultaneously contentious policy issues, they will attract the attention and involvement of interested groups.

A related development is the rise of single-issue groups. These single-issue groups have had a major impact in the political arena, and—not surprisingly—in the judicial arena as well. Interest groups whose concerns are addressed in court rulings have a stake in the composition of the state bench, and they try to influence its composition no matter what the selection system. Thus, after the Florida Supreme Court in 1990 struck down a state law requiring minor girls to obtain parental consent before obtaining abortions, the Florida Right to Life Committee sought to defeat Chief Justice Leander Shaw, the author of the majority opinion. And after the Ohio Supreme Court struck down the state's tort reform statute, the Chamber of Commerce in 2000 targeted Justice Alice Resnick. This does not mean, of course, that single-issue groups are always successful in their opposition—Chief Justice Leander Shaw was re-elected with 59 percent of the vote, and Resnick with 57 percent. However, the opposition to their candidacies certainly changed the intensity and basic character of the re-election process..[31]

Given the strength of such single-issue groups, political figures may be tempted to court such groups by seizing upon a single controversial ruling as a weapon to attack a judge, regardless of the legal merits of the ruling. As former Justice Hans Linde of the Oregon Supreme Court has observed, "Voters are invited to feel angry at a decision and to vent that anger against any judge who participated in it."[32] In addition to using court bashing as a means of scoring points with voters, politicians can also employ this tactic to defeat judges seeking re-election. This has occurred most often with rulings that involve the death penalty. Thus, victims' rights groups targeted White based on an opinion that she joined, which held that rape was not in all cases an aggravating factor in murder cases. Mississippi's state prosecutors' association spotlighted an opinion by Justice James Robertson that noted that the death penalty could not be imposed on rapists whose victims survived the attack.[33] The prospect of an election in

---

[31] It may be that the effectiveness of an interest group will depend on whether the judicial election is a statewide race, which makes it more expensive and more difficult to reach the electorate, or a district race (as in the defeat of Justice Lanphier of the Nebraska Supreme Court).

[32] Linde, *supra* note 11, at 7.

[33] Jeannine Bell, *The Politics of Crime and the Threat to Judicial Independence*, 6, in JUSTICE IN JEOPARDY: REPORT OF THE ABA COMMISSION ON THE 21st CENTURY JUDICIARY 10-11 (2003). (See appendix F.)

which a single decision can be taken out of context and used to attack a judge may have a chilling effect on judicial independence. In a series of interviews conducted with judges who ran in retention elections from 1986-1990, 15 percent indicated that as the election approached, they sought to avoid controversial cases and rulings, while another 5 percent indicated that they became more conservative in sentencing in criminal cases.[34] Even judges who seek to avoid being influenced by the prospect of a re-election campaign worry that they cannot be sure that it does not influence their judgments. Finally, the debate over judicial accountability and judicial independence has been transformed in recent decades by changing public perceptions of law and of judges. Advocates of judicial independence insist that judges remain accountable to the law and that their responsiveness to law, rather than to public opinion or personal values, is crucial to ensuring an even-handed administration of justice. Implicit in this rule-of-law argument are the assumptions that the law provides a standard that can guide judicial decisions and that it is possible to assess judicial fidelity to the law. Yet both these assumptions have become less widely accepted. In part, this skepticism may reflect the more general decline of confidence in the major institutions of American society. But in part it reflects developments within the legal community and their filtering down to the general public. Within the legal community, assessment of judicial fidelity to law has been complicated by a breakdown of consensus about how one interprets the law or, indeed, what constitutes interpretation as opposed to lawmaking. This is true not only with regard to constitutional interpretation—consider the debates over constitutional theory during the 1980s—but also with regard to statutory interpretation and the development of the common law.[35] More broadly, the American public has learned—perhaps all too well—the lessons of legal realism. Although most Americans have never witnessed state judges in operation nor read judicial opinions they have written, poll data reveal a deep skepticism about the impartiality of state courts and the even-handed administration of justice.[36] Whatever the accuracy of this perception, it has important implications. As Deborah Hensler has noted, the perception that judicial decisions are not regularly deter-

---

34 Larry T. Aspin & William K. Hall, *Retention Elections and Judicial Behavior*, 77 JUDICATURE 312, tab. 4 (1994).

35 For an overview of the constitutional theory debates, *see* Michael J. Gerhardt, CONSTITUTIONAL THEORY: ARGUMENTS AND PERSPECTIVES (1993); for differences over statutory interpretation, compare William N. Eskridge, DYNAMICS OF STATUTORY INTERPRETATION (1994), with Antonin Scalia, A MATTER OF INTERPRETATION: FEDERAL COURTS AND THE LAW (1997).

36 These studies are collected and analyzed in Deborah R. Hensler, *Do We Need an Empirical Research Agenda on Judicial Independence?* 72 SO. CAL. L. REV. 707, 710-714 (1999).

mined based on their legal merits tends to weaken the rule-of-law argument for judicial independence.[37]

CONCLUSIONS

The broad political and legal developments sketched out here provide some of the context within which the battle over judicial independence will be fought in the early twenty-first century, but they are not the whole story.

First, it appears that the politicization of judicial elections, particularly retention elections, in a state tends to be episodic rather than endemic. Lanphier was denied re-election in 1996, but he remains the only justice of the Nebraska Supreme Court ever unseated in a retention election. Since the removal of three justices of the California Supreme Court in a 1986 retention election, California has not experienced a high profile, contentious retention election. Even controversial rulings of the California Supreme Court—for example, its determination that a state statute requiring parental consent for abortion violated the state constitution—have led to only token opposition when justices came before the voters for retention.

Second, controversial judicial rulings do not inevitably lead to political reprisals or to threats to judicial independence. The orientation of a state's political leaders is crucial. Over the period of two decades, the New Jersey Supreme Court issued a series of dramatic and, in some instances, unpopular rulings dealing with school finance, exclusionary zoning, the right to die, the rights of defendants, and other issues.[38] Yet these rulings did not lead to efforts to curtail the court. As John Ferejohn has noted, "The independence of the judiciary, as opposed to that of individual judges, is dependent on the `willingness' of the popular branches of government to refrain from using their ample constitutional powers to infringe on judicial authority."[39] The commitment of a state's political leaders to judicial independence can, as in New Jersey, set the tone for political debate in the state and can prevent the politicization of judicial selection, even in a state with strong two-party competition.

---

[37] Frances Zemans has noted: "Though attacks may be focused on individual judges, their impact is generalized and magnified. It is generalized because the public makes little distinction among judges (or even among different jurisdictions).... Reporting possible suspect behavior becomes magnified because typically it is the only information the public has received. There is not a base of knowledge about individual judges or the judiciary as a whole against which the public can evaluate reports of judicial misbehavior." Frances Kahn Zemans, *The Accountable Judge: Guardian of Judicial Independence,* 72 SO. CAL. L. REV. 625, 640 (1999).

[38] For an overview of the New Jersey Supreme Court's jurisprudence, *see* G. Alan Tarr & Mary Cornelia Aldis Porter, STATE SUPREME COURTS IN STATE AND NATION Ch. 5 (1988).

[39] John Ferejohn, *Independent Judges, Dependent Judiciary: Explaining Judicial Independence,* 72 SO. CAL. L. REV. 353, x382 (1999).

Third, states can take steps to create a sense of nonpartisanship (or bipartisanship) with regard to their judiciaries that will foster judicial independence. Delaware, for example, has established a constitutional requirement that a politically balanced judiciary be maintained.[40] Long-standing practice in New Jersey has produced the same effect. This in turn has encouraged support for judicial independence among public officials and members of the general public.

This creation of public and elite opinion in support of judicial independence is ultimately the crucial factor. As Chief Justice Shirley Abrahamson of the Wisconsin Supreme Court has observed, even though she has had to run for re-election on two occasions, Wisconsin's attachment to judicial independence meant that this posed no serious threat to judicial independence. She did not have to change her behavior to court re-election because she knew her arguments for the importance of judicial independence would resonate with the state's electorate.[41] Not surprisingly, she concludes that persuading public officials and the general public of its importance, rather than changing election systems, remains the crucial task confronting advocates of judicial independence.

---

[40] Del. Const., Art.IV, sec.3.

[41] Shirley S. Abrahamson, *The Ballot and the Bench*, 76 N. Y. U. L. Rev. 873 (2001).

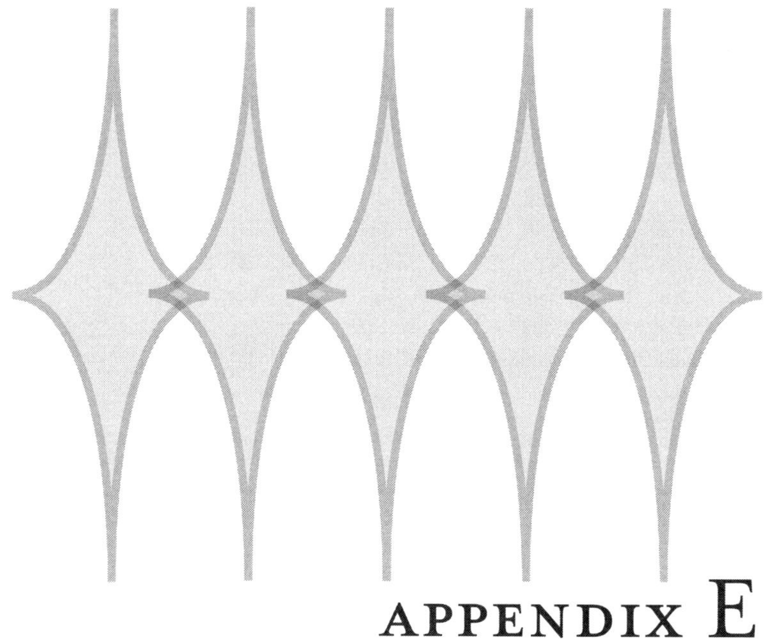

APPENDIX E

CHALLENGES TO CONSTITUTIONAL DECISIONS OF STATE COURTS AND INSTITUTIONAL PRESSURES ON STATE JUDICIARIES

Emily Field Van Tassel [*]

This paper addresses the issues that arise from the politicization of constitutional decision making by state judges, resulting in efforts to use the selection/election process to remove judges for unpopular opinions and the related use of institutional means such as the removal of funding and disciplinary measures to influence judicial outcomes in particular classes of cases.

Historically, state and local judges have been powerful and influential members of their communities, often wielding disproportionate power for good or ill. In some places and at some times judges have aggregated or been delegated all of the powers of government in our tripartite system, without even a nod to the separation of powers so central to our theory of government. For instance, some states gave their courts the power to set taxes and determine road and bridge placement. In other places, judges undertook executive functions and stepped beyond current norms to assume a prosecutorial role, as early federal judges did when instructing local grand juries to seek out particular criminal activities against the United States. Exploring the cultural echoes of these practices and attendant attitudes towards judges with their varying implications for either reining in judicial power or taking a less strict view of separation of powers is beyond the scope of this paper. What this paper will describe are the ways in which contemporary state judges and judiciaries are being challenged, threatened, or rewarded for the exercise of legitimate judicial power and the possible impact on desirable judicial independence such challenges or rewards have.

The buzz words in contemporary as well as historical battles over the shape and function of both state and federal judiciaries are "independence" on the one hand and "accountability" on the other. But these terms have taken on different meanings depending on whether one is talking about federal, life-tenured judges, or elected, limited-term state judges. On the federal level, independence most often refers to the ability of judges to make decisions independent of pressures from either the executive or the legislative branches. Because federal judges are appointed for lifetime tenures, subject to their

---

[*] Historian and legal scholar.

"good behavior," accountability tends to refer to whether judges can be disciplined or removed for actions that stray from appropriate judicial behavior (for instance, corruption or drunkenness on the bench). Since the failed removal by impeachment of Justice Samuel Chase in 1804, Congress has generally accepted the tenet that federal judges should not be removed for unpopular or even erroneous decisions.[1]

On the state level, however, the definitions of independence and accountability seem more fluid. State judiciaries are understudied relative to the federal judiciary, but recent controversies and the rhetoric surrounding them suggest that in many states, accountability is historically a more expansive concept than on the federal level and that many would argue for a more restrictive meaning for judicial independence.

The range of behaviors for which the public wishes to hold judges accountable includes bribery, coercion, laziness, ignorance of the law (incompetence), and ignoring the law (bias and legislating from the bench, also called "activism"). The last area is the current battleground where the legitimate accountability of public servants for their actions comes into most obvious conflict with the opposing value of judicial independence from either punishment or reward when legitimately exercising judicial power to decide cases. The problem lies in devising some means for determining when a judge or group of judges has ignored the law and what is the appropriate means of holding such judges accountable without compromising the ultimate value of independence in judicial decision-making.

The means used to hold state judges accountable for their behavior range from reversal by higher courts to disciplinary actions to removal from office and criminal indictment. Those able to hold judges directly accountable include the public through elections and recalls; the judiciary itself through the appellate process, disciplinary actions, case assignments, and allocation of resources within the court's purview; the executive branch through appointment powers; and the legislative branch through impeachment, censure, rule making, jurisdiction stripping, and funding. All of these hold some dangers to the judicial independence value. The question is how much and what is an acceptable or even desirable amount?

The purpose of this paper is to categorize and catalog the methods being used to attempt to hold judges or the judiciary accountable for

---

[1] Charles Gardner Geyh, *Book Review: Courts, Congress, and the Constitutional Politics of Interbranch Restraint*, 87 GEO L. J. 243, 260 (1998).

their constitutional decision-making, the reasons for these attempts, and their possible impact, both actual and perceptual, on judicial independence. The major areas of concern are the politicization of constitutional decision making through the selection and retention process and the use of legitimate powers to make indirect or implied attacks on independence by the other branches of government.

The politicization of state constitutional decision-making coincides with the "new federalism" of the Reagan era and the willingness of many state appellate courts to look to their own constitutions for guidance in many areas of law previously left to the federal constitution.[2] For instance, state judiciaries have used independent state grounds to expand equal protection beyond that sanctioned by the U.S. Supreme Court under the federal constitution. They have enhanced freedom of speech and of the press; they have utilized educational mandates within their own constitutions that are lacking in the federal constitution; they have applied other specific state protections unavailable at the federal level, such as "little ERAs," rights to privacy, criminal procedures, civil liberties generally, and protections of property rights.[3] One result of this shift from federal to state constitutional decision making has been to raise the profile of state court judges and make control over state judgeships seem more significant to a greater range of interest groups than in the recent past (i.e., to more than the local bar and party politicians).

Because, unlike federal judges, many state judges are subject to some form of popular election to gain or retain their seats, these interest groups often (and not unreasonably) regard judicial accountability in the same manner as the accountability of other public officials subject to the democratic process. As a consequence, it is not surprising to find judicial decision-making politicized in the same fashion as executive and legislative decision making, with attempted ouster from office the result when decisions don't meet with popular approval.

Although many states initially select their judges through gubernatorial appointment to fill midterm vacancies or through nominating commissions that submit a selection of names for gubernatorial appointment, forty-one states require at least some of their judges to stand for election to remain in their offices. Some of these are partisan elections, some are nonpartisan, and some are simply retention elections (asking voters "should judge X remain in office").[4] Historically, the rate of turnover due to defeat in election was

---

[2] G. Alan Tarr, *State Judicial Selection and Judicial Independence, in Justice in* JEOPARDY: REPORT OF THE ABA COMMISSION ON THE 21ST CENTURY JUDICIARY 10-11 (2003). (See Appendix D.)

[3] HARRY STUMPF, AMERICAN JUDICIAL POLITICS 367-76 (2d ed., 1998).

[4] Erwin Chemerinsky, *Judicial Elections and the First Amendment*, 38 TRIAL 78 (Nov. 2002).

exceedingly low. One study of judges in Texas covering the period from 1940-1962 found a 96 percent retention rate. A study of retention elections covering ten states in the years 1964-1984 found only 1.2 percent of judges were defeated. As of 1978, one researcher estimated that contested judicial elections "probably constitute no more than five to seven percent of the total."[5]

Since the nationally publicized ouster of three California appellate judges in 1986, however, the politicization of judicial elections, based not on professional qualifications or overall quality of performance, has appeared to increase significantly. One notable aspect of this increased contention is the focus on single opinions or classes of opinions by sitting judges. Among the constitutional decisions that have attracted the most notable challenges are opinions covering school funding, abortion and parental consent, application of the death penalty, and tort reform.

Criticism (even vitriolic and vituperative criticism) of judges and the judiciary is nothing new.[6] What seems novel about recent developments is the amount of money being expended in elections that have historically been so low key as to be virtually invisible.[7] California provides an excellent case in point. California's governor appoints the justices of its supreme court to twelve-year terms. At the conclusion of the term, a retention election is held. In 1986, Chief Justice Rose Bird and two associate justices lost retention because of a public perception that they were soft on the death penalty.[8] Twelve years later, two other justices were under attack from two groups for their vote in a case involving parental consent for a minor seeking an abortion. The stark contrast in this case is presented by the fact that the targeted justices, Chief Justice Ronald George and Associate Justice Ming Chin felt compelled to raise $1.3 million dollars to defend against the attack—while the two other justices on the ballot, who voted the opposite (and favored) way in the parental consent case, did not feel the need to raise any money or campaign at all.[9]

School funding has been a contentious issue for judges in several states since the Supreme Court took federal constitutional protections out of the picture in Rodriguez. The issue has been the

---

[5] Henry R. Glick, *The Promise and Performance of the Missouri Plan: Judicial Selection in the Fifty States*, 32 MIAMI L. REV. 510 (1978).

[6] *Defending Justice: The Courts, Criticism and Intimidation: The Report of the Citizens for Independent Courts Task Force on the Distinction Between Intimidation and Legitimate Criticism of Judges*, in UNCERTAIN JUSTICE: POLITICS AND AMERICA'S COURTS 130-37 (2000).

[7] AMERICAN BAR ASSOCIATION, REPORT OF THE A.B.A. COMMISSION ON PUBLIC FINANCING OF JUDICIAL CAMPAIGNS 9 (2002).

[8] John H. Culver, *The California Supreme Court Turnabout on Capital Punishment*, 59 ALB. L. REV. 1693 (1996).

[9] Dion Haynes, *Interest Groups Politicizing State Court Balloting: Jurists Forced to Chase Money*, CHI. TRIBUNE, Nov. 2,

inequities in funding across individual states created by using local property taxes as the primary means for supporting schools. Wealthy districts with stronger tax bases have much higher per pupil dollars available than poor districts. After the Supreme Court ruled that the equal protection clause of the federal constitution did not protect school children from disparities in educational quality, a number of state supreme courts looked to their own constitutions to find protections denied by the U.S. Supreme Court's interpretation of the federal constitution. Constitutional mandates such as those in New Jersey and Ohio, which required a state to provide a "thorough and efficient education," have led a number of state supreme courts to invalidate their state's method of school financing. In Ohio, Justice Alice Robie Resnick was targeted for replacement for her constitutional opinions on school funding.[10] She retained her seat but only after an extremely expensive campaign.

Non-elective systems don't necessarily protect judges from assaults on independence. In New Hampshire, the state supreme court (whose judges are appointed and serve until age 70) was under attack for nearly a decade as a consequence of a constitutional decision involving school funding.[11] The weapons used in that dispute include attempted removal by address, impeachment, jurisdiction stripping, term limits, switching to an elective judiciary, and constitutional amendment. Although the impeached chief justice was acquitted by the state senate, he now has an estimated $1 million dollars in legal bills. In at least two other cases, judges were targeted for removal through disciplinary processes after pressure from the political branches over unpopular decisions by those judges.[12]

Examples of other election attacks for particular constitutional interpretations include the following:

- In Georgia, the comments of Justice Leah Sears in her dissent in an alimony case were mischaracterized by her opponent in a bid to unseat her.[13] Judge Gary B. Andrews was challenged over a single reversal of a criminal conviction.

---

[10] Mike Wagner & Scott Elliott, *This is About Politics...Not Kids and Schools*, DAYTON DAILY NEWS, June 3, 2001. Justice Resnick was also targeted for her opinion on tort reform, an issue addressed by Andrew Spalding and Carl Tobias in *Civil Justice and Judicial Selection* (see appendix G).

[11] *ABA Commission on the Twenty-first Century Judiciary*, Phila., Pa. 147-153 (Sept. 27, 2002) (testimony of Andru Volinsky, Lawyer).

[12] Judge Kline of California was brought before the California Commission on Judicial Ethics for a dissent in which he refused to follow what he considered to be an erroneous decision of the state supreme court. *See*, Notice of Formal Proceedings in *Inquiry Concerning J. Anthony Kline*, No. 151, Before the State of California Commission on Judicial Performance 2 (filed June 30, 1998). Judge Duckman of Brooklyn's Criminal Court was removed by New York's Court of Appeals following pressure from the governor; however, the disciplinary charges against him did not stem solely from unpopular decisions. *See*, Gary Spencer, *Court of Appeals Removes Duckman; Dissents Stress Threats to Independence*, N.Y.L.J., July 8, 1998 p.1.

[13] Bill Rankin, *Campaign Flier Targeting Judge Criticized by Legal Ethics Experts*, ATLANTA CONSTITUTION, June 19, 1998, at 6F.

- Justice Cathy Silak lost her bid for re-election in Idaho primarily due to attacks over a single case involving federal water rights.[14]
- Death penalty cases prompted challenges to Justices Penny White and Adolpho Birch in Tennessee.[15]
- In Florida, Justices Leander Shaw and Rosemary Barkett were challenged for re-election because of opinions regarding abortion and protections of criminal defendants.[16]

The opinion-based attacks on these and many other judges have been justified, either explicitly or implicitly, on the grounds that judges should be accountable to the public for their decisions in particular cases. In many more cases, opponents in election campaigns have politicized whole classes of constitutional decision-making, attempting to hold judges democratically accountable for overall legal interpretations in general subject areas such as criminal rights and abortion. In the wake of the U.S. Supreme Court's recent decision in Republican Party of Minnesota v. White, such politicization of constitutional decision-making is likely to accelerate.

Although public attention has been most drawn to attacks on the decisional independence of individual judges because of the visibility and obviousness of such attacks in the election process, attacks on the institutional independence of state judiciaries also appear to have increased as litigants have sought protections under state constitutions that have been limited or foreclosed under the federal constitution. These attacks are manifested in (1) constitutional amendments intended to limit or strip state courts of the authority to interpret their own constitutions; (2) threats to use funding powers to coerce stances more in accord with the legislative and executive branches; (3) moves to change judicial selection to bring courts into line with popular opinion; (4) use of removal or impeachment power to serve as a warning to the judiciary as a whole; and (5) stripping the judiciary of control over its rules. What follows are examples of attacks on the judiciary as a political response to constitutional disagreements. Classified as separate issues are attempts to limit or dictate constitutional interpretation and attempts to strip jurisdiction entirely. The former appears to be a response to the expansion of civil liberties protections under state constitutions versus the federal constitution; the latter are echoes of attempts made at the federal level to completely remove certain subjects from the scrutiny of the judicial branch.

---

[14] Dan Popkey, *Trout Says Politics Had Nothing to Do with Ruling*, IDAHO STATESMAN, Oct. 28, 2001, at IA.

[15] Kirk Loggins & Duren Cheek, *Activists Target Tennessee Judge*, THE TENNESSEAN, July 9, 1998, at IA.

[16] *Governor Bush Taps New State Supreme Court Justice; Trial Judge Kenneth Bell Was Named to Replace Retiring Justice Leander Shaw*, ORLANDO SENTINEL, Dec. 31, 2002.

1) Constitutional Amendments Intended to Limit or Strip State Courts of the Authority to Interpret Their Own Constitutions:

During the 1970s and 1980s, the California Supreme Court extended protections to criminal defendants under the California Constitution that exceeded those that the U.S. Supreme Court had construed to be available under the federal constitution. An initiative intended to insure that criminal defendants could never be given broader protections than the federal constitution provided resulted in a constitutional amendment that declared the thirteen different state constitutional rights of criminal defendants "shall be construed by the courts of this state in a manner consistent with the Constitution of the United States." It added: "This Constitution shall not be construed by the courts to afford greater rights to criminal defendants than those afforded by the Constitution of the United States." In Raven v. Deukmejian, the California Supreme Court struck down the amendment on the grounds that the initiative power had been taken too far, saying the amendment was "so far reaching as to amount to a constitutional revision beyond the scope of the initiative process." Only the more deliberative process of either a constitutional convention or a legislative process followed by popular ratification could achieve such significant change in the constitution. The court noted: "In essence and practical effect, new article I, section 24, would vest all judicial interpretive power, as to fundamental defense rights, in the United States Supreme Court."[17]

- In Florida, a "forced linkage" amendment required state search-and-seizure provisions to be "construed in conformity with the 4th amendment to the United States Constitution, as interpreted by the United States Supreme Court." Political scientist Barry Latzer noted: "Before forced linkage, Florida Supreme Court cases rejected U.S. Supreme Court interpretations in favor of broader rights 80% of the time; after forced linkage the rejection rate dipped to 18%."

- In 1997, Washington state legislators sought a constitutional amendment that would give final authority to the legislature on issues of constitutional interpretation.

2) Attempting to Strip the Judiciary of Its Rulemaking Authority or Its Jurisdiction over Particular Subject Areas

- After the Florida Supreme Court stayed the implementation of the Death Penalty Reform Act, the governor and legislature threatened to shift rule-making authority from the supreme court to the legislature.[18]

---

17 Raven v. Deukmejian 52 Cal.3d 336, 276 Cal.Rptr. 326, 801 P.2d 1077 (1990).
18 Editorial, *Respect the Court*, ST. PETERSBURG TIMES, April 20, 2000.

- In both Ohio and New Hampshire, decisions invalidating the states' school-financing schemes met with attempts to remove school-funding jurisdiction from the courts and give the legislature sole authority to determine what constitutes a "thorough and efficient education" under the state constitution.[19]

- New York's Governor George Pataki attacked the state's high court for a strict interpretation of the exclusionary rule. He then introduced jurisdiction-stripping legislation that would preclude the court from authority to decide cases on unlawfully seized evidence under the state constitution.[20]

3)   Threats to Use the Funding Power to Coerce Judicial Stances More in Accord with the Other Branches

- Prior to oral arguments in a case involving Florida's Death Penalty Reform Act, the chair of the Florida House council in charge of court appropriations sent a note to members of the Florida Supreme Court stating that "your decisions continue to be a mockery to the victims and their families." The vote identified him as chairman of appropriations and was interpreted by one newspaper as a budgetary threat.[21]

- The president of the Maryland Senate threatened to cut the budget of the state's highest court because of a constitutional decision. This occurred after the legislature had voted for two years running to withhold millions of dollars from the state budget for Baltimore's courts until court reforms requested by Baltimore's mayor were implemented.[22]

- A recent survey of state court administrators and some legislative and executive budget officers found that over 36 percent of court administrators (fifteen respondents) and 28.9 percent of legislative budget officers (thirteen respondents) believed that their legislatures had threatened (directly or indirectly) to reduce the judiciary's budget to "influence or protest court rulings or policies." Eleven court administrators and eight legislative budget officers responded that the legislature had actually reduced the judiciary's budget at least once for those reasons.[23]

- New Hampshire's governor proposed cutting court funding in response to the court's school-funding decision.[24]

---

[19] Catherine Candisky, Two Senators Propose to Amend State Constitution School Funding Debate, Columbus Dispatch, March 4, 1999; Shirley Elder, Supreme Court Controversies Have Staying Power, Boston Globe, June 24, 2001; Randy Ludlow School Call: Skip Courts Lawmakers Want Funding Control, Cincinnati Post, March 4, 1999.

[20] *The Governor's Attack on the Judges*, N.Y. TIMES, Feb. 3, 1996, at A-14.

[21] Martin Dyckman, *Courts at Mercy of Legislative Purse*, ST. PETERSBURG TIMES, March 23, 2000.

[22] Thomas Waldron, *O'Malley Insists Funds for Court Woes Be Denied*, SUNSPOT, Feb.12, 2000.

[23] Douglas & Hartley, *The Politics of Court Budgeting in the States: Is Judicial Independence Threatened by the Budgetary Process?* 63 PUBLIC ADMINISTRATION REV. 441, Table 7 (July/August 2003).

[24] ABA Commission on the Twenty-first Century Judiciary, *supra* note 11.

4) Moves to Change Judicial Selection to Bring Courts into Line with Popular Opinion or the Other Branches.

- In response to state supreme and superior court rulings involving abortion and gay marriage, Alaska legislators proposed amending the state constitution to require legislative confirmation for appointees to the supreme court, court of appeals, and the nominating commission charged with recommending potential judges to the governor. A state senator sponsoring the amendments stated: "The court needs to be a reflection of Alaskan society and our values. And if it isn't, then we need to get hold of it."[25]

- Florida's legislators responded negatively to state supreme court decisions adverse to school funding, limits on death penalty appeals, and pro-business limits on civil lawsuits by proposing to expand the number of gubernatorial appointees to the judicial nominating commission. A proposal was also made to shift control of state courts from the supreme court to the legislature.[26]

5) Use of Impeachment or Removal Power as a Warning to the Judicial Branch

- After the Vermont Supreme Court ruled Vermont's system of funding state schools unconstitutional, opponents sought removal of the justices of that court. Vermont's system gives the legislature the power over re-appointment to the courts. Former Senator John McClaughry led the charge against the court, arguing that the court's reasoning in the school-funding case was enough "to fire [Justices] Dooley, Johnson and Morse."[27]

- In New Hampshire, Chief Justice David Brock faced down an attempted ouster by bill of address in 1999 only to be impeached in 2000. Although the charges had to do with lax enforcement of the court's recusal rules, the removal attempts apparently had their roots in the court's school-funding ruling. Justice Brock was acquitted on the impeachment charges but amassed an estimated $1 million legal bill.[28]

- In another school-funding case, a Wyoming senator threatened to begin impeachment proceedings against the state's supreme court justices for their decision in that case.[29]

Although the judicial selection process is the most visible point at which judicial independence is either being threatened or leaving the public with the impression of a judiciary beholden to money or politics for tenure in office, it may be that threats directed at the judicial

---

[25] Liz Ruskin, *A Question of Balance: Court Rulings Ignite Conservative Backlash, Debate Over Judge Selection,* ANCHORAGE DAILY NEWS, March 29, 1998.

[26] Joe Follick, Bar, *Lawmakers Battle over Judge Selectors,* TAMPA TRIBUNE, March 14, 2001.

[27] Ross Sneyd, *Senators Seek to Open Retention Process,* ASSOCIATED PRESS, Feb. 10, 1999.

[28] Shirley Elder, *Supreme Court Controversies Have Staying Power,* BOSTON GLOBE, June 24, 2001.

[29] *Senator Ready to Impeach Judges,* CASPER (WY.) STAR-TRIBUNE, June 9, 2001.

branch itself are at least as inimical to independence. The impression that state judiciaries must by their very localism be less than ideally independent (which dates back to the 1787 Constitutional Convention and subsequent ratification debates) may well be correct. A primary reason for calling a federal judiciary into being was founded in a perception—later reinforced by the Jacksonian introduction of elective judiciaries—that the culture of judicial accountability in the states is a democratic rather than punitive notion and reflects a less than complete or at least highly ambivalent attachment to the concept of judicial independence as understood on the federal level.

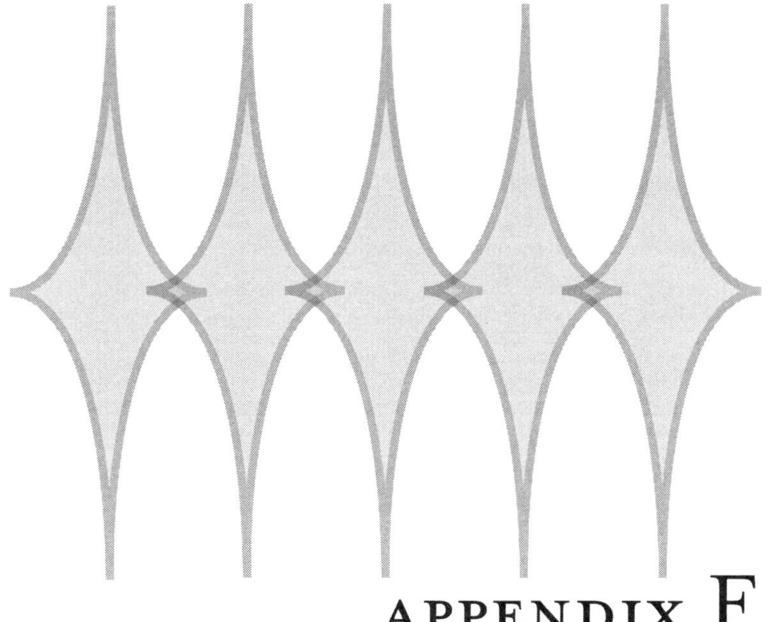

APPENDIX F

THE POLITICS OF CRIME AND THE THREAT TO JUDICIAL INDEPENDENCE

Jeannine Bell[*]

The "higher authority" to whom present-day capital judges may be "too responsive" is a political climate in which judges who covet higher office—or who merely wish to remain judges—must constantly profess their fealty to the death penalty. Alabama trial judges face partisan election every six years. The danger that they will bend to political pressures when pronouncing sentence in highly publicized capital cases is the same danger confronted by judges beholden to King George III.

Harris v. Alabama, 513 U.S. 504, 519 (1995) (Stevens, J. dissenting)

The threat to judicial independence that Justice Stevens notes in his dissent in *Harris v. Alabama* has recently been eliminated. In 2002, the Supreme Court ruled 7-2 in *Ring v. Arizona*[1] that juries, not judges, must make the determination that a defendant will be sentenced to death. Before the Court's decision in *Ring*, judges were ultimately responsible for sentencing in capital cases in nine states. In these states, elected judges faced pressure to demonstrate their support for the death penalty either by overruling a jury verdict or by imposing it with or without a jury's advisory opinion. By taking the ultimate decision regarding whether a defendant will be sentenced to death out of the hands of the judge, *Ring* removed what Stevens identified as a significant threat to state court judges' ability to make unfettered decisions.

Though this particular threat to the independence of state court judges has been eliminated, across the nation the politics of crime still matter for state court judges, the vast majority of whom are elected. Challenged by interest groups and opponents, state court judges face the prospect of election defeat because of rulings they have made in capital cases. Governors have also criticized judges for their rulings in capital cases. The death penalty case is not the only political stumbling block that judicial candidates have faced. Judicial candidates have often felt pressure to demonstrate to constituents that they are not soft on crime.

---

[*] Associate Professor, Indiana University School of Law.
[1] *Ring v. Arizona*, 536 U.S. 584 (2002).

This white paper addresses factors that judges and some scholars argue threaten the ability of state trial court and appellate judges to make independent decisions in criminal cases. Part I discusses the particular issues of concern to judges who must make decisions in the area of criminal law and the sway that the "politics of crime" holds for elected judges. Next, Parts II and III address two types of difficulties that judges face—those that stem mainly from the fact that the vast majority of judges must run for reelection, and those that constitute more direct attempts to limit judges' power. The white paper concludes in Part IV with a brief discussion of some of the consequences of placing such limits on judicial power.

Part I. Why Criminal Law Is Different

All elected judges may be sanctioned by voters who dislike decisions they have made while on the bench. Increasing judicial accountability by increasing citizens' power to remove judges from office is one justification for this form of judicial selection. As judicial elections have become more politicized, elected judges have had to raise money for their election campaigns. Judicial elections have become increasingly expensive, and judges must worry about raising money to run election campaigns. During the 2000 judicial elections, candidates for state supreme court raised $45.6 million, double the figure raised just four years earlier.[2] The need to raise money presents judges with ethical dilemmas when potential or past donors appear before them.

A related issue concerns the need to seek votes. Judges may be concerned that controversial decisions made on the bench will alienate voters and donors, causing them to lose an election or to fail to raise enough funds to mount a successful campaign. Finally, judges may be tempted to take policy positions to distinguish themselves from their challengers during the campaign. While articulating policy positions is a valuable part of the political process for other elected officials, promises are problematic for judges. A judge might be tempted to live up to her campaign promises and ignore the applicable law for fear of not being re-elected. For these reasons, making promises or pledges are ethical violations under the American Bar Association's Model Code of Judicial Conduct, which most states have adopted.[3]

For trial court judges who preside over criminal dockets and appellate judges who must hear appeals in criminal cases, the politics of crime and the public fear of crime add to other threats to judicial inde-

---

[2] Larry Bivens, *Coalition Wants to Reform State Judicial Campaigns*, GANNETT NEWS SERVICE, Feb. 22, 2002.

[3] Penny White, *Judicial Independence: Judging Judges: Securing Judicial Independence by the Use of Judicial Performance Evaluations*, 29 FORDHAM URBAN L.J. 1053, 1061 (2002).

pendence. Though it has always been a concern in America, fear of crime increased and became a more salient issue in the late 1980s and early 1990s for the public and in American politics.[4] Though some statistics suggested the number of actual crimes committed was decreasing, citizens' perception of the amount of crime increased. From 1989-1992, a greater number of Americans indicated in polls that they believed more crimes had occurred that year than the year before. From 1985-1992, the number of individuals claiming to be victims of crime more than doubled.[5]

In the 1980s and 1990s, politicians capitalized on fear of crime by demonstrating that they believed in taking a serious approach to ending crime—that they were tough on crime.[6] One way politicians have chosen to demonstrate that they are tough on crime is by attacking judicial decisions. Judges who make decisions in criminal cases are especially vulnerable.[7] Fear of crime makes decisions in criminal cases of greater interest to the public. Rulings in the defendant's favor in death penalty cases often serve as fodder for criticism from law-and-order politicians. Similarly, judges in criminal cases are required to make thousands of decisions regarding the suppression of evidence and bail.[8] While it is impossible to predict who will commit a crime while released on bail, it is easy for politicians in hindsight to criticize a judge who granted bail to the defendant who re-offends while out on bail.[9] Politicians have also chastised judges for their decisions to suppress evidence and other rulings unfavorable to the prosecution. The sections below describe and provide examples of the myriad ways in which judicial independence is threatened for judges who must make decisions in criminal cases.

Part II. Election-related Challenges to Judicial Power

A. The Public, Special Interest Groups and the Death Penalty

The public interest in crime makes judges most vulnerable to attack when they are running for election. One area of criminal justice to which the public pays close attention is the death penalty. Public support for the death penalty, though it has recently fallen, remains high. Two-thirds of Americans support the imposition of the death

---

[4] Ann Lin, *The Troubled Success of Crime Policy, in* THE SOCIAL DIVIDE: POLITICAL PARTIES AND THE FUTURE OF ACTIVIST GOVERNMENT 313 (1998).

[5] *Id.*

[6] *Id.*

[7] Stephen B. Bright, *Political Attacks on the Judiciary: Can Justice be Done Amid Efforts to Intimidate and Remove Judges from Office for Unpopular Decisions?*, 72 N.Y.U.L. REV. 308, 316 (May 1997).

[8] *Id.* at 319.

[9] *Id.*

penalty, at least in theory.[10] Public support for the death penalty was even higher in the mid-1990s when polling data showed 80 percent of Americans supported the imposition of the death penalty and has remained higher in some states, such as Texas, than it has in the country as a whole.[11]

The high level of public support for the death penalty has meant that judicial candidates' views on the death penalty are often very important. Judges' rulings in death penalty cases and judicial candidates' views on the death penalty have been a minefield for those facing elections. Judges face election or retention elections in all but six of the states that have the death penalty.[12] Candidates are aware of the likelihood of discussions of their views on the death penalty and may try to avoid discussing the issue on the campaign trail for a variety of reasons. For example, one candidate for a local judgeship in California skipped a television debate because he was concerned that his responses to questions about the death penalty and the "three-strikes" law might violate judicial ethics rules.[13] Sometimes their views or rulings in death penalty cases prevent them from being appointed. According one news story, legal experts contend that in an attempt to show he is conservative, Governor Gray Davis of California has appointed judges who enthusiastically support the death penalty.[14] Davis subjected potential justices to a lengthy questionnaire regarding their views in a variety of areas, including the death penalty.[15]

State court judges around the country have faced election defeat because of rulings made in capital cases. When an interest group, challenger, political actor, or governor publicize a judge's behavior in a death penalty case, generally the decision made or vote cast by the judge favors the defendant in some way. The most damaging of these attacks use brochures or ads that describe, in gory detail, the murder for which the defendant received the death penalty. Voters are urged to show their support for the death penalty or sympathy for the victims by not re-electing the judge. The legal basis for the judge's decision is never given.

The best publicized of these attacks was leveled at Tennessee Supreme Court Justice Penny White. In 1996, White was targeted by a pro-

---

[10] Jennifer L. Harry, *Death Penalty Disquiet Stirs Nation*, 62 CORRECTIONS TODAY (Dec. 1, 2000).

[11] *Id.*

[12] Stephen B. Bright and Patrick J. Keenan, *Judges and the Politics of Death: Deciding Between the Bill of Rights and the Next Election in Capital Cases*, 75 B.U.L. REV. 760, 779 (1995).

[13] *Dawson, Citing Ethics Worries, Skips Taping of TV Debate as Opponents Spar Over Experience*, METROPOLITAN NEWS COMPANY, Feb. 24, 2000.

[14] Harriet Chiang, *Defense Attorneys Accuse Davis of Bias in Handing Out Judgeships*, S.F. CHRONICLE, Feb. 21, 2000 at A1.

[15] *Id.*

death penalty group, the Tennessee Conservative Union (TCU), after she and four other justices on the court voted to overturn a convicted murderer's death sentence. White was the only justice sitting for retention that year. TCU and the Republican Party transformed White's retention election into a referendum on the death penalty by sending out flyers describing the murder in grisly detail and advising voters that the murderer had not received punishment he deserved— "[t]hanks to Penny White."[16] The Republicans' brochure advised voters to vote for capital punishment by not voting for White.[17] White, who had spent just nineteen months on the court, lost her bid for re-election.

White is not the only judge to lose an election because of a ruling made or a vote cast in a death penalty case. In 1992, Justice James Robertson of the Mississippi Supreme Court lost his seat after a challenger who ran a law-and-order campaign and was supported by the state prosecutors' association spotlighted an opinion the judge wrote.[18] At issue was Justice Robertson's statement that the Constitution did not allow the death penalty for rape when the victim survived the attack, a view consistent with the Supreme Court's ruling in *Coker v. Georgia.*[19] One ad used by Robertson's opponents advised, "[V]ote against Robertson because he's opposed to the death penalty and he wants to let them all go."[20]

Though the prevalence of such referenda on the death penalty is not precisely clear, judges either faced more difficult elections or lost their seats because of the rulings on the death penalty in Texas and in North Carolina.[21] Judicial independence in capital cases seems especially threatened in Texas. After a 1994 decision to reverse a conviction in a notorious capital case, Texas Republicans responded to a call to take over the Texas Court of Criminal Appeals, and the Republicans won in every judicial election that year.[22] In a similar story also from the Texas Court of Criminal Appeals—Judge Charles Baird was the lone dissenter in the appeal of famed death row inmate Karla Faye Tucker. He cites this as a reason for his defeat in the next

---

[16] Stephen Bright, *Political Attacks on the Judiciary*, 80 JUDICATURE 165, 168 (Jan.-Feb.1997).

[17] *Id.*

[18] *Id. at* 170.

[19] *Id.*

[20] John Blume & Theodore Eisenberg, *Judicial Politics, Death Penalty Appeals, and Case Selection: An Empirical Study*, 72 S. CAL. L. REV. 465, 466 (1999).

[21] In elections in 1986 and 1990 in North Carolina, challengers castigated Chief Justice Exum for voting to reverse several death sentences. Anthony Champagne, *National Summit on Improving Judicial Selection: Interest Groups and Judicial Elections*, 34 LOY. L.A. L. REV. 1391, 1394 (June 2001).

[22] Bright, *supra* note 7, at 320.

election.[23] In recounting his experiences, Baird told of another Texas judge, an eight-year incumbent, who granted a motion to suppress a weapon in a capital case and was defeated in a primary election that occurred immediately after he handed down the decision.[24]

B. Politicians and the Politics of the Death Penalty

Public support for the death penalty and the graphic nature of many of the crimes for which murderers receive the death penalty make calling attention to any of a judge's rulings in death penalty cases that can be construed as favorable to the defendant an especially effective way for politicians to dramatize their own firm commitment to law and order. State supreme court judges have drawn fire from other elected officials—governors, state legislators and, in a few cases, candidates for federal office. During their 1994 election campaigns, opponents of Senators Charles Robb, Edward Kennedy, and Diane Feinstein castigated each for voting to confirm former Chief Justice Rosemary Barkett of the Florida Supreme Court to a seat on the Eleventh Circuit. At issue were Barkett's votes to overturn death sentences in several cases while she was on the Florida high court.[25] For example, one television ad for Feinstein's opponent, Michael Huffington, charged, "Feinstein judges let killers live after victims died."[26]

In addition to candidates for state and national office, state supreme court justices have drawn fire from governors for their rulings in death penalty cases. In 1986, three California supreme court justices were defeated in retention elections after Governor George Dukemejian withdrew his support for them because of their votes in death penalty cases. In Florida, perhaps in response to the justices' striking down his plan to speed up executions by limiting death penalty appeals in 2000, Governor Jeb Bush publicly accused the state supreme court of hurting crime victims by adding "unnecessary delay and legal gamesmanship" in their consideration of death penalty cases.[27]

---

[23] Stephen Bright, et. al, *Breaking the Most Vulnerable Branch: Do Rising Threats to Judicial Independence Preclude Due Process in Capital Cases?*, 31 COLUM. HUMAN RTS. L. REV., 123, 153 (Fall 1999).

[24] *Id.*

[25] Though in his ads Huffington made the comparison between Justice Rosemary Barkett and former Justice Rose Bird, it is important to note that while she was on the Florida Supreme Court, Barkett reportedly voted to uphold more death sentences than she voted to reverse. By contrast, between 1977 and 1986, the California Supreme Court under Rose Bird reviewed seventy-one death penalty convictions and upheld only four death sentences. John Culver, *The Transformation of the California Supreme Court, 1977-1997*, 61 AL. L. REV. 1461 (1998).

[26] Bright, *supra* note 12, at 790.

[27] Jo Becker & Charles Lane, *Florida's Top Court Has Been GOP Target*, WASH. POST, Nov. 15, 2000.

In Tennessee, Republican Governor Dan Sundquist opposed the retention of White, a Democratic appointee, and promised that he would appoint only judges who support the death penalty. In a statement that dramatically illustrates gubernatorial control of the supreme court, Sundquist reportedly said immediately after White lost her seat, "Should a judge look over his shoulder about whether they're going to be thrown out of office? I hope so."[28]

Voters clearly cede to governors the ability to appoint judges who the governors believe best able to adjudicate matters before the court. In addition, governors may believe that the voters elected them with the mandate to carry out particular policy positions and that the best way to do this is to select judges who are more likely to enforce the law from the governor's policy perspective. The actions described above also seem to suggest that these governors assume that the state supreme court is an extension of the governor's mansion. In other words, judges should make decisions in line with the governor's policy perspective, irrespective of the law or the facts in the case.

C. Accusations of Being Soft on Crime

State court trial and appellate judges' ability to make unfettered decisions is compromised when they must be concerned about challengers accusing them of being soft on crime. Such attacks are most troubling to judges when they focus, as they have recently, on the judge's actual decisions. In 1999 Chief Justice Shirley Abrahamson of the Wisconsin Supreme Court faced a challenger who ran ads focusing on her dissent in a case in which she wrote that the Wisconsin's sexual predator law was not constitutional. The challenger's ads suggested that if Abrahamson were re-elected, sexual predators would be free to prey on children.[29] In California, Judge Patricia Gray of the Sonoma County Superior Court sent out brochures maintaining that her opponent, a former public defender, defended the actions of cop killers, violent criminals, and child molesters.[30] In another case, this time from Alabama, the Judicial Inquiry Commission charged Justice Harold See with using ads during his 2000 campaign that accused his opponent of being soft on drug defendants.[31]

---

[28] Bright, *supra* note 7, at 166.

[29] Shirley S. Abrahamson, *The Ballot and the Bench*, 76 N.Y.U. L. REV. 973, 985 (2001).

[30] Mike McKee, *Nasty Election Fight Spurs A Probe By CJP*, THE (S.F.) RECORDER , Dec. 29, 2000. Gray lost the retention election and the California Commission launched a formal inquiry into Gray's campaign practices.

[31] Larry Bivens, *Coalition Wants to Reform State Judicial Campaigns*, GANNETT NEWS SERVICE, Feb. 22, 2002.

In addition to challengers, interest groups may also use media cam-
paigns during elections to criticize judge for decisions they have
made that the group believes to conflict with its views. Florida's
Barkett serves as an excellent example. Though an analysis of
Barkett's opinions showed that she voted with the majority of the
court more than 90 percent of the time, a variety of groups opposed
Barkett's retention in 1992 because she was supposedly soft on crime.
Groups opposed to Barkett's retention included the National Rifle
Association (NRA), which spent more than $30,000 opposing her.
The NRA criticized Barkett because she had not upheld enough death
sentences, despite the fact that she had voted to uphold the death
penalty in more than 200 cases since she was appointed to the court
in 1985.

Not all of the interest groups who attempt to defeat judges because
they are soft on crime are conservative. Gay rights groups, victims'
groups, and activists who represent the black community have also
opposed judges who the groups believed did not adequately punish
criminals who committed crimes against women, gays and lesbians,
and people of color. Protests frequently occur in reaction to what the
community considers too lenient of a sentence for an offender who
has committed a high-profile crime. For instance, Soon Ja Du, a
Korean-American grocer shot and killed Latasha Harlins, an
unarmed black teenager, in 1991. The shooting, which allegedly
occurred because Du believed that Harlins had shoplifted a bottle of
orange juice, was well publicized. After newly-appointed Judge Joyce
Karlin of the Los Angeles Superior Court sentenced Soon Ja Du to
probation, the black community in Los Angeles held numerous
protests.[32] Members of the African-American community filed formal charges with the California Judicial Commission and demanded
Karlin's recall.[33] Karlin's sentence was upheld on appeal, and the
effort to recall her failed. Karlin won reelection against three challengers the next year, but retired from the bench before completing
her term.

In some cases, groups organize around a particular judge who has
made a series of decisions that the groups consider unfavorable.
Women's and gay rights groups came out against Judge David S.
Young of Utah's Third District , accusing him of bias when gays and
women were crime victims. In 1996, Young held onto his seat by a
slim margin, but was unseated when he lost a retention election in
2002.[34]

---

[32] Rene Lynch, *Shooting sentence focuses attention on state's judiciary*, ORANGE COUNTY REGISTER, Dec. 2, 1991.

[33] *Id.*

[34] Elizabeth Neff, *Judge's Removal Causes Stir; Some support Young, his rulings; others laud retention vote system; Young Is First State Judge to Be Ousted*, THE SALT LAKE TRIBUNE, Nov. 7, 2002, at B1.

Judges who are perceived as not being tough on crime may also face opposition from prosecutors and law enforcement groups during their reelection or retention campaigns. For example, Citizens for a Responsible Judiciary, a group composed of police officers and state's attorneys organized to publicly oppose Barkett's retention in 1992.[35] In both Mississippi and Oklahoma, prosecutors have organized similar organizations to oppose judicial candidates they believe to be soft on crime.[36]

Though the charge that a judge is soft on crime can and has been used to characterize decisions made by judges from a variety of political perspectives, the Republican Party has leveled this charge in a number of cases at judges who are Democrats. In addition to the takeover of the Texas Court of Criminal Appeals described above, the Republican Party has accused candidates who are Democrats of being pro-defendant or soft on crime in several different states. In a state where no sitting supreme court justice had been challenged in over 100 years, Justice Jean Hoefer Toal, South Carolina's first female justice, ran for reelection by the legislature in 1995 and was attacked by the state Republican Party, which called her a liberal judge who was soft on crime.[37] In Michigan, the Republican Party ran television commercials in which the word "pedophile" was quickly shown adjacent to the name of one Democratic appeals court judges, along with an announcement indicating that he had voted to uphold a light sentence for a pedophile.[38]

Part III: Direct Attempts to Limit Judicial Power

Many (though not all) of the limitations on judicial power described above are offshoots of the process of electing judges, rather than selecting them by appointment. Judges who face reelection are vulnerable to attacks by politicians, challengers, and interest groups. In other words, any threat to the judicial independence that exists can be viewed as one cost of the system of accountability most states have chosen. Some view this as a fitting price for allowing citizens to have an opportunity to be involved in electing their state's judges.

The independence of state court judges has been also challenged in ways which have little to do with elections. A judge's freedom to make decisions is compromised when judicial commissions or ethics

---

[35] Diane Rado, *Fiery debate rages ever hotter over chief justice's keeping job,* ST. PETERSBURG TIMES, Sept. 9, 1992.

[36] In 1986, the Oklahoma District Attorneys Association came out against a Court of Criminal Appeals judge because they believed he did not support the death penalty. Prosecutors in Mississippi have also organized to oppose candidates who are soft on crime. See Champagne, *supra* note 21, at 1399.

[37] Blume, *supra* note 20, at 471.

[38] Randall T. Shepard, *Judicial Independence and the Problem of Elections: 'We have met the enemy and he is us,'* 20 QUINNIPIAC L. REV. 753, 757 (2001).

boards sanction judges for having made unpopular decisions. While it is important that judges be disciplined for unethical behavior, their ability to make independent decisions is threatened when public outcry leads to charges filed against a judge, especially when the particular decision lies within the scope of the judge's discretion.

Perhaps the most widely reported case of a judge being sanctioned for an unpopular decision involved Judge Howard Broadman of the Tulare County (California) Superior Court. The California Commission on Judicial Performance charged Broadman with willful judicial misconduct in 1995 and 1996. At issue was Judge Broadman's widely publicized 1991 order that a defendant in a drug case agree to the implantation of the birth control device Norplant as a condition of probation. The defendant had previously lost custody of her five children. In another very controversial case, Broadman delayed sentencing of an HIV-positive rapist to investigate the possibility of prison officials' withholding medical treatment from the defendant.[39] Though some of the charges of improper sentencing against him were dismissed, Broadman, who was supported by the California Judges Association, argued that the charges against him interfered with his exercise of judicial independence.[40]

Removing a judge from a particular jurisdiction because of an unpopular decision that he or she has made demonstrates a related threat to judicial decision-making. Significant public outcry over a particular judge's decision can lead for calls for the judge's removal or transfer to another jurisdiction. Such was the case in Los Angeles after Karlin sentenced Du, the Koren-American grocer, to probation. After the decision, Los Angeles District Attorney Ira Reiner attempted to prevent Karlin from hearing new criminal cases by filing for affidavits of removal on all of her pending cases. In a move that was heralded as striking a blow for judicial independence, the head judge of the court declined to transfer Karlin to a noncriminal court outside out of the area. This signaled a defeat for the Los Angeles District Attorney's office—which had succeeded in having judges prevented in at least two earlier occasions in 1985 and 1990 from hearing criminal cases after they made decisions with which the district attorney's office did not agree.[41]

Judicial independence is directly threatened by legislation or other actions that attempt to limit the scope or range of judicial decision making. A relatively little known example occurred in Texas in 1989

---

[39] *A Career Under Fire*, THE (S.F.) RECORDER, JAN. 5, 2000.

[40] Steven Lubet, *Judicial Discipline and Judicial Independence*, 61 LAW & CONTEMP. PROB. 59, 67 (Summer 1998).

[41] Lynch, *supra* note 32.

when the Texas District County Attorneys Association—dissatisfied with what it believed were the liberal, pro-defendant decisions of the Texas Court of Criminal Appeals—put forth a legislative proposal to amend the Texas Constitution to restrict the court's decisions. Prosecutors argued that the court, an intermediate court with supervisory authority over criminal appeals, was interpreting the Texas Constitution in a way that gave defendants more rights than the U.S. Constitution did. The proposed constitutional amendment, which ultimately died in House committee, would have prevented the court from independently construing provisions of the Texas Constitution having to do with defendants and thus removed judges' interpretive independence.[42]

Sentencing guidelines, three-strikes law, and mandatory minima are more commonly used legislative initiatives to limit judicial discretion. Judges, who are often opposed to sentencing guidelines, argue that guidelines requiring mandatory sentencing for particular crimes violate the separation of powers and impede their ability to render justice.[43] One Florida judge remarked that sentencing guidelines result "in the truly evil avoiding punishment and the technically guilty being senselessly incarcerated more often than should be tolerated in a free society."[44]

Three-strikes laws, which are in force in the majority of states, require judges to impose a long sentence on any defendant guilty of three felonies. Under California's three-strikes laws, which were passed in 1994, defendants with two previous convictions for violent felonies had to receive a sentence of twenty-five years to life for their third felony.[45] This sentence is required irrespective of whether violence was used during the commission of the third felony. A second strike requires a doubling of the normal sentence. Judges complain that these types of laws comprise judicial independence by taking the power away from judges to decide whether the defendant should been shown mercy or if rehabilitation is possible and would serve the public interest more than meting out a long sentence. The California Supreme Court agreed and handed down a controversial decision in 1996, which indicated that three-strikes laws limit judicial discretion and in doing so violate the separation of powers.[46] In that decision, judges were given the power to dismiss felonies if there is a low likeli-

---

[42] George E. Dix, *Judicial Independence in Defining Criminal Defendants' Texas Constitutional Rights*, 68 TEX. L. REV. 1369, 1376-79 (1990).

[43] *Keep Politics Out of Justice*, FLA. SUN-SENTINEL, Nov. 4, 2001.

[44] *Id.*

[45] *See* Michael Vitiello, *Three Strikes and the Romero Case: The Supreme Court Restores Democracy*, 30 LOY. L.A. REV. 1643, 1647 (1997).

[46] People v. Superior Court (Romero), 13 Cal. 4th at 529-30, 917 P.2d at 647, 53 Cal. Rptr. 2d at 808.

hood of the defendant committing further crimes.[47] The California Supreme Court further expanded judicial discretion the following year when it decided that judges had broad authority to reduce felony convictions in crimes that were "wobblers," crimes such as petty theft that are nonviolent felonies.[48] In the event of wobblers, judges were given the authority to reduce the third conviction to a misdemeanor conviction, thereby avoiding the three-strikes law.

Part IV. Conclusion: Consequences of Politicization

All of the actions described above—criticism of judges' decision by the public, interest groups, prosecutors, challengers, and governors; sanctions issued to judges; and legislative attempts to limit judges' power to decide cases have changed the judicial landscape. The most obvious change is the politicization of campaigns has made judicial campaigns much more expensive, forcing judges to raise large sums of money to defend themselves against attacks.

Judges may also find it harder to keep their seats. Even if a judge is able to comment on a decision that is being scrutinized, he or she may have a hard time defending his or her actions. In the area of criminal law, judges who are responsible for sentencing make many decisions, often with incomplete information. If a defendant out on bail commits a crime, the judge may find it particularly difficult to defend his or her decision to grant bail. Judges who are accused of letting violent killers go free are frequently defeated at the polls because the crimes for which defendants are sentenced to death are often grisly and the procedural protections on which judges base their decision may seem inadequate to the public.

Judges and some scholars believe that the message the defeat sends to judges who remain constitutes an even more significant threat to judicial independence. They argue defeat of a judge who lost because he or she was targeted by a governor, interest group, or challenger for making an unpopular, yet legally defensible, decision suggests to all the remaining judges and judicial candidates that if one is to remain a judge, policy preferences must guide decision-making rather than the law.

Politicization of crime may have led some judges who are eager to keep their seats to inject politics into the race by dramatizing their

---

[47] Maura Dolan, *Court Widens Judges' Leeway on Three Strikes*, L.A. TIMES, Jan. 17, 1997.
[48] *Id.*

records[49] or by accusing their opponents of opposing the death penalty.[50] Judge Mike McCormick of the Alabama Tenth Circuit Criminal Court ran advertisements during his re-election campaign bragging: "Some complain that he's too tough on criminals, and he is....We need him now more than ever."[51] In an attempt to appear tough on crime, candidates have also made promises regarding future conduct—a clear violation of judicial ethics rules. One candidate for the Texas Court of Criminal Appeals, Judge John Devine of the Harris County Civil District Court, announced his candidacy by declaring that he believed in "being short on words but long on sentences."[52] Another candidate for the same court promised during her campaign that if elected she would never vote to reverse in a capital murder case.[53]

The politicization of the death penalty and other criminal justice issues may have had an impact on how judges make decisions. The independence on the judiciary is limited if judges are more likely to make particular decisions because they feel that their tenure would be threatened if they were to decide otherwise. Several types of evidence—anecdotal evidence showing that particular judges have fulfilled campaign promises never to reverse death sentences, studies of death penalty relief rates after politicization, and surveys of judicial attitudes—suggest that the politicization of criminal justice issues and attaching consequences to unpopular rulings affect judicial decision making.

Researchers have attempted to evaluate systematically the degree to which judges feel pressured to vote to uphold death sentences. Using data that compared appellate reversal rates before and after events in

---

[49] There is evidence from around the country that judges may advertise the number of cases in which they upheld the death penalty. For instance in his retention election campaign for the Nevada Supreme Court, Justice Cliff Young ran an advertisement in which he demonstrated how tough he was on crime by giving the number of cases in which he had voted to uphold the death penalty. Steven Bright, *Judicial Review and Judicial Independence: Can Judicial Independence Be Attained in the South? Overcoming History, Elections, and Misperceptions about the Role of the Judiciary*," 14 GA. ST. U. L. REV, 817, 847 (1998).

[50] In the race for the First District Court of Appeals in 1996, incumbent Judge Lee Hildebrant ran misleading television advertisements accusing his opponent of opposing the death penalty. The opponent, who lost, filed a grievance. The offending judge was found to have violated the judicial code of conduct. *In re* Judicial Campaign Complaint Against Hildebrandt, 675 N.E.2d 889 (1997). In a similar case from Georgia, George M. Weaver distributed a brochure that accused his opponent in the race for the Georgia Supreme Court of calling the electric chair silly. Like Hildebrandt, Weaver was found to have violated the state code of judicial conduct. Shepard, *supra* note 38, at 762. Weaver appealed to the federal courts, and in October 2002, a three-judge panel of the United States Court of Appeals for the 11th Circuit found unconstitutional portions of Georgia's judicial canons that restrict misrepresentations in judicial campaign speech and that prohibit judges from personally soliciting campaign contributions. Weaver v. Bonner, 309 F.3d 1312 (11th Cir. 2002).

[51] Bright, *supra* note 7, at 320.

[52] Julie Mason, *Judge Devine enters Court of Criminal Appeals race*, HOUSTON CHRONICLE, July 28, 1999.

[53] Bright et. al., *supra* note 23, at 133. One of her former colleagues maintains that in five years on the court, she had kept that promise and never voted to reverse a capital case.

which the death penalty was highly politicized, John Blume and Theodore Eisenberg found that in California, Tennessee, and South Carolina, politics did have an impact on outcomes in death penalty cases.[54] In California, the event was the removal of Chief Justice Rose Bird; in Tennessee, the event was the removal of White. In South Carolina, the focal event was the pro-death penalty campaign of the state's attorney general. In each of these three states, the authors found a statistically significant decrease in reversal rates following these highly politicized pro-death penalty events.[55] The authors cautioned that politicization might not affect reversal rates in all states, however. Data from Texas and Mississippi did not show decreases in relief rates following highly publicized pro-death penalty events.[56]

A third measure of the impact of the politicization on appellate and trial courts is the way judges feel about making unpopular decisions. There is some evidence that judges—and not necessarily judges who make decisions in the area of criminal law—feel the affect of politicization of their jobs. For instance, one recent study of Florida judges by the League of Women Voters found that close to 95 percent of the judges surveyed indicated they are conscious of the consequences that will follow from an unpopular ruling; a quarter of the respondents said this happens frequently.[57] Though the judges denied that being aware of the consequences affects their ruling, the vast majority, some 83 percent, indicated that they believed that their colleagues were affected by the consequences. As a reason for their concerns, judges in the survey cited recent attacks on courts and the likelihood that they would not be re-elected.[58] Even if the survey is correct and the knowledge that some decisions may have negative consequences does not affect a judge's final decision, the survey revealed that at least some judges behave differently when they are worried how a decision will be received. Some judges insisted they often spend more time drafting an opinion or order they fear will be unpopular.[59]

---

[54] John Blume & Theodore Eisenberg, *Judicial Politics, Death Penalty Appeals, and Case Selection: An Empirical Study,* 72 S. Cal. L. Rev. 465, 499 (1999).

[55] *Id.* at 500-501.

[56] *Id.*

[57] Amy K. Brown, *Judges Say Politics Are Interfering with Independence,* 28 Fla. Bar News, Oct. 15, 2001 at 1.

[58] *Id.*

[59] *Id.*

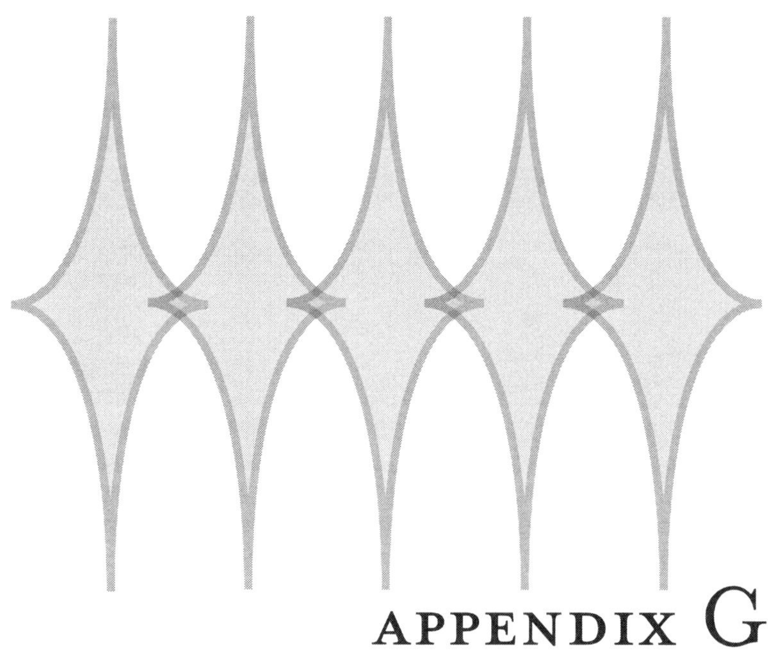

APPENDIX G

CIVIL JUSTICE AND JUDICIAL SELECTION

Andrew Spalding* and Carl Tobias**

I. INTRODUCTION: CIVIL JUSTICE REFORM IN CONTEXT

Over the last quarter century, critics have periodically expressed concerns about a so-called "litigation explosion" and have sought substantive and procedural reforms to remedy or ameliorate the difficulties that they perceive. One definition of litigation explosion is that too many civil cases that lack merit are filed. During this two-and-a-half decade period, critics have periodically suggested that there have been crises in specific substantive areas. Some important areas for concern include health care delivery generally and medical malpractice specifically, products liability, as well as insurance coverage for these areas and others, such as local governmental subdivisions and school districts.

One major concern of these critics is that the substantive rules respecting liability are too flexible or liberal and expose defendants to open-ended and substantial liability. Illustrative is the strict liability in tort under the Restatement of Torts Section 402A for design defects. Another significant concern is that the procedural rules regarding liability are too flexible or liberal as written or as applied. Illustrative are personal jurisdiction and venue as well as joinder and class action devices—which plaintiffs purportedly use against defendants to require them to litigate in unfriendly fora before hostile judges and juries. Critics concomitantly maintain that these substantive and procedural advantages enable plaintiffs to extract substantial settlements from institutional defendants, who are unwilling to risk imposition of even greater liability by pro-plaintiff judges and juries. The critics have argued that these crises have imposed detrimental economic impacts and increased the costs of goods and services for all consumers. The critics have sought substantive and procedural reforms for the problems, which they have identified primarily as coming from Congress and state legislatures, but they have also sought relief from courts and from procedural rulemaking entities.

Congress and most of the state legislatures have responded to these criticisms by passing statutes that have instituted certain substantive reforms. For example, numerous states have imposed caps on the recovery of non-economic damages in the area of medical malpractice or caps on the recovery of punitive damages for medical malprac-

---

* J.D William S. Boyd School of Law, University of Nevada, Las Vegas, PhD., political science, University of Wisconsin - Madison.

tice and products liability. Some jurisdictions have shortened their statutes of limitation or modified provisions for joint and several liability.

The federal and state legislative and judicial branches also have implemented numerous procedural reforms that are intended as responses to the substantive and procedural problems identified above generally and to the litigation explosion specifically. The principal focus of these reforms has been the pretrial process in general and discovery specifically. The 1983 amendments in the Federal Rules of Civil Procedure and their state analogues were intended to limit discovery, increase judicial control of the pretrial process through judicial case management, and expand lawyer responsibility by prescribing sanctions for improper behavior. Congress correspondingly passed the Civil Justice Reform Act of 1990 that required all ninety-four federal districts to experiment for seven years with procedures for reducing expense and delay in civil litigation. Emphasis was placed on judicial control of discovery, judicial case management, and alternative dispute resolution. Most of the procedural reforms that Congress prescribed had already received application or experimentation in many states. The 1993 amendments to the Federal Rules of Civil Procedure imposed mandatory prediscovery or automatic disclosure and substantially limited the sanctioning provision in the 1983 amendments, which proved controversial principally by facilitating satellite litigation unrelated to merits resolution of cases. The 2000 amendments to the Federal Rules of Civil Procedure narrowed the 1993 amendment's provision for automatic disclosure and narrowed the scope of discovery generally. One important aspiration of the rule revisors who drafted the 2000 amendments was to encourage greater judicial involvement in discovery disputes.

The precise effects of these federal and state substantive and procedural reforms on the putative problems delineated remain unclear. However, despite these efforts at reform, numerous observers contend that plaintiffs and defendants have continued seeking to extract substantive and procedural advantages from the civil justice system. For example, certain jurisdictions, which allegedly have plaintiff-friendly judges and juries, have become focal points for plaintiffs and lawyers who pursue extraordinary awards. Defense interests have responded by seeking to persuade the state legislatures to enact tort reform or by attempting to retain and elect judges whom they perceive as more favorably inclined to their interests. Individual plaintiffs and groups, as well as plaintiffs' trial lawyers, have concomitantly responded by opposing these tort reform efforts in state legislatures and by attempting to retain and elect judges whom they perceive are favorably disposed to them.

II. NEW EXCESSES OF MASS TORT LITIGATION: PROBLEM JURISDICTIONS

In Jefferson County, Mississippi, there had never been a punitive damage verdict that surpassed $9 million prior to 1995. Since then, there have been at least nineteen, totaling more than $2 billion,[1] five of them exceeding $100 million.[2] Between 1999 and 2001, the total number of plaintiffs (more than 10,000) who pursued tort litigation exceeded the county's population (9,740).[3] In February 2001, jurors in Copiah County, Mississippi, returned what would have been a record-breaking verdict of $75 billion, only to later realize that they had written too many zeroes. They meant $75 million.[4] Jeffrey Jackson, a professor at Mississippi College School of Law, said Mississippi jurors have difficulty finding a frame of reference. "On a scale of one to 10 billion, how bright is the light in your office? That's the kind of thing jurors have to decide."[5] Most of these cases have been class actions.[6]

News of Mississippi's spectacular punitive awards has attracted lawyers from across the country—particularly the nearby states of Texas and Alabama, where tort reform laws have limited punitive damages. The Mississippi rules of civil procedure, unlike those in forty-eight other states, do not technically permit class action lawsuits. Plaintiffs with claims that involve a common question of law or fact, however, can be joined. Mississippi's jurisdictional laws require only that one plaintiff live in the county, regardless of how many other plaintiffs might be joined; no in-state plaintiff is necessary if a single in-state defendant can be found.[7] Mississippi has another unique rule that allows plaintiffs to go to trial ninety days after filing suit, which severely limits defense discovery.[8] Some lawyers now refer to the courthouse in Jefferson County—a county where half the people live below the poverty line and fewer than half of the jury pool is secondary school graduates,[9] and which has consistently suffered from double-digit unemployment[10]—as "the center for the redistribution for wealth."[11]

---

[1] *Jackpot Justice?*, THE CLARION-LEDGER, June 19, 2001.

[2] Jimmie E. Gates, *Critics Link Lawyer Ads, Big Awards*, THE CLARION-LEDGER, June 18, 2001.

[3] Jerry Mitchell, *Out-of-State Cases, In-State Headaches*, THE CLARION-LEDGER, June 17, 2001.

[4] *Id.*

[5] *Id.*

[6] *Id.*

[7] *Id.*

[8] Mark Ballard, *Mississippi Becomes a Mecca For Tort Suits*, NAT'L LAW JOURNAL, Apr. 27, 2002.

[9] Amity Shales, *A Tobacco Lawsuit Stranger Than Fiction*, NAT'L POST, May 29, 2002.

[10] Mitchell, *supra* note 3.

[11] *Id.*

Mike Hotra of the American Tort Reform Association says that the jurisdiction has become a "hell hole" for corporate defendants, leading at least two companies to leave the state because of its reputation as a "mecca for suits."[12]

There is apparently a connection between the growth of the class action suit in Jefferson County and local restrictions on lawyer advertising. In 1995, most restrictions on lawyer advertising were lifted, and now advertisements frequently appear in local newspapers. According to Chip Reno, executive director of Stop Lawsuit Abuse of Mississippi, these ads "just invite people to sue."[13]
Similarly, in rural Madison County, Illinois, population 259,000,[14] the number of class actions increased from two to forty-three between 1998 and 2001. Lawyers and litigants pursue more class action suits in this county than any other jurisdiction except Los Angeles County and Cook County, which includes Chicago.[15] Most of the class actions are filed on behalf of multistate or nationwide classes. Madison County judges have been more willing than federal judges to certify such classes. Two Chicago-based law firms filed a majority of these cases. Paul Weiss, an attorney with the Chicago-based firm of Freed and Weiss, has pursued 30 such cases in Madison County.[16] These firms have principally relied on a strategy of filing separate cases that attack multiple companies in a single industry, with each lawsuit challenging the same practice. For example, eleven of the cases filed in 2001 challenged the method employed by automobile insurers for calculating the value of "totaled" vehicles. Another ten cases challenged optional insurance policies used in conjunction with credit cards, mortgages, or automobile loans to pay the consumer's debt in the event of disability or death. Connections between the suits and the county are often tenuous. One suit challenged energy fees that the Wyndham hotel chain charged customers. A plaintiff, who spent two nights in a Wyndham hotel and was allegedly charged $2.87 per night, represented a nationwide class. Wyndham owns no hotels in Madison County.[17]

According to Paul Simon, former U.S. Senator from Illinois, "it's a working-man and working-woman kind of area. The steel industry has gone down a great deal, but you still have the memory of the steel

---

[12] John Porretto, *Rural County Known for Huge Verdicts*, MISSISSIPPI SUN HERALD, July 2, 2001.

[13] Gates, *supra* note 2.

[14] Christi Parsons, *Downstate County is a 'Plaintiff's Paradise;' Class-Action Suits Rising Dramatically, Critics Complain*, CHICAGO TRIBUNE, June 17, 2002.

[15] Dennis Conrad, *Lawyers with Class-Action Suits Find State Courts More Generous*, SAN DIEGO UNION-TRIBUNE, June 6, 2002.

[16] *Id.*

[17] John H. Beisner & Jessica Davidson Miller, *Class Action Magnet Courts: The Allure Intensifies*, CIVIL JUSTICE REPORT, June, 2002, *available at* http://www. manhattan-institute.org.

mills there. The attitude of family members and former workers is still very much a part of the culture of the area."[18] William Schroeder, a law professor at Southern Illinois University, says that these conditions contribute to a pronounced "pro-plaintiffs environment."[19]

These two jurisdictions afford particularly egregious examples of the excesses that attend some mass tort litigation from the plaintiffs' perspective. Similar, albeit subtler, excesses have been manifested from a defense perspective. For example, judges have rejected plaintiffs' efforts to pursue litigation by refusing to find jurisdiction or venue or to certify class actions as well as by liberally granting motions to dismiss or for summary judgment. When states have instituted efforts to curb these excesses, however, a new, but related, set of problems has arisen.

III. TORT REFORM AND JUDICIAL CAMPAIGNS

Campaign expenditures for state supreme court candidates increased 61 percent between 1998 and 2000, and more than 100 percent since 1994.[20] The most hotly contested, and most expensive, judicial elections occurred in the states of Alabama, Michigan, and Ohio.[21] In these states, supreme court justices had ruled against their respective legislatures' efforts at tort reform. In response, business interests organized to elect more "business-friendly" judges. This reaction was predictable and understandable. These interests, having persuaded legislative bodies to adopt tort reform and having experienced judicial rejection of these reforms, may have believed that the principal recourse left to them was changing the judiciary's composition. Their political adversaries, such as the plaintiffs' trial bar, frequently responded by contributing to campaigns of candidates whom they perceived were more favorably inclined to plaintiffs' interests.

A. ALABAMA

The Brennan Center reports that the 2000 supreme court races in Alabama were the costliest judicial elections in the nation, with candidates raising over twice as much as the national average. The National Institute on Money and Politics found that seven of the top ten fund-raisers in state judicial elections across the country were from Alabama.[22] These expenditures dramatically escalated when

---

[18] Parsons, *supra* note 14.

[19] Conrad, *supra* note 15.

[20] Deborah Goldberg, Craig Holman & Samantha Sanchez, *The New Politics of Judicial Elections*, *available* at http://bennancenter.org/resources/resources_books.html#ji, at 4.

[21] *Id.* at 8.

[22] Mary Orndorff, *State Justice Races Most Costly in U.S.*, BIRMINGHAM NEWS, Apr. 1, 2002.

judges affiliated with the Democratic Party invalidated that state's tort reform legislation in 1987.[23] According to some local commentators, supreme court elections have become referenda on the trend of the court—which is dominated by judges affiliated with the Republican Party— toward favoring defendants over plaintiffs in tort cases.[24] An Alabama Democratic Party advertisement, which aired immediately before the 2000 elections, blamed Republican supreme court justices for the inability of Alabama citizens to sue Ford and Firestone over a tire recall. The justices have similarly been blamed for the prevalence of binding arbitration clauses that Alabama car buyers have signed, even though federal law authorizes the practice.[25]

Concerns about the partiality of judges who accept contributions from business groups surfaced in a recent case involving a couple who had purchased a new home on their realtor's assurance that the buyer of their old home had proper financing. The couple subsequently learned that the financing structure left them with two mortgages and sued. They secured a $1.5 million verdict at trial, which the Alabama Supreme Court overturned. After the couple's attorney publicly castigated the court for being beholden to business interest groups, the court reconsidered the case and awarded the couple $1 million.

A study by Stephen J. Ware, a professor at the Cumberland School of Law, similarly found that justices who received campaign contributions from trial attorneys ruled against arbitration, while those who received contributions from corporations ruled in favor of arbitration. He concluded that "[a]rbitration law in Alabama seems to have no doctrine at all that is purely legal, as opposed to political."[26]

A candidate in the 2000 election, Judge Pam Baschab of the Alabama Court of Criminal Appeals, walked the length of the state to symbolize the harm big money contributions inflict on Alabama's judicial system. She claimed to be the only one of the four candidates who had not accepted contributions from interest groups and pledged to spend no more than $110,000 on her campaign.[27] Her protest apparently fell on deaf ears because she was defeated.

---

[23] Stan Bailey, *Bench Hopefuls Get Lawyers' Donations*, BIRMINGHAM NEWS, Oct. 6, 2000. For a more thorough scholarly account of the impact of state courts overturning tort reform legislation, see Symposium, *Thirteenth Annual Issue on State Constitutional Law*, 32 RUTGERS L.J. 897 (2001).

[24] Sean Reilly, GOP *Justices Stomp Democrats in Fundraising*, MOBILE REGISTER, Feb. 2, 2000.

[25] Alan Choate, *Ads Link Supreme Court Justices to Firestone Controversy*, MOBILE REGISTER, Nov. 2, 2000.

[26] *Who Holds the Gavel in Alabama?*, BIRMINGHAM NEWS, Apr. 1, 2001. *See generally* Stephen J. Ware, *Money, Politics and Judicial Decisions: A Case Study of Arbitration Law in Alabama*, 15 J.L. & POL. 645 (1999).

[27] Stan Bailey, *Baschab: 'Big Money' Shouldn't Determine Chief Justice*, BIRMINGHAM NEWS, May 22, 2000.

Tort-related campaign contributions may not be all powerful in Alabama. Former Chief Justice Harold See, who was a prodigious fundraiser with substantial support from business groups, nonetheless, lost the Republican primary to Alabama Circuit Court Judge Roy S. Moore. Moore's notoriety derives principally from his refusal to remove a plaque of the Ten Commandments from his courtroom.[28] Despite this aberration, in the final elections conducted during 2000, all candidates supported by the Chamber of Commerce won their races.[29]

B. MICHIGAN

In 1995, James Barrett, president of the Michigan Chamber of Commerce, declared that "it is becoming increasingly apparent that to win both the battle and the war to improve Michigan's business climate, job providers must become more focused on judicial elections, providing financial assistance to responsible judicial candidates when necessary."[30] Over the past decade, the price of a court race has risen from $300,000 to $5 million.[31] In the most recent election, the Chamber of Commerce alone spent $3.2 million.[32] Among the tactics employed by the Chamber was an advertising campaign that promoted Michigan over Ohio as a place in which the "judicial restraint of the Michigan Supreme Court and fair laws have helped create a healthy economic climate." A radio advertisement similarly claimed, "The Ohio Supreme Court has rejected reasonable legal reform," whereas in Michigan, "consumers are confident, jobs are safe and business thrives."[33] As private contributions have escalated, so have contributions from political parties. In Michigan, justices must secure nomination at political party conventions, only to then compete in an ostensibly nonpartisan final election.[34] Recent practices call into question the nonpartisan nature of these final elections; although the Republican Party spent only $100,000 on the races ten years ago, this year it spent nearly $10 million.[35] The three politically conservative justices who sought re-election, Clifford Taylor, Robert Young, and Stephen Markman, retained their seats.

The involvement of insurance companies is a particular interest in Michigan. In 2000, the Supreme Court issued a 5-2 decision in

---

[28] Kevin Sack, *Ten Commandments' Defender Wins Vote*, N.Y. TIMES, June 8, 2000.

[29] Katherine Rizzo, *Chamber Ads Failed in Ohio, Worked Elsewhere*, ASSOCIATED PRESS WIRE, Nov. 8, 2000.

[30] Curt Guyette, *Justice at Any Price?* DETROIT METRO TIMES, Oct. 10, 2000.

[31] David Shepardson, *Stakes Rise in Court Race*, THE DETROIT NEWS, Oct. 31, 2000.

[32] Sheila Schimpf, *Report Sees Big Growth, Problems in Spending on Michigan Judicial Races*, MONEY & POLITICS REP., May 14, 2002.

[33] *Chamber Ads Court Business, Not Fairness*, DETROIT FREE PRESS, June 21, 2000.

[34] Jeffrey Haden, *Supreme Court in Partisan Catch-22*, THE DETROIT NEWS, Jan. 18, 2000.

[35] Kathy Barks Hoffman, *Expensive Bitter Supreme Court Races May Be Just Beginning*, GRAND RAPIDS PRESS, Nov.

favor of Daimler Chrysler after four of the justices received contributions from the company.[36] The Michigan Democratic Party subsequently sponsored advertisements which suggested that Republican candidates were beholden to insurance companies, even though the candidates have received only about $15,000 from those companies.[37] Despite these modest sums, some of the companies' tactics have drawn national attention. Three insurance companies sponsored a cocktail party in which they invited attorneys to hear three Republican state supreme court justices speak, after which the attorneys were asked to make campaign contributions. One attorney said that "you can't say no. That's not far from extortion."[38]

Reflecting on the dynamic in Michigan, a columnist observed that "if you had only the candidates' rhetoric and TV ads to go by, you might conclude that the plaintiffs' bar and the insurance industry were the only parties with a stake in this year's contest."[39]

As testament to the expanding interest in judicial elections, a study by the National Institute on Money in State Politics showed that 94 percent of donors in Michigan judicial campaigns did not appear before the court.[40] However, the Michigan Campaign Finance Network reported that between 1990 and 1999, 86 percent of the cases heard by the Michigan Supreme Court involved either lawyers or litigants who had contributed to the campaigns of at least one of the justices.[41] Nonetheless, the National Institute insists that those who did contribute enjoyed the same likelihood of success before the court as noncontributors.[42]

C. OHIO

In Ohio, tort reform has been the major issue that has galvanized numerous groups to support particular judicial candidates. Trial lawyers and trade unions have aided the Democratic candidates, while insurance companies, businesses, and medical interests have assisted the Republicans.[43] Supreme Court Justice Alice Robie Resnick, who authored the majority opinion in the court's decision that overturned legislative tort reform, was the target of an especially aggressive campaign by the Ohio Chamber of Commerce.[44] After issuance of the

---

[36] *Id.* at 23.

[37] Thomas J. Bray, *Rule of Law Is at Stake in Court Race*, DETROIT NEWS, Nov. 5, 2000.

[38] Nancy Perry Graham, *The Best Judges Money Can Buy*, GEORGE, Dec. 21, 2000.

[39] Brian Dickerson, *Every Voter Has a Stake in Outcome of State Court Race*, DETROIT FREE-PRESS, Sept. 29, 2000.

[40] Dawson Bell, *Good News About Judicial Fairness Gets Overlooked*, DETROIT FREE-PRESS, Mar. 25, 2002.

[41] Brian Dickerson, *What Money Can — and Can't — Buy*, DETROIT FREE-PRESS, May 3, 2002.

[42] Bell, *supra* note 40.

[43] James Bradshaw, *Typical Backers Enter High-Court Campaigns*, Aug. 4, 2000.

[44] Joe Hallett, *High Court Race Conjures Low Blows*, THE COLUMBUS DISPATCH, Apr. 2, 2000.

decision, the Chamber hired the political consultants who had helped elect conservative judges to the Michigan Supreme Court. The consultants reportedly told the Chamber that "playing dirty was a necessity."[45] The Chamber alone spent over $4 million attacking Resnick.[46] Although Resnick and her opponent agreed to abide by a recently overturned statute that capped judicial election spending at $500,000, no restriction is imposed on third-party campaign spending in judicial elections.[47] Andrew Doehrel, president of the Ohio Chamber of Commerce, defended this level of involvement by invoking the language of pluralism: "[U]ntil recently, the power of elected state Supreme Courts has been understood and harnessed by only one special-interest group: personal-injury lawyers."[48] Doehrel added that the Chamber intends to offset that group's influence.

Another pro-business group, Citizens for a Strong Ohio, raised $3 million for the 2000 judicial elections. Although Citizens describes itself as an issue advocacy group, Common Cause of Ohio alleges that Citizens is a political action committee because it is attempting to influence the outcome of the election and thus should be bound by disclosure and spending limit laws.[49] One example of the advertisements which created this controversy featured an image of Lady Justice peeking around her blindfold while the voiceover asks, "Alice Resnick: Is Justice for Sale?" The advertisement never mentioned Resnick's opponent or the election.[50] The Ohio Elections Commission rejected the Common Cause argument.[51]

Despite the Chamber's opposition, Resnick secured re-election. Similar dynamics are likely to attend the 2002 election, however, as two candidates are competing for the seat that Justice Andrew Douglas is vacating. Like Resnick, Douglas was a member of the four-person majority who invalidated Ohio's tort reform legislation.

IV. OTHER METHODS FOR ATTEMPTING TO INFLUENCE THE JUDICIARY: JUDICIAL EDUCATION AND EVALUATION

In addition to making campaign contributions, certain interests have organized to promote particular theories of judicial interpretation and to orchestrate public evaluations of judges premised on related

---

[45] Doug Oplinger, *Supreme Court Race to Alter Ohio Politics*, AKRON BEACON-JOURNAL, Nov. 3, 2000.

[46] *Id.*

[47] Randy Ludlow, *Big Business Goal: Oust Ohio Justice*, CINCINNATI POST, Sept. 9, 2000.

[48] Andrew Doehrel & Anne Valentine, *Bias Favors Lawyers, Public Interest at Heart*, USA TODAY, Sept. 1, 2000.

[49] William Hershey & Mike Wagner, *Group Files Complaint about Anti-Resnick Ads*, DAYTON DAILY NEWS, Oct. 18, 2000.

[50] Jim Provance, *Panel Won't Stop Anti-Resnick Ad from Being Aired*, TOLEDO BLADE, Oct. 20, 2000.

[51] Joe Hallett, *Free Speech Protects Attack Ads, Ruling Says*, COLUMBUS DISPATCH, Apr. 5, 2001.

criteria. The fountainhead of the judicial education and evaluation movement has been the Law and Economics Center (LEC) at Virginia's George Mason University School of Law. The principal mission of the LEC, which was founded in 1976 by Henry Manne, is to educate federal judges; it claims over 600 alumni.[52] Although primarily economic in focus, its course list from the last several years is a survey in the pillars of modern intellectual conservatism. "The Economics of Private Law" and "The Economics of Public Law" predominate over humanities-based complements, such as "Aristotle and the Virtues," "The Idea of America," "Individual Responsibility and Culture," and "The Challenge of Civil Society."[53] Former McGill University Professor Francis H. Buckley, in conjunction with the law school's dean, Mark F. Grady, now directs the program.

LEC achieved recent notoriety in connection with the confirmation process of D. Brooks Smith, chief judge of the U.S. District Court for the Western District of Pennsylvania, whom President Bush nominated and the Senate has since confirmed to the U.S. Court of Appeals for the Third Circuit. Between 1992 and 2000, Smith attended twelve seminars, incurring more than $30,000 in expenses paid for by LEC.[54] Locations for the seminars included Amelia Island, Florida, and Montana's Gallatin Gateway Inn.[55] Questions of judicial ethics were widely debated in the popular press,[56] creating a spotlight that was quickly seized by Senators John Kerry and Russell Feingold, who sponsored a bill that would have banned these trips for federal judges.

LEC has been linked with other efforts to influence the judiciary, however, before the recent controversy. Richard Fink, an economics professor at George Mason University, left his position in the early 1980s and founded a pro-business lobby in Washington called Citizens for a Sound Economy.[57] The lobby was financed with seed money from the Koch family foundations. Koch Industries hired Fink in 1990 to manage its Washington office and promote the company's "market-based management" philosophy. From this position, Fink recruited another George Mason professor, Henry N. Butler, to fill the Koch Distinguished Teaching Professor of Law and

---

[52] Law & Economics Center, George Mason University School of Law *at* http://www.gmu/departments/law/lawecon (last visited July 1, 2003).

[53] *Id.*

[54] Edward Walsh, *Judge Defends Role in Seminars, Bank: Senators Questions Appellate Nominee*, THE WASHINGTON POST, Feb. 9, 2002.

[55] Ann McFeatters, *Appeals Court Nominee Targeted Groups Oppose Pick for 3rd Circuit Seat*, PITTSBURGH POST-GAZETTE, Feb. 9, 2002.

[56] *See, e.g., A Questions of Ethics*, THE WASHINGTON POST, May 23, 2002; *Ethical Programs for Judges*, THE WASHINGTON POST, June 2, 2002.

[57] John J. Fialka, *How Koch Industries Tries to Influence Judicial System*, WALL STREET JOURNAL, Aug. 9, 1999.

Economics position at the University of Kansas. Butler's principal task was to develop a series of seminars for state judges, educating them in "Kochian" economics. Since 1995, over 550 judges have attended Economics Institutes for State Judges. The seminars would typically last two weeks at such locations as Snowbird, Utah, with nearly the entire $5,000 bill paid by the institute. The general focus of these seminars was to teach basic microeconomics, according to Butler, who feels he is performing an important public service by "keeping judges intellectually alive."[58] Subjects have included "the costs of overdeterrence" by judges who hold companies liable for harming people or the environment. According to the institute's syllabus, "many potentially hazardous activities offer great benefits to society."[59] Mr. Butler has since left the university, and the institute has disbanded.

Many participants may have enrolled in the seminars because of judicial evaluation, another mechanism that has allegedly influenced judicial elections. The Koch family foundations have also partially financed this measure. In numerous states, including Texas, Louisiana, Alabama, Mississippi, West Virginia, Michigan, and Kansas,[60] pro-business organizations have attempted to evaluate the performance of state judges. The entities claim to help inform the electorate about the impact of the judicial process on the state's economy by distributing surveys to members of the state bar, tallying the results, and distributing them to the community at large.

In Oklahoma, the judicial evaluation process has been perhaps the most sophisticated and has generated the most publicity. Ron Howell, a former executive with Koch Industries, left the company in 1987 to create a Tulsa political consulting firm with Koch support.[61] He developed Oklahomans for Judicial Excellence (OJE) to ascertain and publicize judges' "clear pro-economy, anti-economy impact." [62] Howell was joined on the board by James Milner, director of Oklahoma Citizens for a Sound Economy; Scott Mitchell, director of the Oklahoma Retailers Association; and John Brock, president of Tulsa-based Rockford Exploration and former member of Citizens Against Lawsuit Abuse, which pushed for tort reform in 1994. OJE was a nonprofit corporation with 9,000 members and was comprised of Oklahoma businesses, including oil and gas companies, insurance

---

[58] *Id.*

[59] *Id.*

[60] *Id.*

[61] *Id.*

[62] Leigh Jones, *Scoring Well in Scorned Tests,* available at http://www.statesource.com/leigh.htm (last visited July 1, 2003).

companies and manufacturers.[63] OJE's web page announced that "no area of business cost has grown faster in recent years than legal litigation costs." The organization considers itself a counterbalance to the trial lawyers, whose vested interests, OJE claims, have "manipulate[d] both the laws and the selection of Oklahoma's state judges."[64] The organization's web site went on to claim that the election process is uninformed, because "business-minded citizens go to the polls and have no valid information to make a judicial retention or selection decision." OJE sought to "stimulate voter interest"[65] and enlighten that decision.

To that end, OJE mailed a questionnaire to 2,500 members of the Oklahoma Bar Association who in the previous year had cases before judges on the ballot.[66] The questionnaire included mostly multiple-choice questions on all district, appellate, and supreme court judges as well as the state's workers compensation judges. The questions were intended to address "overall fairness, docket control, pro-employer/employee bias and the inclination to 'send everything to the jury.'"[67] The results were then systematically distributed to interested Oklahoma organizations. The list of targeted presentations was impressive in its thoroughness, including industry associations (banking, medical, agricultural, retail, manufacturing, and other associations); civic associations (political parties, interest groups); all state daily and weekly newspapers; and Chambers of Commerce in communities larger than 15,000.[68]

The origin of the questionnaire raised additional separation-of-powers issues. The polling company was the Oklahoma-based Cole, Hargrave, Snodgrass & Associates, Inc. When the questionnaire was being completed, Tom Cole, a named partner of the company, was Oklahoma's secretary of state.[69] He is now running for the congressional seat to be vacated by J.C. Watts. Cole denied any intent to influence the judiciary and defended his firm's conduct in terms of voter education: "[I]t's extraordinarily difficult for a voter to have information on judicial performance. . . . I find it hard to believe it's inappropriate."[70]

---

63 Oklahomans for Judicial Excellence, *Executive Summary,* at http://www.statesource.com/summary.htm (last visited July 1, 2003).

64 *Id.*

65 Jay F. Marks, *available at* http://www.statesource.com/enid.htm (last visited July 1, 2003).

66 Jim Campbell, *State Judges Get 'Report Cards,' available at* http://www.statesource.com/OPA.htm (last visited July 1, 2003).

67 Oklahomans for Judicial Excellence, *Research Methodology,* at http://www.statesource.come/research.htm (last visited July 1, 2003).

68 Oklahomans for Judicial Excellence, *Presentations & Distributions,* at http://www.statesource.come/present.htm (last visited July 1, 2003).

69 John Greiner, *Senator Claims Judicial Ratings Try to Influence,* THE DAILY OKLAHOMAN, Apr. 10, 1998.

70 *Id.*

The reports were not well received by the Oklahoma bar or trial lawyers association. Howell claims that the resistance to publicizing judicial evaluations is essentially elitist: "[T]hese organizations have members (being attorneys in the state) that have the benefit of knowledge of judicial performance that most Oklahomans do not have available to them."[71] A better response, according to Howell, would be for such groups to "join the effort to get quality information to all of their fellow citizens."[72]

Approximately 1,000 members returned the surveys, representing about 11 percent of the Oklahoma bar.[73] Mr. Howell found the response "astounding," because most mail surveys generate less than a five percent return. He felt the high response levels indicated the perceived need for evaluations among bar members.[74] At least one district court judge in Oklahoma, however, spoke publicly of his uneasiness with public evaluations being based on the opinions of so few attorneys: "one in ten is not a very good survey result," said Judge John W. Michael of the Garfield County District Court.[75]

The results ranked the judges on a scale of one to one hundred, with higher numbers supposedly indicating a stronger "pro-business" philosophy. The average was just above 58. OJE published a list of all judges, their scores, and a plus or minus sign beside their names, indicating whether they were above or below average. A separate organization called Oklahomans for Jobs and Economic Growth, which describes itself as a political action committee formed to promote judicial reform, published a hierarchical ranking of all judges at each level of the court system.

Judges who faired poorly in the surveys rushed to defend themselves and typically did so cloaked in the language of apolitical arbiters of a neutral law that has more to do with justice than economics.[76] "I can't think of any case where I would make a decision based on the economic impact it would have on the community," said Richard M. Perry, an associate district judge of the Garfield County District Court who received a below-average score. "I always try to do the right thing in a case, regardless of the implications."[77] Another judge with below-average marks, Judge Keith Rapp of the Oklahoma Court

---

[71] *Judicial Survey Brings Mixed Response*, Tulsa Daily Commerce and Legal News, June 24, 1998.

[72] *Id.*

[73] *Id.*

[74] *Id.*

[75] Marks, *supra* note 65.

[76] David Gerard, *District Judges Receive Mediocre Evaluations*, Muskogee Daily Phoenix and Times-Democrat, June 22, 1998.

[77] Marks, *supra* note 65.

of Civil Appeals Division Two and Four, insisted that judges decide cases on the merits, not on "special agendas. We're not to be biased toward individuals or one group.[78] If someone is, that person shouldn't be on the bench."[79] Yet others accepted the principle of judicial evaluation, but thought that a neutral group should, and could, perform evaluations. The only supreme court judge to receive an unfavorable ranking, Justice Alma Wilson, subsequently enrolled in the Economic Institutes at the University of Kansas. The evaluations prompted at least one local journalist to call for a re-examination of Oklahoma's judicial selection process. [80]

V. CONCLUSION

Concerns that plaintiffs and plaintiffs' trial lawyers were extracting substantive and procedural advantages from the civil justice system have led defense interests to seek substantive and procedural reforms from Congress, state legislatures, courts and rulemaking entities. Plaintiffs' interests have opposed these reforms and sought to retain and elect state judges whom they perceived as favorably inclined toward them, while defense interests have responded by seeking to retain and elect judges perceived as favorably disposed toward them. These two groups of interests supported their candidates' campaigns principally through monetary donations. From the defense perspective, plaintiffs' interest groups have also sponsored judicial education seminars and judicial evaluations as means for promoting their viewpoints.

---

[78] Gerard, *supra* note 76.

[79] Marks, *supra* note 65.

[80] Chuck Ervin, *A Better Way to Judge*, TULSA WORLD, Nov. 21. 1999

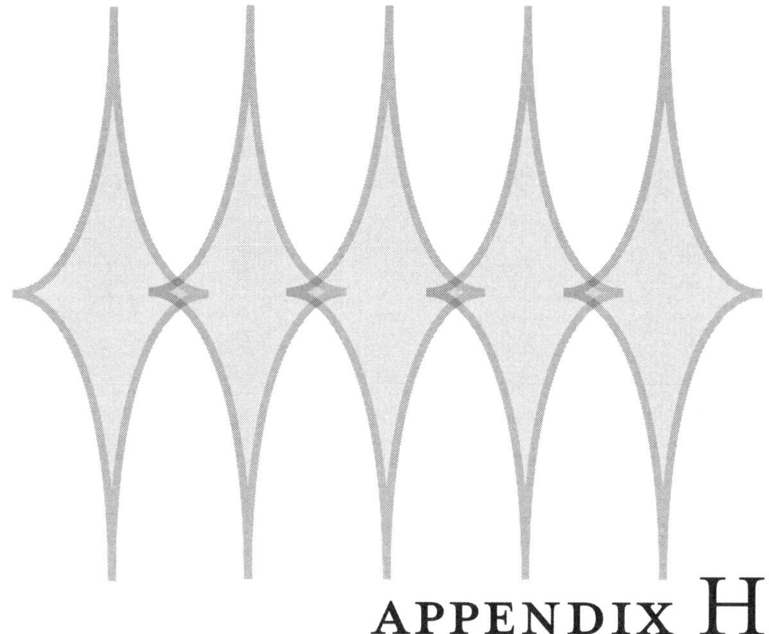

APPENDIX H

JUDICIAL INDEPENDENCE IN FAMILY COURTS

Barbara A. Babb[*]

Judith B. Moran[**]

I. Introduction

Judicial independence has become an increasingly important area of concern forcourt reformers, academics, the bench, and the bar.[1] Professional associations, such as the American Bar Association and the American Judicature Society, have begun initiatives to focus on the issue, as have citizens groups.[2] Several law journals have published symposia on the topic, as well.[3]

Court reform initiatives are an integral part of judicial independence in the family court context, and, in fact, they have the potential to facilitate an autonomous family court judiciary. Professor Barbara Babb has written extensively on family court reform.[4] She posits that some statewide family court reform projects, notably one that recently was implemented in Maryland, have supported improved judicial selection processes. This process now includes a focus on the candidate's background in and temperament for handling family law matters. Arguably, judges who are familiar with and interested in family law will be less subject to the political and social forces that influence family law decision-making.

The independence of the family court judiciary is influenced by multiple factors, which encompass some of society's most deeply held beliefs.[5] These include issues such as the age at which minors should be subject to criminal responsibility and punishment, the grounds for marital dissolution, gender-related issues in child custody awards, and child rearing standards that define child abuse and neglect. In addition to these philosophical and moral judgments, family law decision-making also is influenced by the method of judicial

---

[*] Associate Professor of Law and Director, Center for Families, Children and the Courts, University of Baltimore School of Law.

[**] Consultant, Center for Families, Children and the Courts, University of Baltimore School of Law.

[1] *See* Charles Gardner Geyh, *Why Judicial Elections Stink*, 64 OHIO ST. L.J. 43 (2003).

[2] *See id.*, at 47.

[3] *See id.* (noting those journals as publications associated with the following law schools: Georgia State University, Mercer University, St. John's University and the University of Southern California).

[4] *See generally* Barbara A. Babb, *Fashioning an Interdisciplinary Framework for Court Reform in Family Law: A Blueprint to Construct a Unified Family Court*, 71 S. CAL. L. REV. 469 (1998) (advocating the adoption of a therapeutic jurisprudence and holistic perspective for family court reform, which provides an interdisciplinary approach to family law decision-making).

[5] See Steven H. Hobbs, *In Search of Family Value: Constructing A Blueprint for Jurisprudential Discourse*, 75 MARQ. L.

selection, the scope of a particular family court's subject matter jurisdiction, community norms and concerns, the expectations of society for judicial decision-making, and the manner in which judges conduct their personal lives.

Most discourses on judicial independence focus on judicial elections and the adverse consequences of selecting judicial officers via this method. The presumption is that when a judge is appointed, she will be freer to make decisions notwithstanding political forces. This assumption, however, may not be particularly relevant in the family court context. In this context, the decisions made are affected not only by external forces, such as community norms and political issues, but by internal factors resulting from a judge's personal experience in her own family. Each judge, after all, is herself the product of a family, and, presumably, she relates to many of the issues that bring families to court. Personal biases borne out of particular circumstances are bound to impact a judge's thinking.

Even if these internal forces are managed, the appointment process as opposed to the election process in and of itself does not support judicial independence. Consider the family court judge appointed by a state or local government official who has an interest in lowering the juvenile crime rate. When faced with a delinquency case, that judge is likely to be influenced by the person to whom she "owes" her seat on the bench. Overall, the most important factor regarding judicial independence in the family court context, however, may be that we do not want judges to have so much discretion in family law matters. As a result of our ambivalence, we tether their decisions to statutes, which circumscribe their roles.[6]

This paper will discuss the particular factors that influence judicial independence in the family court context. First, the paper addresses procedural mechanisms by which an individual becomes a judge. Second, family court jurisdiction and its relationship to the issue of judicial autonomy are addressed. Third, the paper discusses the impact of social norms and political forces on particular aspects of family law decision-making. Finally, the effect of the media, the expectations the public has for judges, and legislative influences on judicial discretion are noted.

---

[6] *See* John J. Sampson, *Bringing the Courts to Heel: Substituting Legislative Policy for Judicial Discretion*, 33 FAM. L. Q. 565 (1999) (noting the trend towards legislative control over family law decision-making).

II. Factors Influencing Judicial Independence in the Family Court Context

Method of Judicial Selection

The way in which an individual becomes a family court judge varies from state to state. In Maryland, for example, judges are appointed by the governor for a one-year term and then are subject to a "retention election"[7] for the remaining fourteen-year term of office. Judges who survive the election process are then selected by the administrative judge in each Circuit Court to sit in that court's Family Division for an eighteen-month period. In contrast, New York City's Family Court judges are appointed by the mayor. As John Sampson has noted, "We now have in this country a patchwork quilt of judicial selection methods."[8] The most popular selection method appears to be the electoral process.[9]

Although reformers criticize the election of judges in so far as it has the potential to erode judicial independence, appointing family court judges does not guarantee an independent judiciary. Family court judges are not immune to outside influences, as they are susceptible to political pressures brought to bear by the elected officials who make decisions about the composition of the family court bench. As stated above, in New York City the mayor determines the make-up of the Family Court judiciary. A recent analysis of Family Court judicial appointments by former Mayor Giuliani has highlighted the extent to which his Family Court appointments have reflected his crime control agenda. Daniel Wise states in a recent New York Law Journal article that "[s]omewhat more consistently than his predecessors, practitioners said, Mr. Giuliani has appointed lawyers who spent a large part of their careers as prosecutors, either of criminal cases against adults or juvenile delinquency cases in Family Court."[10]

Family Court Jurisdiction

The breadth of a family court's jurisdiction varies from state to state. In some states[11] family courts have the authority to decide all matters relating to family law.[12] In others, family court subject matter juris-

---

[7] *See id.* at 584.

[8] *See id.*

[9] *See id.* (noting that about forty-two states utilize this process).

[10] See Daniel Wise, *Lawyers Find Smart, Committed Judges in Court Defined by Tension*, N.Y.L.J. March 19, 2002 at 1.

[11] *See* Babb, *supra* note 4, at 471 [citing DEL. CODE ANN. tit. 10 §§ 921-928 (Supp. 1996); D.C. CODE ANN. § 11-1101 (1995), §§ 16-2301 to 16-2365 (1997); HAW. REV. STAT. §§ 571-11 to 571-14 (1993)].

[12] *See id.* (Defining family law as cases involving divorce, annulment and property distribution; child custody and visitation; alimony and child support; paternity, adoption, and termination of parental rights; juvenile delinquency, child abuse and child neglect; domestic violence; criminal non-support; name change; guardianship of minors and disabled persons; and withholding or withdrawal of life-sustaining medical procedures, involuntary admissions and emergency evaluations).

diction is limited to deciding matters relating to child protection and dependency, juvenile delinquency, child custody and visitation.[13] Conceivably, the scope of a family court's jurisdiction affects the degree to which a judge is influenced by the community at large and by discrete political constituencies, as well as the extent to which the public has confidence in family court decisions or outcomes.

Family courts whose primary jurisdictional mandates are juvenile causes attract attention from communities focused on crime control and prevention. Consequently, judges may be influenced by anti-crime initiatives that cause them to detain delinquent youth, rather than sentence them to probation and community-based rehabilitation programs. Conversely, family courts with more expansive jurisdiction may be scrutinized on many levels, including issues of divorce, child custody, and family violence. One legal scholar opines that the more comprehensive the jurisdiction of the family court, the greater the public interest.[14]

A family court with comprehensive jurisdiction, however, may support an independent thinking judiciary and promote consumer confidence in the court system. In her discussion of unified family courts, Professor Babb suggests that one of the values of the unified family court model is that it supports informed judicial decisions by making available to judges support staff with backgrounds in mental health and social work.[15] These individuals assist the judge by assessing families, thereby helping to ensure that the court issues decisions that are appropriate for the family's particular circumstances. Arguably, the result may be an increased public trust in the judges who decide family law cases, which, in turn, promotes their independence.

Community Norms/Political Forces

Community norms and political forces influence nearly every area of family law. The more notable influences on particular family law case categories are discussed below.

Child Protection

Judicial decision-making in child protection matters clearly is influenced by public policy. Laws reflective of how best to safeguard the welfare of children, while protecting the integrity of the family, guide family court judges to decide the critical issue of where to place a

---

[13] N.Y. Fam. Court Act §115 (2001).

[14] *See* Interview with Barbara A. Babb, Associate Professor of Law, University of Baltimore School of Law, in Baltimore, MD (June 10, 2002).

[15] *See* Barbara A. Babb and Judith D. Moran, *Substance Abuse, Families and the Courts: The Creation of a Caring Justice System*, 3 J. HEALTH CARE L. & Pol'y 1, 18 (1999).

neglected or abused child. "During certain periods in this century, emphasis has been placed on family integrity and the inviolability of parents' fundamental rights to the child in all but the most extreme circumstances of maltreatment. However, in other periods considerations of the child's best interest have been used to justify high levels of state intervention in the parent-child relationship, including removal of the child and placement in foster care."[16]

Currently, the trajectory of public policy has veered toward more state intervention in the lives of children and families. Permanency for children, the clarion call of the late 1990's, continues into the new century, resulting in less judicial discretion as to when to terminate parental rights and to free a child for adoption.[17]

Prior to the passage of the Adoption and Safe Families Act of 1997, the law[18] guiding family court judges in cases of child abuse and neglect, although premised on permanency for children, allowed for considerable judicial discretion in determining when to permanently remove a child from her family. "Permanency planning meant that the state would make reasonable efforts to avoid the removal of children from their parents through service plans, would closely monitor children in placement, and work to reunite parents and children through supportive services if placement occurred."[19] This allowed judges to make more independent decisions about when to terminate parental rights.

The Adoption and Safe Families Act of 1997[20] heralded an era "of shorter and more stringent time requirements before actions would be taken to place children in permanent homes through adoption."[21] The 1997 law curtailed judges by imposing strict timelines on foster placement, as policymakers reacted to what they believed was an overreliance on preservation and reunification efforts.[22] Thus, the family court judge was divested of discretion to determine when parents must demonstrate they are fit to retain or regain custody of their child or permanently lose their parental rights.

Cultural norms, as they relate to child rearing, also affect the adjudication of child abuse and neglect cases and circumscribe judicial

---

[16] *See* Robert F. Kelly, *Family Preservation and Reunification Programs in Child Protection Cases: Effectiveness, Best Practices, and Implications for Legal Representation, Judicial Practice, and Public Policy,* 34 Fam. L. Q. 359 (2000).

[17] *See* Adoption and Safe Families Act of 1997, Pub. L. No. 105-89.

[18] *See* Adoption Assistance and Child Welfare Act of 1980, Pub. L. No. 96-272.

[19] *See* Kelly, *supra* note 16, at 364.

[20] Adoption and Safe Families Act of 1997, Pub. L. No. 105-89.

[21] *See* Kelly, *supra* note 16, at 364.

[22] *See id.*

independence. Although state statutes ideally objectify parenting standards reflective of social norms, these laws can and do clash with child rearing practices in minority cultures.[23] A judge, although aware of the clash of cultural norms, may be forced to rule that certain behavior constitutes child neglect, dismissing evidence that a parent's particular ethnic orientation has influenced his behavior.

Child Custody

As there have been dramatic policy shifts in child welfare, there have been varying perspectives on child custody, as well. A review of the case law demonstrates the ebb and flow of judicial decision-making in this area of family law. The earliest cases devoted to custody decisions demonstrate a paternal preference.[24] By the late nineteenth century,[25] the cases reflect judicial reliance on the "tender years presumption," supporting routine custody awards to mothers of young children, as well as an inclination toward a maternal preference, regardless of the child's age.[26] At the 20th century's mid-point, history notes that courts craft decisions allowing for custody awards to the "psychological parent," yielding to social science research demonstrating the value of a child residing with the parent with whom the child has the strongest emotional bond. Concurrently, the "best interests" standard, which continues to guide judges in custody decision-making, also has been favored.

Although the "best interests" of the child is the overarching principle for custody decisions,[27] "[t]oo often, gender stereotypes play a role in custody determinations."[28] With the advent of the father's rights movement in the 1970s, yet another perspective on which parent is the preferable custodian has become part of the child custody debate. Owing to the substantial political activism stemming from the father's rights movement,[29] the political ramifications of a custody award, rather than the "best interests" of the child, may influence judges faced with a custody dispute.

Juvenile Delinquency

With the advent of the crime control agenda, which has gained momentum over the last several decades, many state legislatures have

---

[23] *See* Yilu Zhao, *Cultural Divide Over Parental Discipline*, N.Y. TIMES, May 29, 2002, at B3.

[24] *See* Shannon Dean Sexton, *A Custody System Free of Gender Preferences and Consistent with the Best Interests of the Child: Suggestions for a More Protective and Equitable Custody System*, 88 KY. L.J. 761, 765 (1999–2000) (noting that under English common law the father was the preferred custodian and that this perspective permeated colonial American jurisprudence).

[25] *See id.* at 768.

[26] *See id.*

[27] *See id.* at 771.

[28] *See id.* at 762.

[29] *See id.* at 770 (describing the movement to influence state and federal legislators to retool custody laws so that they are more favorable to fathers).

responded by enacting laws to impose stiffer punishments on youthful offenders. Howard N. Snyder and Melissa Sickmund state in their report on juvenile offenders that "[p]erceptions of the juvenile crime epidemic in the early 1990's fueled public scrutiny of the system's ability to effectively control violent juvenile offenders. As a result, states have adopted numerous legislative changes in an effort to crack down on juvenile crime."[30]

The sweep of changes in juvenile crime legislation between 1992 and 1997 encompassed nearly every state in the country.[31] These revisions to existing statutes resulted in the following: making it easier to prosecute juveniles in adult criminal courts, expanding sentencing alternatives, decreasing restrictions on the confidentiality of juvenile proceedings, increasing the role of victims, and modifying correctional programs.[32]

The manner in which the courts handle juvenile offenders is based on two approaches, both of which involve judicial discretion. In each instance, the issue is whether the juvenile is tried in an adult court and, if so, how that occurs. Two states, Tennessee and New York, are illustrative of the differences. In New York,[33] the crime committed and the age of the child are automatic determinants of where the youth is tried. For example, commission of murder in the second degree at age thirteen compels a trial in an adult criminal court. The statute does, however, provide for transfer to juvenile court if "the court determines that to do so would be in the interests of justice."[34] The statute lists factors for the court to consider, but, clearly, judicial discretion is operative in this circumstance. Judges in Tennessee also are called upon to use discretion in determining whether a juvenile offender is tried in an adult criminal court. In a departure from New York law, judges in Tennessee have the discretion to transfer the case to the adult criminal court after a hearing on the issue.[35]

Notwithstanding the different mechanisms for applying adult criminal justice procedures to juvenile causes, judges are likely to be held accountable by the community for the kind of justice—juvenile or adultt—to which the youthful offender is subject. Because the focus of juvenile courts is rehabilitation and not punishment, allowing a juve-

---

[30] *See* Howard N. Snyder and Melissa Sickmund, *Juvenile Offenders and Victims: 1999 National Report,* NATIONAL CENTER FOR JUVENILE JUSTICE, September 1999 at 85.

[31] *See id.* at 89 (noting that all but three states changed at least one aspect of the laws governing the adjudication of juvenile criminal offenders).

[32] *See id.*

[33] *See* NY CLS CPL § 1.20, § 210.43 2. (a)-(i) (2002).

[34] *See* NY CLS CPL § 210.43 1.(b) (2002).

[35] *See* TENN. CODE ANN. § 37-1-134. (2) (3) (4) (2001).

nile offender to remain in the juvenile system or returning her to it could cast the judge in a "soft on crime" light. Arguably, given society's crime control agenda, judges resist being independent decision-makers in this circumstance.

Marital Dissolution

Some of the most difficult decisions judges make in family law cases are those relating to the legal severance of the marital relationship. The difficulties arise from the fact that marital dissolution, particularly when children are involved, presents a plethora of issues. The legal outcomes have substantial long-term consequences, such as how and by whom the children are cared for, the economic well-being of a financially dependent spouse, and the fate of extended family relationships with children when grandparents and other relatives wish to maintain contact with them.

The granting of the divorce itself, despite any of the aforementioned issues, is fraught with our national ambivalence about the sanctity of the marital bond. The most notable examples are the recent state statutes providing for "covenant marriage," where those contemplating marriage enter into agreements that make a divorce more difficult to obtain.[36] In Louisiana, for example, the covenant marriage law limits the dissolution of the marital relationship to circumstances involving mostly fault-based grounds.[37]

Although covenant marriage as a legislative phenomenon is a rarity, many state statutes governing marital dissolution reflect our conflicted attitudes about divorce. The fault grounds enumerated in these laws provide insight into the national psyche surrounding the relationship that "no man shall put asunder." An examination of fault grounds for divorce actions across several states reflects our collective wisdom—that only the most egregious acts or the most difficult of circumstances substantiate dissolving the marital relationship. In Maine, for example, the grounds for divorce include: "adultery; impotence; extreme cruelty; utter desertion continued for three consecutive years prior to the commencement of the action; and gross and confirmed habits of intoxication from the use of liquor or drugs."[38] Even when irreconcilable differences exist, Maine provides for judicial discretion to order the couples to counseling.[39] It appears

---

[36] *See* ARIZ. REV. STAT. ANN. § 25-901 (2001), ARK. CODE ANN. § 9-11-202 MICHIE (2001), LA. REV. STAT. ANN. § 9:273 (WEST 2001).

[37] *See* LA. REV. STAT. ANN. 9:237(c) (WEST 2001).

[38] *See* MAINE, 19-A M.R.S. § 902 1 A-E (2001).

[39] *See* MAINE, 19-AM.R.S. § 902 2 (2001): Irreconcilable Differences; Counseling. "If one party alleges that there are irreconcilable marital differences and the opposing party denies that allegation, the court upon its own motion or upon motion of either party may continue the case and require both

that Maine favors reasonable efforts to preserve the marriage, or at least a demonstration, with objective evidence that the marriage cannot be saved.[40]

Maryland reveals that its public policy supports maintaining marital relationships by requiring the court's due diligence as to evidentiary findings. Maryland's evidentiary requirements for substantiating a divorce action include similar grounds as those numerated in the Maine statute, with the additional stricture of a corroborating witness to testify as to the grounds[41] and a showing that "there is no reasonable expectation of reconciliation."[42]

"The prevailing wisdom on divorce . . . has, like other cultural attitudes, changed along with the times."[43] It is, however, difficult to gauge these shifting winds of change—whether they are favorable to divorce, as evidenced by no fault laws, or whether our values support making divorces more difficult to obtain. With a backdrop of fault-based grounds for divorce in many states,[44] judges base their decisions on laws with insidious moral underpinnings. The wiggle room in many statutes with fault-based grounds, such as what constitutes "cruelty of treatment,"[45] gives judges discretion in decision-making both as to the form and substance of the divorce action. As noted above, in Maine a judge may compel the parties to attend marriage counseling. The decision to grant a divorce, or at least how to order the parties to proceed in obtaining one, is undoubtedly influenced by community norms. But divining those norms is difficult—judges who are too quick to grant a divorce may suffer reprisals from constituents whose moral compass veers in the direction of preserving the marital union, while judges who resist granting a divorce may be judged harshly, as well. In such a climate of uncertainty, it is not unreasonable to conclude that independent judicial decision-making is threatened by moral and social forces..

Family Violence

Violence between spouses, or other domestic partners, accounts for a substantial caseload in most family courts. These cases present judges with immediate safety issues for women and children. The result of seeking a protective order can place the vulnerable party in danger no matter what the legal outcome. There have been many cases where the

---

[40] *See id.* "The counselor shall give a written report of the counseling to the court and to both parties. The failure or refusal of the party who denies irreconcilable difference to submit to counseling without good reason is prima facie evidence that the marital differences are irreconcilable."

[41] *See* MD. FAMILY LAW CODE ANN. § 7-101 (1999).

[42] *See* MD. FAMILY LAW CODE ANN. § 7-103 (1999).

[43] *See* Daphne Merkin, *Can this Divorce Be Saved?*, THE NEW YORKER, April 22, 2002, at 192.

[44] *See* CODE OF ALA. § 30-2-1. (2001); NY CLS DOM. REL. § 170 (2002); VA. CODE ANN. § 20-91 (2001); NORTH CAROLINA § 50-5.1.

[45] *See* MD. FAMILY LAW CODE ANN. § 7-103 (7) (1999).

petitioner is killed leaving the courthouse after obtaining a protection order. Conversely, women whose petitions have been denied have suffered at the hands of their abusers. These high-stakes outcomes are fodder for the media to cast a bright light on judicial decision-making in family matters. It is not surprising that judges themselves may feel besieged, as they are second-guessed about the wisdom of their decisions in these most difficult cases. Furthermore, there is anecdotal evidence from domestic violence advocates that political influences taint the judiciary regarding these matters. This appears to be true, particularly in small rural jurisdictions, where a judge's relationships in the community may impact whether to grant an order that will shed an unfavorable light on a family's private affairs.

III. Other Influences

Media Pressures

A judge's worst nightmare may be to read that a youth she sentenced to probation committed a subsequent crime, or that a woman whose petition for an order of protection she denied was further harmed by her alleged batterer. The pressures of community norms and values are brought to bear in a more dramatic way when the news media reports the adverse consequences of a judicial decision. Although there may be no objective measurement to determine the effect of publicity, the independence of the judiciary clearly is compromised by media attention.

In addition to family court decisions that spawn subsequent violent criminal acts, other family court matters are also grist for the media mill. High-profile divorce cases make good copy, and they frequently contain specific judicial decisions, such as custody awards, child support mandates, and findings of fault.[46] As the wisdom of these decisions often is debated in the public arena, the potential for this public controversy to influence a judge is very real, indeed.

Changing Expectations of Judicial Roles

With the advent of a problem-solving approach to judicial decision-making,[47] spawned by the growth of specialized courts such as drug

---

[46] *See* Susan Saulny, *18 Months After Giuliani, Hanover Files for Divorce, Citing Adultery*, N.Y. TIMES, June 21, 2002, at B 3 (describing the specifics of the judge's decision regarding child support and spousal maintenance).

[47] *See* National Conference of State Court Administrators, Resolution 4, Conference of Chief Justices, Resolution 22, *In Support of Problem-Solving Courts*, Conference of Chief Justices, at http://cosca.ncsc.dni.us/resolutionproblemsolvingcts.html (resolving to spearhead the problem-solving model for judicial decision-making).

courts,[48] community courts,[49] and mental health courts,[50] a judge's role has changed dramatically. Criminal court judges presiding in drug courts may find themselves imposing sentences fashioned to rehabilitate a drug involved felon and monitoring his treatment regime. The expectations for family court judges, particularly those involved with child protection matters, often include a quasi-social work function. The judge is responsible to ensure that the family receives services, with the hope of keeping children in the home or facilitating their swift return to the family unit.

There is burgeoning evidence that society's expectations of the judiciary have taken on another dimension. A recent news article devoted to the issue of an Arizona judge's marijuana use during the period of time within which he imposed two death sentences highlights the extent to which a judge's private life should be in the public domain.[51] The federal appellate court challenge to one of the sentences has resulted in the court's upholding the defendant's death penalty appeal. Commenting upon the intrusive aspects of the decision, Judge Alex Kozinski has noted in his dissenting opinion that "the decision invited intrusion into judges' personal lives."[52] Echoing the concerns of the dissent, an Arizona Assistant Attorney General has opined that the decision could support inquiries about "all sorts of matters that might influence judicial decision making," including divorce.[53]

If the foregoing case promotes a trend toward the exploration of a criminal court judge's personal background, then the independence of the family court bench also may be at risk. Family law matters relate to issues affecting a significant percentage of the population. Professor Babb notes that family law cases account for more than 35% of the civil case filings in the nation's state courts.[54] In light of the high volume of this category of cases, it is likely that many family court judges, and/or their family members, have themselves been involved in a family court case. Consider the divorced judge presiding in a marital dissolution case. Will her decision be subject to challenge based upon that aspect of her personal history? Further, con-

---

[48] *See* Honorable Peggy Fulton Hora, Honorable William Schma and John T.A. Rosenthal, *Therapeutic Jurisprudence and the Drug Court Movement: Revolutionizing the Criminal Justice System's Response to Drug Abuse and Crime in America*, 74 NOTRE DAME L. REV. 439 (1999).

[49] *See* Michele Sviridoff, David Rottman, Brian Ostrum and Richard Curtis, *Dispensing Justice Locally, The Implementation and Effects of the Midtown Community Court*, HARWOOD ACADEMIC PUBLISHERS, (2000).

[50] *See* Leroy L. Kondo, *Therapeutic Jurisprudence, Issues Analysis and Applications: Advocacy of the Establishment of Mental Health Specialty Courts in the Provision of Therapeutic Jurisprudence for Mentally Ill Offenders*, 24 SEATTLE L. REV. 373 (2000).

[51] *See* Adam Liptak, *Judge's Drug Use at Issue in 2 Death Sentences*, N.Y. TIMES, May 16, 2002, at A1.

[52] *See id.*

[53] *See id.* at A1, A22.

[54] *See* Barbara A. Babb, *Fashioning An Interdisciplinary Framework for Court Reform in Family Law: Application of an Ecological and Therapeutic Perspective*, 72 IND. L.J. 775 (1997).

sider the presiding judge in a delinquency case, whose own child has been involved with the juvenile justice system. Does that fact preclude him from being impartial, thereby exposing the decision to appellate review? Holding judges accountable is a hallmark of our judicial system; however, in the quest for accountability, we may jeopardize judicial independence in the family courts of this country.

Judicial Discretion

The crux of the entire judicial independence dilemma may be society's increasing reluctance to allow for judicial discretion in family law decision-making. Professor John J. Sampson comments that the "establishment of basic family law policies by our elected representatives is preferable to leaving those decisions to lawyers, especially gubernatorially appointed lawyers."[55] He argues that "even when judges are elected, judicial elections virtually never turn on real policy issues, to say nothing of family law policies."[56] In discussing the evolution of Texas' joint custody statute, Professor Sampson notes the legislative trend to enact detailed custody directives.[57] He predicts a legislative trend toward reducing judicial discretion in family law matters.[58]

Although Professor Sampson speaks from his experience in one state, the issue he raises regarding who should decide what is best for families resonates with much of the previous discussion of the factors influencing judicial decision-making. With all the private and complicated matters involved in family law cases, it is not unreasonable to assume that few of us want a judge to decide them. If the judge is authorized to do so, we hold her accountable in ways that constrain her independence, whether through detailed legislative directives, media publicity, or the power of appointment or election.

IV. Conclusion

The resolution of the issue of judicial independence in the family court context involves addressing an array of factors that influence a judge's decision-making. To be sure, the appointment-election conundrum is one important concern; however, its resolution is not dispositive of the issue. As discussed earlier, under either selection process, family court judges are not free of political concerns, whether they are related to an appointment made by a public official or the result of election by their local constituents. Furthermore, the

---

[55] *See* John J. Sampson, *Bringing the Courts to Heel: Substituting Legislative Policy for Judicial Discretion*, 33 FAM. L. Q. 565 (1999).

[56] *See id.*

[57] *See id.* at 580 *See also* Robert J. Levy, *Trends in Legislative Regulation of Family Law Doctrine*, 33 FAM. L. Q. 543 (1999).

[58] *See* Sampson, *supra* note 55.

volatility of family law matters stems from the fact that these issues lie at the heart of what we hold most dear, our privacy, our homes, our spouses or partners, and our children. The beliefs that accompany the issues are closely held, as well, resulting from our own experience with a family and our reluctance to allow a third party to decide such private matters.

The context for family law decision-making, thus, is vulnerable to scrutiny of the judges' decisions, whether they involve which parent is awarded the custody of a child, how the courts handle a juvenile delinquent, or whether a marriage is dissolved. This public scrutiny constrains the actual independence of the family court judge because family law decisions frequently are subject to collective second-guessing.

The solution proposed to this problem is a relatively simple one, but it requires a concerted commitment to change the procedures for placing judges in family court and providing support for them while they are there.

First, family court judges should be scrutinized aggressively *before* they become judges. A rigorous standard for judicial selection can be implemented, "regardless of whether a given state is an elective state or an appointive state."[59] Most states require that family court judges have backgrounds that are particularly suited to family law.[60] This directive should be taken seriously, as it impacts the capacity of a judge to make the critical decisions involved in family law adjudication. It also would further the interests of "professionalizing the judiciary," with the hope of convincing the public that "judges ought to be selected differently than public officials in the political branches."[61] Arguably, if the public has confidence in the wisdom of judges, the conflict about judicial discretion[62] in making family law related decisions would be reduced.

Second, family court structures and procedures should be optimized to promote independent judicial decision-making. Professor Babb suggests that family court reform initiatives promote more informed and more independent thinking judges.

Finally, sitting judges should receive regular and on-going education and training in such subjects as family dynamics, domestic violence,

---

[59] *See* E. Norman Veasey, *The Many Facets of the Judicial Independence Diamond*, 20 QUINNIPIAC L. REV. 779, 787 (2000).

[60] *See* MD. CTS. & JUD. PROC. §3-806 (2002 Replacement Volume).

[61] *See* Geyh, *supra* note 1, at 33.

[62] *See* Sampson, *supra* note 55.

and child development in order to promote more public confidence in the courts. This, in turn, facilitates the public's willingness to allow judges to judge—unhampered by political second guessing and personal bias.